Market Know How: Finance and Markets

Market Know How: Finance and Markets

Francesca Taylor

Financial Times
Prentice Hall
is an imprint of

Harlow, England • London • New York • Boston • San Francisco • Toronto • Sydney • Singapore • Hong Kong
Tokyo • Seoul • Taipei • New Delhi • Cape Town • Madrid • Mexico City • Amsterdam • Munich • Paris • Milan

PEARSON EDUCATION LIMITED

Edinburgh Gate
Harlow CM20 2JE
Tel: +44 (0)1279 623623
Fax: +44 (0)1279 431059
Website: www.pearsoned.co.uk

First published in Great Britain in 2009

ISBN: 978-0-273-72378-3

British Library Cataloguing-in-Publication Data
A catalogue record for this book is available from the British Library

Library of Congress Cataloging-in-Publication Data
Taylor, Francesca.
Market know how : finance and markets / Francesca Taylor. -- 1st ed.
p. cm.
Includes bibliographical references and index.
ISBN 978-0-273-72378-3 (pbk. : alk. paper) 1. Finance. I. Title.
HG101.T39 2009
332.6--dc22
2009027935

10 9 8 7 6 5 4 3 2 1
13 12 11 10 09

Designed by Sue Lamble
Typeset in 9.5pt/13.5pt by 30
Printed by Ashford Colour Press Ltd, Gosport, UK

The publisher's policy is to use paper manufactured from sustainable forests.

Contents

Preface

This book has been incredibly hard to put together. Every time a chapter was written, the financial markets shifted – requiring re-writing, in practice this is the third or fourth edition before the first one was even published.

So much has happened in the past year; esoteric terms such as credit crunch, subprime mortgage debt and the LIBOR disconnect are almost in everyday language, even taxi drivers are discussing them.

Derivatives used for hedging purposes and structured products – for so long the exotic playthings of the commercial and investment banks – are now affecting the high street, our mortgages, our house prices and our investments.

To date, in June 2009, the banks have written down (admitted) losses of about $650 billion, yet the total amount of losses linked to the credit crunch has been estimated to be in excess of $3 trillion. For those of you not used to these types of numbers, that is $3,000,000,000,000. Based on those figures we have only had about a fifth of the bad news so far!

We read about the possible creation of a 'bad bank' to take on some of this debt, which may ameliorate the situation. Have we seen the worst of the credit crunch? Is it all over now? What do you think?

What about the value of the US dollar and the euro? With plummeting oil and commodity prices it was still expensive to fill up a car with petrol.

Some of our strongest global financial institutions have been or are currently under threat. Where did it all go wrong?

Everyone seems to be walking on eggshells. Can we tell jokes in the office? What if someone is offended? Can we invite the staff out for team meetings? Can we offer alcohol? Will we be sued?

In financial markets and businesses linked to financial markets you are expected to understand these things, yet too often we either have no direct experience to draw on, or we have become overly specialised. For example, the bond market or flotation specialist who has only a sliver of knowledge about the foreign exchange markets, or the relationship manager who has only a fleeting acquaintance with derivatives, yet is being asked questions by his clients, or the new entrant who is feeling daunted by all the terminology and market jargon. Or, as I heard recently a software engineer coding a piece of option software without understanding the terms 'put' and 'call'! To reflect this, I have included a substantial glossary of terms; a word that appears in bold type indicates a glossary item. However, this book is not intended to replace a full text book for each of the subjects – of which there are many, and I have noted additional reading at the end of many of the chapters for anyone who would like it.

This book is designed for anyone who feels that they may not have all the pertinent facts. It is a 'cross-over' book because it is becoming increasingly important to see how all the markets inter-relate together, i.e., debt and equity securities markets, derivatives and foreign exchange, compliance and risk. How these products are then valued to establish if we are making money or not, this is known as marking-to-market, or if you are feeling really cynical, marking-to-myth!

What goes on in the front office of a bank or financial institution? What distinguishes a good trader from one not so good? Can you 'learn' to be a trader? What happens after the deal is done – then we are in the mysterious world of 'operations' – nothing to do with hospitals.

Risk and risk management is critical, so learn from the experts about what to watch out for.

I am often accused of being too gloomy in these troubled times, but let me pose one question: 'If someone is going to default on his mortgage payments (or has already), isn't he now going to be defaulting on his personal loans and his credit cards?' We have financial products linked to all of these things too…

FST
June 2009

About the author

FRANCESCA TAYLOR is the founder and chief executive of Taylor Associates (International) Ltd. The company is based in London and specialises in providing learning and education to regulators, asset managers, hedge funds, banks, information providers, government bodies, IT professionals, exchanges, infrastructure providers, corporates and private individuals. This makes Francesca ideally placed to write user-friendly, technical books and to offer independent training to a range of clients.

Francesca started in the group treasury of one of the UK's largest firms, BICC plc, where she honed her corporate treasury skills and became a member of the Association of Corporate Treasurers. She has also enjoyed a number of years as a banker, broker and consultant, concentrating on currency and interest rate risk management.

She moved into derivatives and has since written a number of bestsellers, *Mastering the Derivatives Markets*, now in its third edition and *Mastering Foreign Exchange and Currency Options*, now in its second edition, both published by Financial Times Prentice Hall.

Francesca also has extensive experience of post-trade activities, working with market providers of infrastructure services, notably, Capco, CLS, DTCC Deriv/Serv and Omgeo, both in the UK and North America. She has also been working with government bodies in the UK and overseas to facilitate the understanding of highly technical subject matter, by the legislative authorities. She has spoken at conferences in London, New York, Hong Kong, Singapore, Malaysia and Australia.

Francesca lives in Surrey with her family. Her dog, Storm, was the first dog in the world to have a prosthetic paw fitted; unfortunately he succumbed to cancer in 2008. She is now the owner of two rescue cats, Star and Shadow. Her academic qualifications include a BSc (Hons) in geology from London University, an MBA from Imperial College and an AMCT from the Association of Corporate Treasurers.

About the contributors

TONY BLUNDEN is head of consulting and a board member of Chase Cooper.

Tony's areas of focus are the identification and development of clients' needs, the development of Chase Cooper's profile and product set, and the provision of training, both internally and to clients. Tony's previous client engagements have included advising and guiding clients on risk and compliance frameworks and governance, ARROW visits and pre-visit awareness sessions, corporate governance expectations of regulators, prospects and the outlook for regulation, modelling of risk and risk reporting.

Tony has worked in the City of London for more than thirty years, primarily within risk management, compliance and related areas in financial services. Before joining Chase Cooper, Tony spent four years as a director in Ernst & Young's financial services risk management practice.

Tony has spoken at around sixty international risk and compliance conferences and has appeared on television and radio. He is also a well known author of articles and chapters on risk management and compliance having published some twenty five documents.

SUE COOPER is a business behaviour specialist, coach and organisational change consultant. She spent the first twenty years of her career with blue-chip retail organisations in senior trading and change management roles. Sue spent her career in Tesco and Kingfisher at a time of profound change and rapid growth in each company. During this time, she did everything from tramping potato fields (don't ask) and master-minding the biggest shipment of Christmas trees to the UK (as a buyer and trading director) to developing corporate strategy, with spells in human resources and information technology in between. She moved into management development ten years ago when she co-founded Enigma Management Development. She also lectures in workplace psychology at the University of Westminster.

Sue now spends her time coaching and training individuals and groups and advising organisations, helping them to take a fresh look at the way they are operating and to make the changes they need to succeed and expand. She has a broad client portfolio and has worked on every continent (except Antarctica).

Sue has a MA from Cambridge University, a foundation certificate in psychotherapy and counselling and is a member of the Institute of Transactional Analysis. She is qualified to administer a variety of psychological instruments including the Myers Briggs Type Indicator.

She now divides her time between her homes in London and South Florida, depending on her schedule and the UK weather forecast.

BILL HODGSON is director of Sapient Trading and Risk Management, Process Solutions Group. His career has included a variety of businesses including cash registers, children's games, RADAR, oil drilling (although not actually on the rig itself) and for the past fifteen years in the capital markets, especially OTC derivatives. The children's games were sold for the Sinclair ZX Spectrum, now a museum piece, unlike Bill of course. In the drilling business, Bill worked on software to simulate the behaviour of drilling components underground, enabling BP to prove they could drill a hole for thousands of feet underground and watch the drill head pop up back where it started.

In the capital markets, Bill initially worked on developing software to process OTC derivatives at Merrill Lynch, in the days when paper trade tickets were the norm. Subsequently, Bill has worked with banks to improve their OTC processing capabilities, and then with LCH.Clearnet and DTCC to develop the market infrastructure for OTC products. Bill is currently specialising in clearing for OTC derivatives with Sapient, an end-to-end service provider which includes business consulting, technology consulting, process and operations, and software products.

RICHARD MOORE. Until April 2008, Richard enjoyed a successful career with Citigroup. The early part of Richard's time at the bank encapsulated many varied roles in its foreign exchange business culminating in his appointment as global head of foreign exchange in June 2000.

In 2003, Richard's responsibilities were expanded to include the global rates and commodity business and in 2007, in his final role at Citigroup, he was responsible for the fixed-income division in Europe, Middle East and Africa. In this role, Richard reported directly to the regional chief executive and was responsible for 1,800 banking professionals devising and distributing the full range of fixed-income products and services. Richard held this last position until 2008 before leaving Citigroup to pursue his interests in property, student entertainment and film finance.

MICHAEL SIMMONS is an operations specialist, having spent more than twenty years with S.G. Warburg, where he held positions such as head of Eurobond settlements and head of operations. He specialised in debt and equity operations with day-to-day management responsibility across both domestic and international markets. Mike has also worked as a senior business analyst assessing operations business requirements for investment banks, asset managers and retail banks in the UK, US and mainland Europe. He has also been involved with setting up off-shore operations in India, and the assessment of risk in operations and the implementation of controls. In the past twelve years, Mike has delivered hundreds of courses in numerous countries to investment banks, asset managers, consulting companies and software companies. Mike is also the author of two operations books: *Securities Operations* and *Corporate Actions.*

Acknowledgements

I OWE A HUGE THANKS TO MY CONTRIBUTORS who have made a sterling effort to put pen to paper, these are:

Tony Blunden, Chase Cooper
Sue Cooper, Enigma Management Development
Bill Hodgson, Sapient
Richard Moore, ex-Citigroup and FX market legend
Mike Simmons, independent trainer and author

Many thanks also to my colleagues on LinkedIn with their snippets of market jargon – some of which I'm afraid I couldn't publish! I'd also like to thank my publishers Financial Times Prentice Hall and everyone involved in the production of this book.

Finally, my thanks go to everyone at home and at Taylor Associates who kept everything running smoothly whilst I wrote this.

FST

Publisher's acknowledgements

We are grateful to the following for permission to reproduce copyright material:

Figures
Figures 1.1, 1.5, 1.6, 1.7, 2.7 from Thomson Reuters; Figures 1.3, 6.2, 6.3, 6.4 from *Mastering Derivatives Markets*, 3rd ed., Pearson Education (Taylor, F. 2007); Figure 1.8 from First American CoreLogic LoanPerformance data; Figure 2.6 reproduced with kind permission of NYSE Liffe; Figure 3.1 from Federal Reserve Board; Figure 3.2 from European Central Bank (ECB), this picture is available free of charge via the ECB's homepage (www.ecb.europa.eu/home); Figure 3.3 from www.ffiec.gov/nicpubweb/nicweb/Top50Form.aspx, National

Information Center; Figures 5.1, 5.2, 5.3, 5.4, 5.5, 5.6 from Chase Cooper Ltd. The publishers acknowledge permission from John Wiley & Sons to use the following material: Figures 8.1, 8.2, 8.8 and Table 8.5, which are identical or adapted from the originals. These first appeared in *Securities Operations: A guide to trade and position management* (ISBN: 0471497584), published by Wiley. Figures 9.3 and 9.14 reprinted with permission of ISDA © 2008 International Swaps and Derivatives Association.

Tables
Table 4.1 from *Euromoney* (May 2008).

Text
Extract on pages 17–21 from Dr David Gershon, CEO, Super Derivatives.

The Financial Times
Figure 6.1 from Informa Global Markets Calendar, *The Financial Times*, 17 November 2008.

In some instances we have been unable to trace the owners of copyright material, and we would appreciate any information that would enable us to do so.

1

Key concepts, calculations, tools and techniques

There is an element of confusion about financial markets.

- Introduction
- Euro, domestic and offshore markets
- The role and use of LIBOR
- Interest calculations using day counts and business day conventions
- Financial maths: time value of money, compounding, discounting
- Marking to market (MTM)
- Collateral management
- Netting
- Option pricing models
- Forward rates: fair value calculations
- Yield curves
- Technical analysis
- Credit crunch

Introduction

There is an element of confusion about financial markets and a lot of background knowledge is assumed, which is why practitioners are often accused of speaking a different language. When I started in finance I understood the words but not necessarily their meaning. Furthermore, concepts I had been taught at business school were referred to, but I couldn't see the direct application.

Euro, domestic and offshore markets

Start with the assumption that all currency is held in its country of origin, so US dollars are held (in deposit accounts) in the US, sterling is held in the UK, Japanese yen are held in Japan and euros are held in Europe. When this is so, the currencies are known as domestic and are subject to domestic local interest rates. If anyone holds US dollar-denominated instruments outside the US, say in Europe or Asia, they are then subject to international interest rates (not always the same as domestic US rates) and are conventionally known as euro or offshore currencies or instruments. There may also be differences relating to regulation and tax treatment.

EXAMPLE

- Sterling that is outside the UK, e.g. in Europe, is known as euro-sterling.
- Japanese yen outside Japan, e.g. in Australia, are known as euro-yen.
- US dollars outside the US, e.g. in Tokyo, are euro-dollars.
- Euros outside the eurozone are known as euro-euro!!

Consequently, to a US borrower there may be advantages or disadvantages to borrowing the dollars on-shore (domestic) rather than offshore (euro markets).

The role and use of LIBOR

Banks and large organisations have funding linked to **LIBOR** (London Interbank Offered Rate). This is an international, commercial index rate at which banks lend money to each other. It forms a reference rate for a range of borrowings and also for **derivatives**. The formal LIBOR fixing is carried out in London at 11am every business day and rates are available for periods up to one year. Sterling LIBOR is the UK domestic interest rate, but there are also rates available in currencies such as US dollar, Canadian dollar, euro and yen – these then are euro-currency rates.

Almost everything in finance has a **bid** and an **offer**. The bid is the price at which the bank will buy and the offer is the price at which the bank will sell – another word for offer is 'ask'. A two-way price is where the buy and sell prices are shown simultaneously, the trader hopes to buy cheap and sell expensive and make the profit in the middle, known as the **bid-offer spread**.

In the UK, interest rates are displayed as shown below – they look like they are quoted backwards, but this is traditionally the way to do it. Eccentric!

London interbank offer rate – London interbank bid rate

3.70% – 3.60%

LIBOR – LIBID

(offer) – (bid)

used for customer borrowings – used for customer deposits

LIBOR is the rate at which the market-making bank will offer to sell (lend) money. Libid is the rate at which the market-making bank will bid for a deposit.

Note that other countries have their own version of LIBOR such as:

- EURIBOR: Euro Interbank Offered Rate.
- TIBOR: Tokyo Interbank Offered Rate.

There is an element of misunderstanding about these types of fixings. This is because in the UK, the lending rate between two banks is also called LIBOR and this rate will fluctuate with supply and demand throughout the day.

Question: Does that mean that every bank will quote the same LIBOR rate at the same time?

Answer: No, it depends on the bank's position; is it long or short (of money)? In practice, a bank with a lot of money to lend will quote a lower LIBOR rate than a bank that is itself borrowing and would rather be contacted by investors.

LIBOR fix

How can LIBOR be a reference rate if it is a different rate at every bank? A reference point is needed for instruments such as derivatives and loans that is only going to change once a day. This is known as the LIBOR 'fixing', which is set in London, every business day at 11am. The sixteen most active banks in their respective currencies send their current market rates to the **British Bankers Association (BBA)** for the range of time periods shown in Figure 1.1. The BBA is an independent body that takes these sixteen rates for say one month LIBOR and removes the four highest and four lowest rates and averages the eight rates that are left. This process is undertaken for each period, **overnight**, one-week, two-weeks and then every monthly period up to twelve months.

11:45 26JAN09 THOMSON REUTERS BBA LIBOR RATES UK67516 LIBOR01
BRITISH BANKERS ASSOCIATION INTEREST SETTLEMENT RATES Alternative to <3750>
[26/01/09] RATES AT 11:00 LONDON TIME 26/01/2009 Disclaimer <LIBORDISC>
BBA Guide <BBAMENU>

	USD	GBP	CAD	EUR	JPY	EUR 365
O/N	0.23250	1.51750	1.03333	1.11500	SN 0.22188	1.13049
1WK	0.31000	1.58750	1.10000	1.38750	0.25825	1.40677
2WK	0.35000	1.61000	1.20000	1.53625	0.30450	1.55759
1MO	0.40875	1.59563	1.35000	1.80000	0.40813	1.82500
2MO	0.91375	1.98563	1.45000	1.99375	0.56188	2.02144
3MO	1.18375	2.17500	1.57167	2.14250	0.69000	2.17226
4MO	1.37625	2.24000	1.66500	2.18375	0.78063	2.21408
5MO	1.52625	2.29625	1.76500	2.21375	0.81625	2.24450
6MO	1.67250	2.35250	1.87000	2.25000	0.87250	2.28125
7MO	1.72625	2.39188	1.93000	2.27000	0.88913	2.30153
8MO	1.78000	2.42125	1.99167	2.28375	0.91875	2.31547
9MO	1.83625	2.45063	2.05000	2.30125	0.93938	2.33321
10MO	1.87875	2.46563	2.09667	2.31500	0.96100	2.34715
11MO	1.92125	2.48188	2.14667	2.33125	0.98563	2.36363
12MO	1.96625	2.49500	2.19667	2.34250	1.00563	2.37503

<0#LIBORSUPERRICS> RICs for above <0#LIBORRICS> Contributor RICs

FIGURE 1.1 LIBOR fixing for 7 Jan 2009

Source: Thomson Reuters

You cannot physically transact at the LIBOR fix rate, although many banks benchmark their investments against what a particular LIBOR rate is – it is after all a composite rate and it is possible no one bank was quoting that actual rate.

NOTE

The six month LIBOR fix is very popular and may be used for interest rate **swaps**, caps, FRAs and for setting the variable interest rate on a bank loan or security.

There was some criticism of the LIBOR fix during the market upheavals linked to the credit crunch. Notably, that if banks were not actually dealing at their 11am prices, then how accurate was the fix? In addition, of the sixteen banks in the US dollar fix, at one point only two of them were able to access directly the support offered by the US authorities, meaning rates in London did not reflect the government intervention as much as the market hoped. It is a fact that more US dollars are borrowed worldwide linked to the London LIBOR dollar fix than anything else, and this was not showing the effects of the added **liquidity** being pumped into the markets.

NOTE

Banks are not in the business of lending money to their competitors – that is not a good business model. They do, however, normally park their surpluses with each other and the credit crunch made banks nervous of the risk related to this: if I lend it out, will I get it back?

Is LIBOR just for banks?

The short answer is No. A client who wishes to have a borrowing linked to LIBOR but who is not a bank will just have to pay an additional margin, e.g. three-month LIBOR + 0.25% (25 **basis points**). The 25bp is known as the credit spread.

What happens if a client needs to borrow for a longer-term, say five years? How can a short-term rate such as LIBOR be the reference rate? The loan would need to be a variable rate loan and the LIBOR would be set periodically, usually every six months (+ a spread if applicable). LIBOR will therefore fluctuate with the prevailing interest rate sentiment.

Interest calculations using day counts and business day conventions

Interest rates are quoted as annual rates, so a loan rate of 5 per cent is actually 5 per cent a year. A transaction with a maturity of up to twelve months will normally have the interest paid in arrears – on the maturity date. For a longer-term transaction, say eighteen months, interest is likely to be paid every six months, with the last interest payment on the maturity date. As interest rates are quoted as annual rates if a client borrows for only three months the amount of interest is calculated per day then multiplied by the number of days in the period.

EXAMPLE

Assume £5 million is borrowed at 4.94938 per cent per annum (p.a.) for three months. The interest amount must be apportioned for the required number of days in that particular three-month period, it is too imprecise to say that it is just a quarter of a year. Assume there are 91 days in this period of three months. The calculation is:

$$£5,000,000 \times \frac{91}{365} \times \frac{4.94938}{100} = £61,697.75$$

Notice the use of 365 days in this transaction. This is known as the day count convention and is written 'actual/365' or A/365. In the above example, this becomes 91/365.

There is another convention, 'actual/actual' or A/A, where leap years are recognised and 365 becomes 366. This is typically found in the bond markets.

If the loan happened to be in $5 million, at the same rate for the same period, the interest amount would be different. This is because US dollar calculations assume a figure of 360 days for the day count convention:

$$\$5,000,000 \times \frac{91}{360} \times \frac{4.94938}{100} = \$62,554.66$$

This **day count convention** is written 'actual/360', or A/360 or Act/360. It assumes 360 days in the year (every year including leap years) and 91 days in this three-month period. This also means that for a twelve-month transaction, the fraction will become 365/360. For more information on financial calculations, see Robert Steiner's, *Mastering Financial Calculations*.

NOTE

If anyone asks why the Americans and the Europeans use A/360 and the UK and the Japanese use A/365, just say 'it's traditional'. In short, the markets evolved differently.

I have lost count on the number of times I have been asked that question and I have not yet received a plausible answer – lots of very implausible ones though!

Different countries have different 'day count conventions' that determine the number of days per month/year, here are the main ones:

- GBP and NZD, AUD, CAD, JPY: A/365.
- USD and EUR: A/360.

Question: Are Saturdays, Sundays and bank holidays included in the day count calculations?

Answer: Yes, although interest and principal payments must be made and received on 'good days', i.e. when the financial markets are open for business. So if the maturity date happens to be a Sunday or a bank holiday, what happens? The business day conventions set out what happens if the maturity date on a transaction falls on a weekend or public holiday. Assume the maturity date is a Saturday:

- Following business day: go to the next business day, which is Monday, unless Monday is a public holiday, in which case go to Tuesday.

- Previous business day: go to Friday.
- Modified following business day: go to Monday *unless* this puts you in the following month, if it does, go back to Friday.

Question: What happens in Europe where Spain has one set of public holidays and Italy may have another and the euro is supposed to cover the whole of Europe?

Answer: There is a convention for that too; Europe is assumed to be 'open' on every business day except Christmas day and New Year's day.

EXAMPLE

Assume you have a three-month deposit maturing on 31 October 2009, which is a Saturday. Under the normal following business day convention, you would go to Monday. However, Monday is 2 November, which means that if you were using the modified business day convention you would now go back to Friday.

It is important to ascertain which convention is to be used at the beginning of the transaction because it affects the number of days in the calculation period. Ultimately, it is the customer's choice.

Financial maths: time value of money, compounding, discounting

Time value of money (TVM)

The basic tenet of interest is that investors earn interest and borrowers pay interest. The financial markets provide vehicles for investors and borrowers to optimise their risk and return. The rate of interest reflects the fact that cash has a current value and a decision to invest, i.e. not spend the cash today, must mean there will be a reward in the future. When an investor invests in equity or a bond or a money market instrument, he or she is forgoing the benefits of consuming a known value of money today, in return for an unknown value in the future. The investor therefore requires compensation for two things:

- The period the money is invested (unable to be used elsewhere).
- The risk that the money may not be repaid (credit risk).

Generally, borrowers need to compensate investors for both of these factors. This will be in the form of interest income if the investment is a loan or a bond, dividends from equity, rent from property and so on, together with an increase in the value of the original capital over time. The first is known as interest income and the second is known as capital gain. The sum of these two elements is known as the overall rate of return on the investment, or **yield**.

Interest rates are expressed as per annum interest rates. This enables us to compare and contrast the returns on different instruments for different periods. Where there is only a single payment of interest (usually at maturity) this is known as simple interest.

What about earning or paying interest on interest? This is especially important where interim payments are made or received, and is known as compound interest.

Of critical importance is the notion of **time value** of money (TVM). All instruments have a face value (principal), a purchase price and a redemption value (which may be the same) and an interest rate. The way this all links together is time value of money. The inter-relationships between present value, PV, (money today) and future value, FV, (money in the future) are shown below.

Future value (FV)

$$FV = PV \times \left(1 + \left(i \times \frac{d}{y}\right)\right)$$

where: PV = Present value (the principal amount)

FV = Future value

d = Actual number of (calendar) days elapsed

i = Quoted interest rate

y = Standardised year denominator (360 or 365)

EXAMPLE

What is the FV of $10,000,000 in 91 days' time at an interest rate of 4.5 per cent, assuming a day count of 'A/360'?

$$FV = \$10m \times \left(1 + \left(0.045 \times \frac{91}{360}\right)\right) = \$10,113,750.00$$

EXAMPLE

What is the FV of £5,000,000 in 30 days' time at an interest rate of 5.5 per cent, assuming a day count using A/365?

$$FV = £5m \times \left(1 + \left(0.055 \times \frac{30}{365}\right)\right) = £5,022,602.74$$

Present value (PV)

$$PV = FV \times \frac{1}{\left(1 + \left(i \times \frac{d}{y}\right)\right)}$$

where: PV = Present value (the principal amount)

FV = Future value

d = Actual number of (calendar) days elapsed

i = Quoted interest rate

y = Standardised year denominator (360 or 365)

With so many capital market instruments having interest and principal payment/repayment dates in the future, a way of calculating the true worth of the value of those cash flows today is needed. This is known as a present value calculation or discounting back the cash flow. It can be likened to working backwards from the principal plus **accrued interest** to find out what the original principal amount invested should be.

TIP

The present value calculation underlies the concept of marking-to-market for many financial instruments.

EXAMPLE

What is the PV of $10,113,750, assuming an interest rate of 4.5 per cent, over 91 days and a day count of A/360.

$$PV = \$10,113,750 \times \frac{1}{\left(1 + \left(0.045 \times \frac{91}{360}\right)\right)}$$

$$= \$10,000,000$$

EXAMPLE

You are expecting to receive £100,000 in 182 days' time. What is the present value (PV) of this sum, given that current market interest rates are 5 per cent per annum?

$$PV = £100,000 \times \frac{1}{\left(1 + \left(0.05 \times \frac{182}{365}\right)\right)} = £97,567.49$$

This means you would need to invest £97,567.49 for 182 days at a rate of 5 per cent to end up with £100,000.

The present value and future value are related by a **discount** factor. The expression for a discount factor over one year is:

$$Df = [1 + i\,\%]$$

Where the period in question is shorter than one year, this becomes:

$$Df = \{1 + [i\,\% \text{ x days/year}]\}$$

Where the period in question is more than a year, (say two years) this becomes:

$$Df = [1 + i\,\%]^2$$

EXAMPLE

We need to value a security with a future value of US$100,000.

The maturity date is exactly eight years from now and assumes that the annual yield is 4.24 per cent for each year. What is the present value of this security?

$$PV = \frac{\$100{,}000}{(1 + 0.0424)^8}$$

$$= \frac{\$100{,}000}{(1.0424)^8}$$

$$= \frac{\$100{,}000}{1.39403996}$$

$$= \$71{,}733.96$$

Marking to market (MTM)

This is essentially how to value something – a subject that has been foremost in people's minds, since the credit crunch. Marking to market is the way that firms, not just banks, establish the current value of financial assets which they are holding. These assets may be loans, investments in bonds or equity, or holdings in derivatives or structured finance products such as CDOs, swaps or options.

Simplified example

Yesterday, you purchased green apples at 90p a pound, so you are 'long' apples. Today, at close of business, the price for the same green apples is quoted at 92p. Even though you have not sold them – you could have, and at a better price, thus making a 2p profit. This is known as a notional profit or an unrealised profit. You still have the apples. Tomorrow, the closing price may be 93p a pound, and then your notional profit will be 3p and so on. The notional profit (or loss) will fluctuate with market movements. On some days you may lose as the price falls. Today, on a mark-to-market basis you made a notional profit of 2p per pound. The difference between an unrealised profit or loss (**P/L**) and a realised one is this; an unrealised profit or loss will fluctuate for the time you continue to hold the asset, whereas realised profit or loss is fixed when you sell the asset.

However, the closing price used for any valuation must be an independent price, such as one displayed on a Reuters or Bloomberg network or via an independent market provider such as Markit. What if the closing price for your apples was quoted at

89–91; would you have made or lost money? You would have lost 1p because you can only sell the apples where another purchaser will buy them, in this case at 89p. It is important, where possible, to take into account the bid-offer spread when marking to market.

take into account the bid-offer spread when marking to market

With derivatives, another question arises; continuing the same analogy with our green apples, what if the only closing price available is for red apples? Can you use it if there is nothing else? No unless you can construct a relationship along these lines, green apples = red apples + *x* pence.

As derivatives become more complex it is harder and harder to mark to market as there may be no published prices. In addition, many of the derivatives have cash flows stretching over years into the future. These will all need to be given a NPV and compared with current prices to establish whether there is a mark-to-market gain or loss on the transaction.

During the credit crunch, it became impossible to do a mark to market for many sub-prime instruments. There was a huge overhang of people wanting to sell these related financial assets. However, because no-one wanted to buy them, there was no price to benchmark against. Yet everyone knew the products must be worth more than zero, because the mortgages at the core of most products won't all **default** – will they? Some yes – but not all. You start to see the problem.

The logical next step is to construct a mathematical model to calculate what the assets should be worth. This is known as marking-to-model, which is fine as long as you have market confidence in your model. This is often lacking.

Question: How do we get a benchmark price if no-one is buying and we don't believe our financial models?

Answer (1) Get the banks to set up special investment vehicles (SIVs) off-shore in places like the Cayman Islands, then they can buy the questionable assets and then they are 'off-balance sheet'. The market saw through that!

Answer (2) Get the US government and an assortment of central banks worldwide to buy them!

Answer (3) Create a marking-to-hold price, which reflects that the assets may be kept on the balance sheet for some time.

Collateral management

The concept of providing security and collateral against lending or other financial risk is not new. Why is it taken? So that if the client defaults you have something of theirs to sell, *but* taking collateral does not stop the client defaulting, it does, however, improve your rate of recovery. Typical collateral used to include property, precious metals, securities and cash. However, you could argue that this in itself has led to increased operational, documentation, legal and valuation risks. It goes without saying, that if the objective is to have something to sell, the asset itself must be liquid, valuable and legally watertight.

These are the reasons for taking collateral:

- To reduce, not eliminate, credit risk.
- To reduce exposure to do more business when credit lines are under pressure.
- Maybe one party can only deal with another with collateral, because of their own counterparty credit ratings policy.
- To net exposure to achieve regulatory capital savings under **Basel II** regulations.
- To offer keener prices.
- To improve market liquidity by collateralising derivatives exposures.

Under Basel II, which is one of the banking regulations, banks that collateralise their **over the counter (OTC)** derivatives positions, especially their credit derivatives, are allowed to post lower levels of regulatory capital. This is a big incentive. It was the asset management, banks and hedge fund community that wanted to withdraw their collateral, all at the same time, which put huge pressure on Bear Stearns and led to its illiquidity and collapse in March 2008. The OTC market requires that the ISDA documentation for collateral management is put in place, notably the appropriate credit support annexe (CSA) – see Chapter 9.

For details see www.isda.org

Market conditions as the credit crunch continues still require collateral that was linked to the credit ratings of both the buyer and seller in the transaction and the valuation of their respective derivatives positions with each other. Both buyers and sellers will post collateral with each other, which may include these assets:

- cash;
- government securities – often G10 only (Belgium, Canada, France, Italy, UK, Japan, Netherlands, US, Germany and Sweden. Switzerland joined later but the group is still called the G10!);
- mortgage-backed securities;
- corporate bonds;
- letters of credit;
- equities.

Note that about 85 per cent of all collateral is cash or G10 securities – with a huge emphasis on cash.

Those working in the collateral management department of a bank or financial institution may need to:

- record details of the collateral relationship in the system;
- monitor client exposure and collateral received/posted on agreed mark-to-market frequency – often daily;
- call for margin as required, taking into account,
  - collateral already held, thresholds, minimum transfer amounts and rounding;
  - to transfer collateral to the other party if a valid call has been made;

- to check collateral is eligible once it is received;
- to ensure the pledged collateral is transferred within the agreed time period when a custodian involved, under pledge documentation;
- deal with fails, i.e. collateral not delivered;
- call for collateral;
- apply **haircuts** to collateral received/paid;
- re-use collateral where permitted;
- return surplus collateral in accordance with terms of documentation;
- deal with request for substitutions;
- pay over coupons on securities to collateral providers (repos) – may be outsourced to **corporate actions** department;
- pay over interest on cash collateral and monitor its receipt;
- deal with disagreements over valuations as they arise;
- act as valuation agent where agreed;
- reconcile portfolios of transactions at regular intervals;
- co-ordinate exposure and collateral valuations of various branches, if collateral management is centralised;
- deal with default situations (involving legal and credit functions);
- become involved in collateral agreement negotiation;
- perform special projects;
- establish best use of collateral.

collateral management has become big business

As you can see, collateral management has become big business, especially in the derivatives arena with some banks employing hundreds of people for the task.

Netting

Netting is a term used for off-setting similar/reversing trades with the same counterparty. For example:

I buy ten **futures** contracts in the morning from Bank A.

I sell ten futures contracts in the afternoon to Bank C.

Net position = 0

Netting is easy to achieve using **exchange-traded** derivatives because the clearing house is acting as a central counterparty. It is less easy where the products are OTC and banks may all look at this a bit differently. Obviously, if the positions can be netted off it is going to affect the collateral requirements.

Option pricing models

This section was written by Dr David Gershon, chief executive of SuperDerivatives.

Options, which are a derivative product, can be based on underlying assets such as currencies, equities, commodities and interest rates. Their main use is to mitigate the risk of economic loss from changes in the value of the underlying asset – an activity known as hedging. Alternatively, derivatives can be used by investors to speculate and increase the profit arising if the value of the underlying asset moves in the direction they expect.

Derivatives are measured and priced as assets or liabilities at fair value but their complexity requires the best tools and market data from an independent source to price derivatives accurately. Pricing of options depends on factors such as data quality, operational and technology support, models, implementation and skill in using the models. Each of these ingredients is instrumental in producing a verifiable price level.

The price that matters for a trading operation is the execution price, i.e. the price of an actual transaction taking place. Immediately related to execution price are the bid and offer quotes. These depend on factors such as the size of an order, counterparty risk, competitive situation and relationship between the counterparties.

Market conditions mean we also need to look at the accounting price, which is the price of a security when held on the books of a trading entity, rather than the transactional price when the security is changing hands. The accounting price is a much less certain number and depends on additional factors including liquidity levels, similarity to traded securities, available market data, pricing models, documentation and legal considerations.

The current standard is the mark-to-market price, which is the price that an asset would fetch on the market if sold immediately. Recently, however, mark-to-holding has been promoted as an alternative, especially when liquidity is a concern. In the mark-to-holding approach, the price of an asset is derived from an assumption that the asset will be held on the books until maturity. It is argued that this accounting method will avoid penalising financial institutions and corporations, which are engaged in long-term investment in complex assets.

Mark-to-holding value of even a good asset in difficult market conditions is not unlike trying to drive a car on a road full of potholes. Even if the car happens to be in a good condition, the environment renders the value of the car much smaller than its condition implies.

Mark-to-market is the current preferred method of valuation, truly reflecting the market conditions and potential benefits of holding a security. If valuations are done prudently and expertly, it reduces the valuation uncertainty.

Pricing of any financial instrument, derivative or not, depends on many factors, of which quality data is the first critical ingredient. Instrument coverage is almost just as important, as it is desirable to work with a single valuation provider for all instruments. This helps to reduce operational risk and overheads and to keep this option cost effective.

Quality and reliability of the data is the key to good pricing. Together with transparent models and assumptions, this ensures that pricing is done with the best available market information.

Given current market conditions, valuing complex options based on a theoretical model is no longer enough. The need is now acute for institutions to take stock and revisit how they value their portfolios, and the regulators agree.

For many years there has been a danger of over-reliance on standalone models for pricing options, and the credit crunch brought the reality of those dangers home with institutions unable to accurately value their holdings.

A new system is needed to value options as the limitations become all the more profound and more and more institutions have struggled to gauge an accurate picture of their options holdings.

The heart of the issue is that models such as Black-Scholes, for example, assume that everything, apart from the spot rate of the underlying product, is constant through the life of a given option.

This became the initial benchmark and consistent way to price options, which led to exponential growth in the market and liquidity as traders chose to adopt the model not only for pricing and revaluation, but also to develop more advanced options.

In reality, the fluctuation of the underlying spot rate and interest rates change frequently, so many models were unable to provide realistic, real-time pricing for options, which experience volatility changes over their lifetime.

The difficulties of achieving an accurate valuation become even more pronounced when pricing advanced or **exotic options** because of their illiquidity. This means that the price often cannot be corrected through periods of volatility.

the price often cannot be corrected through periods of volatility

Despite all of these limitations, many participants in the market have been reluctant to take a fresh approach to option pricing, or to consider different models or methodologies for valuing derivatives.

In the credit crisis, it transpired that the amount of illiquid products held by financial institutions was so large that uncertainty in the valuation losses was big enough to put a question mark on the financial strength of institutions. Now, we are operating in an environment where regulators are finally advising companies to seek independent valuation services that provide the widest coverage of financial products and deliver pricing that is reflective of the real and current market and not some theoretical estimation.

This is to be welcomed as the right move for an open and orderly options marketplace. The regulators are finally getting it right and this is critical to restore faith in the options markets, and a sense of impartial balance to the way individual options and overall portfolios are priced.

The options market as a whole must now seek to rebuild confidence and trust through more transparent valuations and asset pricing. At its core is the urgent need for institutions to accurately value and manage their options portfolios.

What is now needed is a critical, effective look at methodologies to value both straightforward and advanced derivatives.

The model or methodology used must be independent of any single trading counterparty interest, it must be robust, proven and based on varied market data that truly reflect the market prices of derivatives.

A trusted valuation service can give a wealth of detail and a snapshot of real-time prices of derivatives, providing a clear picture of the value of the **portfolio** at the desired valuation time.

A well thought-out options valuation model should also provide sensitivity analysis for illiquid options products so one can assess the level of price risk that stems from illiquidity when unwinding trades.

The SuperDerivatives methodology's accuracy in generating prices for all types of derivatives has now been empirically proven and validated continuously. The key was to source pricing from the widest range of brokers, banks, central banks and funds, effectively establishing an independent global market data network to feed the pricing model.

This means that institutions using the system are able to gain an unbiased insight into the market and can gain a real-time price or valuation before or after buying an option. Independence and an unbiased approach were key to meeting the need in the market.

There is no substitute for transparency and accuracy throughout the financial services industry.

Forward rates: fair value calculations

Of supreme importance in the financial and derivatives market is the ability to ascertain whether an instrument is trading cheap or trading expensive. This is ascertained by comparing the price of the asset now to the price where it is expected to trade by incorporating all known current market data in the price, arriving at a figure known as **fair value**. This is where it is expected to trade.

All financial instruments are priced by comparing the requested structure with the current market price. Ascertaining the true underlying 'benchmark' for comparison prices means deciding on:

- the benchmark;
- whether to use the forward price or the current spot price;
- how to arrive at 'fair value'.

Calculating forward rates for a commodity

Consider one of the metals, say copper. Assume a customer has asked a bank or a copper trader for a sixth-month forward price. The current spot rate at the time may be $3,150 a tonne. We need to estimate, not where copper will be trading in six months' time (that would be a guess on the spot rate) but what rate the quoting party can live with, if it is asked to guarantee the price. The only way to do this safely is to purchase the copper now at today's known spot rate and factor in all the additional costs (known as cost of carry):

- Financing: how does the bank/trader pay for the copper now if the client is not going to pay for six months? The money will need to be borrowed for six months at $ LIBOR, assume 1.0% per annum.

- Storage: what does the bank/trader do with the copper for six months? Assume it cannot be loaned to anyone else in the meantime.
- Transport and insurance: if appropriate.

Assume the additional costs (per tonne at $3,150) are:

- Finance: $15.84.
- Storage: $15.
- Transport and insurance: $12.
- Total cost of carry is $42.84.

The true cost of this transaction to the bank/trader is therefore:

$3,150 + $42.84 = $3,192.84

This is the fair value of the forward. It is a breakeven price and a profit margin will then be added on top. This pricing relationship can be summarised as:

Spot + Cost of carry = Forward price (theoretical)

There is a drawback with this: it assumes that nothing will change, yet we know it will, so this is not a forecast. Simply, given everything we know today, this is where the asset *should* be trading!

Forward pricing for all assets works in much the same way.

You need to know the spot rate, then gather the data for the cost of carry. The forward rate becomes the rate where everything is included and is a breakeven rate. A profit margin may be added later.

Pricing forward interest rates is more difficult and this is explained below.

Calculating forward interest rates

This is known as a **forward/forward** calculation or an implied forward calculation, or even a 'fair-value' calculation and uses information known today to infer where a particular asset will trade on a date in the future.

EXAMPLE

A client wants to know the rate on a six-month borrowing of £5 million, which will be drawn-down (borrowed) in three months' time. Because financial markets change continuously, the bank is unable to guarantee the rate three months in advance – unless it takes on the risk of moving market rates. However, the bank can calculate where the interest rate should be. It can then advise the client, but unless the client wants to enter into some sort of a hedging derivative, there will be no guarantee.

Strategy: in simple terms, the bank can borrow the money (on behalf of the client) for nine months at today's LIBOR rate, but the client does not want the money until the end of the third month. This gives the bank the opportunity to invest the money for the first three months at LIBID. At maturity in three months' time, the deposit is returned with interest and is then ready and available for the client for the six-month borrowing.

Assume these periods and interest rates are quoted in the market:

- 6-month GBP (181 days);
- 3-month (90 days);
- 9-month (271 days);
- 9-month 4.87-4.84%;
- 6-month 4.84-4.82%;
- 3-month 4.81-4.79%.

Forward/Forward rates are calculated using off-setting LIBOR/LIBID rates. The standard forward rate break-even formula is:

$$(1+r_2t_2) = (1+r_1t_1)(1+r_ft_f)$$

see Figure 1.2 for a graphical representation of the example, using the following terms:

r_2 = interest rate for the long period (LIBOR).

r_1 = interest rate for the short period (LIBID).

r_{gap} = interest rate for the gap period in question.

t_2 = time period from today until end of long period.

t_1 = time period from today until end of short period.

t_{gap} = contract period – forward gap (t_2-t_1).

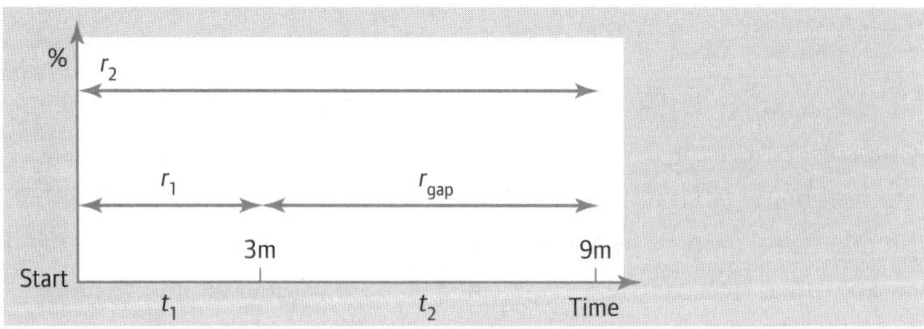

FIGURE 1.2 Calculating implied forward rates

As we shall quote the number of days in the period, we will use '*n*' (days) instead of '*t*' (time period) and re-arrange the formula:

$$r_{gap} = \frac{r_2 n_2 - r_1 n_1}{n_{gap}[1+(r_1 \times n_1/365)]}$$

Substituting the actual data gives:

$$r_{gap} = \frac{(4.87\% \times 271) - (4.79\% \times 90)}{181\ [1+(4.79\% \times 90/365)]}$$

$$= 4.85247\%$$

This, then, is the rate the bank could quote for the transaction commencing in three months' time for a period of six months, finishing at the end of month nine.

Yield curves

A **yield curve** is a graphical representation of interest yields against time. In the US, this is known as the 'term structure of interest rates'. There are different styles of yield curves, e.g. zero coupon curves, swap curves and forward curves. The simplest curve is known as the **par** curve. It is usually drawn using the **gross redemption yield (GRY)** on risk-free instruments such as government bonds, e.g., UK Gilts and **UK Treasury bills**, or US **Treasury bills** and US **Treasury bonds**. The shape of the yield curve (Figure 1.3) is an important consideration when choosing whether or not to use derivatives, and indeed whether to borrow short and lend long, or vice versa. If three-month interest rates are 2 per cent and twelve-month interest rates are 5 per cent, it makes good business to borrow short-term at 2 per cent and lend long term at 5 per cent. However, an interest rate risk arises when at the

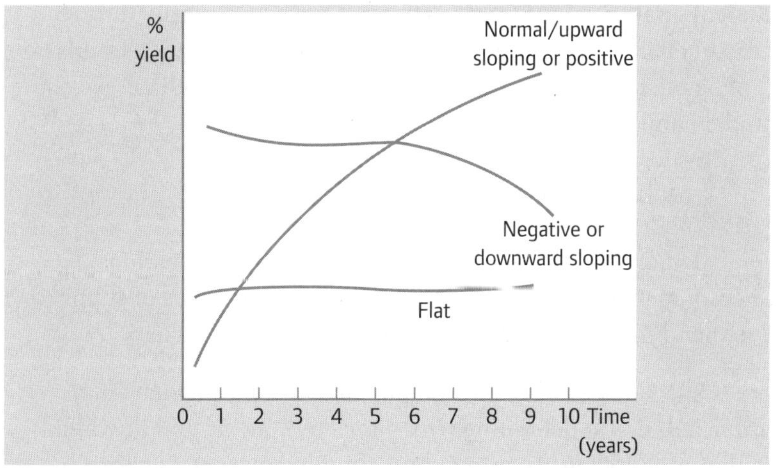

FIGURE 1.3 Yield curves

Source: *Mastering Derivatives Markets* by Francesa Taylor, Pearson Education, 2007.

end of three months, the loan has to be repaid to the lender and another three-month borrowing will need to be arranged – but what will be the new three-month rate? This obviously needs to be managed carefully. An upward sloping yield curve (positive) is one where, as the maturity lengthens, interest rates tend to increase as investors seek higher yields for locking up their money for longer periods at fixed rates. A downward sloping yield curve (negative) is one where as the maturity lengthens, the less reward the investor gets and the cheaper borrowing becomes. This type of curve is usually an indicator of reducing inflationary tendencies. A flat yield curve indicates a stable inflationary environment – not necessarily a zero inflation rate.

Technical analysis

It is estimated that more than half of the trading in US large cap stocks is carried out by computers. Electronic trading platforms have replaced human market makers and computerised models are taking the trading decisions. This has resulted in a mass of electronically reported data, making real-time technical analysis available to everyone. Many of the models are built around traditional technical analysis techniques, such as **momentum**-based models.

Technical analysis is the study of market action, primarily through the use of charts, for the purpose of forecasting future price trends. Do not be misled! Technical analysis is not a 'crystal ball', however, an understanding of the techniques is essential.

technical analysis is not a 'crystal ball'

Technical analysis concentrates on the study of market action, while fundamental analysis looks at the economic forces of supply and demand that cause markets to rise, fall or stay the same.

There is still no substitute for fundamental analysis, which an investor will use to determine why prices will move, and in which direction. But how many people buy, thinking an asset is cheap, only to find that it then gets a lot cheaper? Or take a profit way too early? This is where technical analysis is crucial:

- Timing when to buy or sell.
- Applying a disciplined approach to trading/investing.

Trend analysis

A trend has three directions as shown in Figure 1.4.

The concept of **trend** is essential to the technical approach to market analysis. You may have heard the following:

- The trend is your friend.
- Never buck the trend.

Obvious? But, a 'technician' will identify a rising trend and follow a long-only strategy, meaning looking for levels to buy and then take profit, then maybe buy again, but never short. In an uptrend, 'higher highs and higher lows' is very important. If a peak does not rise above the last peak, then it is an early warning that the trend may be about to fail.

Conversely, if the trend is down, a technician will adopt a short-only strategy. Short sell and look for lower levels to buy back, and then look for opportunities to short again.

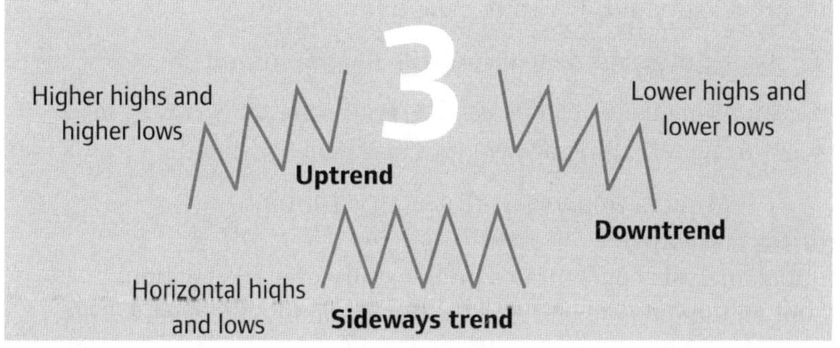

FIGURE 1.4 A trend has three directions

Trend lines

The drawing of 'trend lines' can be very individual. As you can see in Figure 1.5 the only important lines should pick up levels to short (in a downtrend) and levels to buy (in an uptrend). Nothing else is necessary; the trader just needs the trend in place, and, crucially, to look for possible trend breaks. Notice the early warning signal in the downtrend, where the lower low failed, indicated a possible trend change. This was followed by a break, which needs to be confirmed, by:

FIGURE 1.5 Forex chart (GBP/USD)

Source: Thomson Reuters

- The price action needs to break the trendline.
- The closing price needs to be outside the trendline.
- Price and time filters can be used as confirmation (per cent price break through the line, or two days breaking the line).

Moving averages

Moving averages are constructed using the mean of closing prices over different time periods. Figure 1.6 shows five-day and fifteen-day moving averages. The five-day average 'hugs' the price, and the fifteen-day average will 'lag behind' the price. When the averages cross, a signal is generated.

Note that moving averages follow trends and are useless in sideways-trending markets. So, trend analysis first. The moving average should be one of several technical indicators confirming an entry to a trade. Where they excel, is in maximising the profit potential to a trade. The natural human tendency is to grab a profit too quickly, but the averages will allow the position to run until the trend has broken.

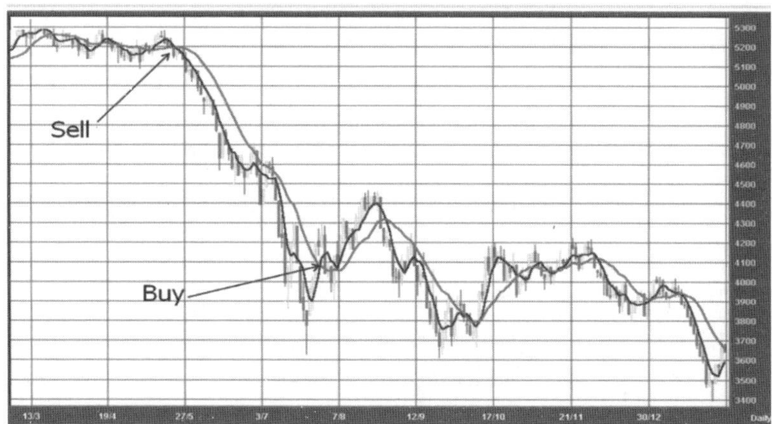

FIGURE 1.6 Moving averages (FTSE 100 chart)

Source: Thomson Reuters

What does the technical analyst see?

Figure 1.7 overleaf shows the FTSE 100 over an eleven-month period in 2001.

The technical analyst will see:

1. Downtrend in place so looking for shorting opportunities, or timing when to **hedge** an equity portfolio.
2. Long term support breaking at 5,300.
3. Moving averages crossing.
4. Trending triangle breakout.
5. Pattern recognition.
6. The timing is narrowed to an exact day for when to trade.

The market has broken on the downside, and hedging is initiated, or a short position instigated. The market goes into freefall, and notice one week later is 11 September 2001. The technicals have already told you not to be long, hedge downside risk or instigate a short strategy, and they have indicated when.

Technical analysis, is a natural companion to fundamental analysis, and should be used as an aid to timing when taking decisions. It helps you get into a trade and also indicates when to get out, and is an important part of trading discipline. Technical analysis is said to be self-perpetuating: as more people use it, then it carries more weight.

What you have to ask yourself is: 'Can you afford not to have a good grasp of the techniques?'

Credit crunch

Much has been written about the credit crunch and this section simply describes how the situation evolved and the main repercussions.

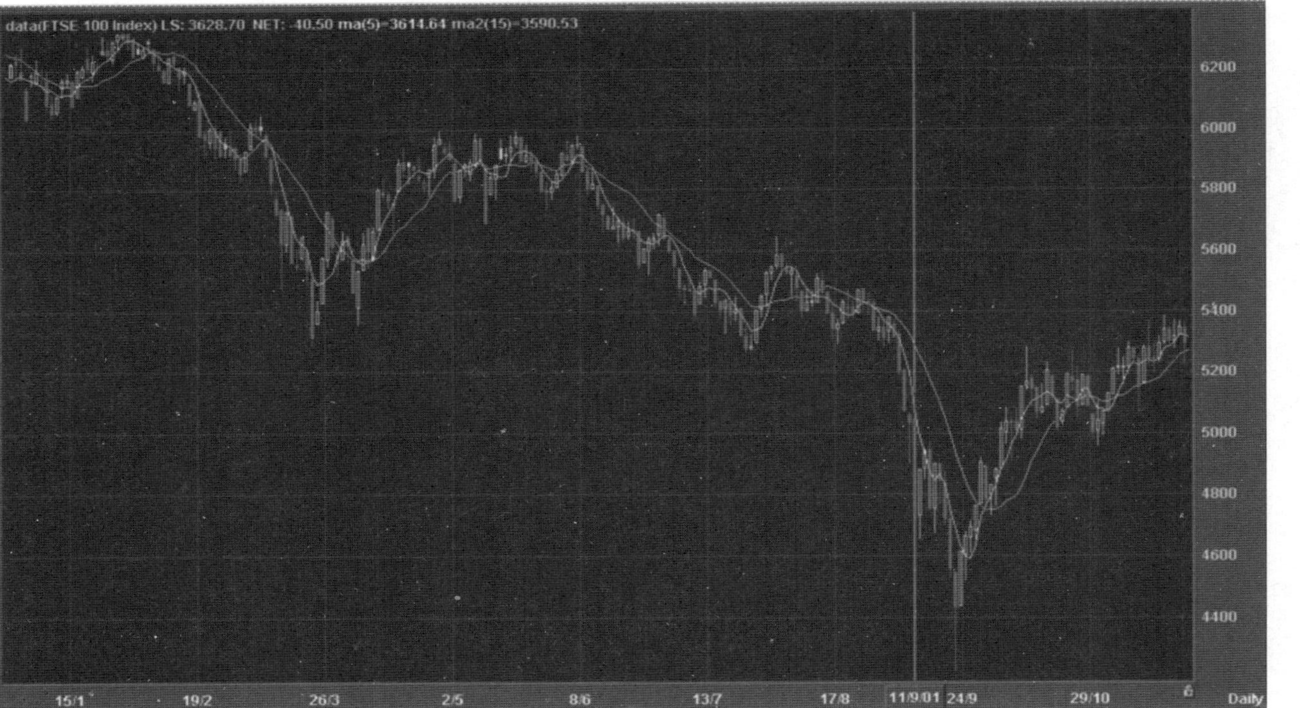

FIGURE 1.7 What does the technical analyst see?

Source: Thomson Reuters

In the mid 1990s – thanks to the US government's drive to increase home ownership, the banks were encouraged to increase mortgage lending to some of the poorer communities. For a number of reasons, these borrowers were known as 'subprime' customers and were often families that had found it hard to get credit in the past. The reasons for their lack of credit included: the fact that they had defaulted on loans before; they had been made bankrupt; were unemployed; had erratic and/or part-time employment; a criminal rocord; no assets – in short they had a high expected rate of default.

Some of the local US banks employed brokers to garner more business. These brokers were paid based on the number of mortgages they signed up. Naturally, the brokers wanted to sign up as many people as possible and they allowed the borrowers to self certify their income when making their loan applications. This meant the potential borrower did not need to supply wage or salary slips.

the potential borrower did not need to supply wage or salary slips

These loans became known as 'Ninja loans' (no income, no job and no assets). During this period a rosy outlook had been forecast for the US housing market. However, it was expected that 5–10 per cent of these borrowers would default and this was factored in to the loans. For some time, this default rate was manageable, but then the loan arrears started to escalate above 15 per cent and beyond, as the economy weakened (Figure 1.8).

The banks that had lent the mortgage funds started to get nervous and wondered how they were going to get their money back – some were concerned as early as the year 2000.

During this period the investment banking community and the big commercial banks had employed staff known as Quants or Structurers. These are individuals with maths, physics or astronomy degrees. The quants designed products that, put simply, allowed the original lenders to package up thousands of these mortgages into products known as mortgage backed securities (MBS) and sell them on to investors. That meant the original lenders could get most of their money out as the investors then

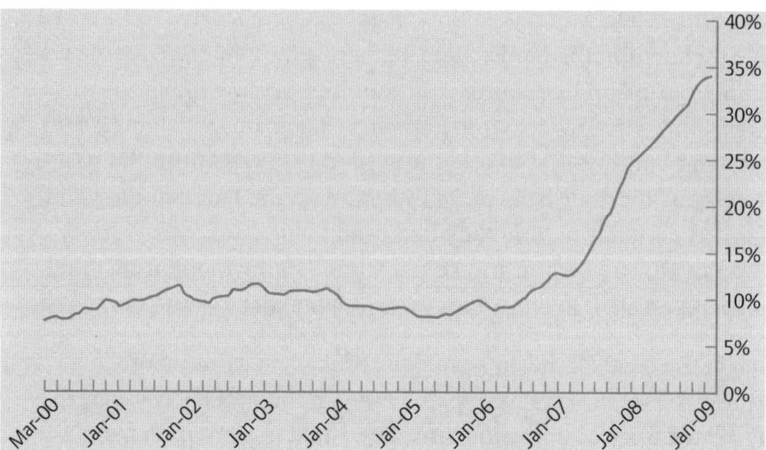

FIGURE 1.8 Share of US subprime loans 60 or more days in arrears, by value

Source: First American CoreLogic, LoanPerformance data

bought the MBS and so took on the **default risk**. The appeal for the investor was a high rate of return. Over the next few years there was an explosion of related products, which all used the basic concept of packaging up assets and selling them to third parties. The more exotic of these used derivatives and one of the most popular ones was the CDO – collateralised debt obligation (collateralised debt as it includes mortgages *and* loans). See Chapter 2 for details of how these work.

To encourage investors, the majority of these structured products had tranches (slices) of debt linked to them, and each slice had an independent credit rating from a rating agency such as Standard and Poor's or Moody's. The investor could buy the slice – or the part of the slice where he felt most comfortable with the risk.

The investment bank that designed the CDO for the original mortgage lenders would have charged a fee. Some of these instruments were also insured with the **monoline** insurers to protect the investor in the case of default.

So, in summary:

1. The broker was paid per mortgage – and is no longer involved.
2. The original mortgage lender is now repaid.
3. The investment bank charged a fee to structure the CDO.
4. The rating agency has charged fees to rate the tranches.
5. The monoline insurer has charged an insurance premium.
6. The investors have bought securities linked to the CDO.

So what happened next?

As the housing situation worsened and defaults spiralled, more and more borrowers were in danger of losing their homes. Many then tried to sell their homes – all at the same time, which depressed house prices further, resulting in a huge overhang of, effectively, un-saleable properties.

The investors who had bought these mortgage-linked assets included banks, hedge funds, pension funds, asset managers, in fact almost everyone around the world had some exposure. And, naturally enough, if the market worsens and the price of your investment starts to fall and you are holding something you don't like, you will try and sell it. Everyone tried to sell at once – depressing the prices again.

Question: How do you value an asset if you cannot sell it as no-one is buying?

Answer: You don't. So is the real answer, it is worth zero? Or do you assume these assets must be worth something because not all the subprime borrowers will default.

This is the crux of the problem with the credit crunch!

No one really knew with any certainty what these assets were worth and the financial community owned a lot of them.

Picture this: two banks that would normally lend money to each other in the LIBOR market, both have exposure to this 'toxic' debt. Each knows it has a lot and cannot value the debt with certainty, so why would it led money to a bank that might be in a worse position? The other bank might be unable to repay the loan because its mortgage-related debt might overwhelm it.

The result of this was that LIBOR funding, which is the lifeblood of business, became more expensive and eventually dried up. This became known as the 'LIBOR disconnect' as LIBOR disconnected from all normal lending rates. It was this phenomenon that led to the downfall of Northern Rock in the UK.

There have been various government initiatives with money being made available to purchase this toxic debt from the banks to give them the confidence to start lending again. So far, none of these initiatives has actually bought any debt and the banks are still facing the same problems.

In 2009, there was a crisis of confidence.

Further reading

Mastering Financial Calculations by Bob Steiner, 2008, Financial Times Prentice Hall, 2nd edition.

British Bankers Association, www.bba.org.

International Swaps and Derivatives Association, www.isda.org.

SuperDerivatives, www.superderivatives.com.

2 Key instruments in the financial markets

...as an analogy, this is for readers who want to know that their car will take them safely from A to B, but who don't neccessarily want or need to know how the engine works!

- Introduction
- Securities markets: money market transactions
- Securities markets: bond markets (fixed income)
- Securities markets: equity
- Repo
- Spot and forward foreign exchange
- Derivatives: OTC and exchange traded instruments
- Financial futures
- Rate swaps (IRS)
- Options
- Credit default swaps (CDS)
- Asset swaps
- Collateralised debt obligations (CDOs)

Introduction

I am often asked for a simple explanation of some of the core financial instruments. Whilst many of these individual products may well have books devoted to them, this chapter covers their main uses and applications. As an analogy, this is for readers who want to know that their car will take them safely from A to B, but who don't necessarily want or need to know how the engine works! They may also be regarded as 'pills' of knowledge – akin to a quick refresher on a topic before going into a meeting. The list is not exhaustive, but the instruments are those that I would have liked to have had an understanding of when I started in finance. Almost all of the complex products that have been subsequently 'engineered' will have originated somewhere here.

Figure 2.1 shows the four building blocks of the capital markets: money markets, medium-term loans, bonds, and equity. These are collectively known as the securities markets. These provide the main ways for borrowing or investing money, with differing time horizons and differing risk/reward profiles.

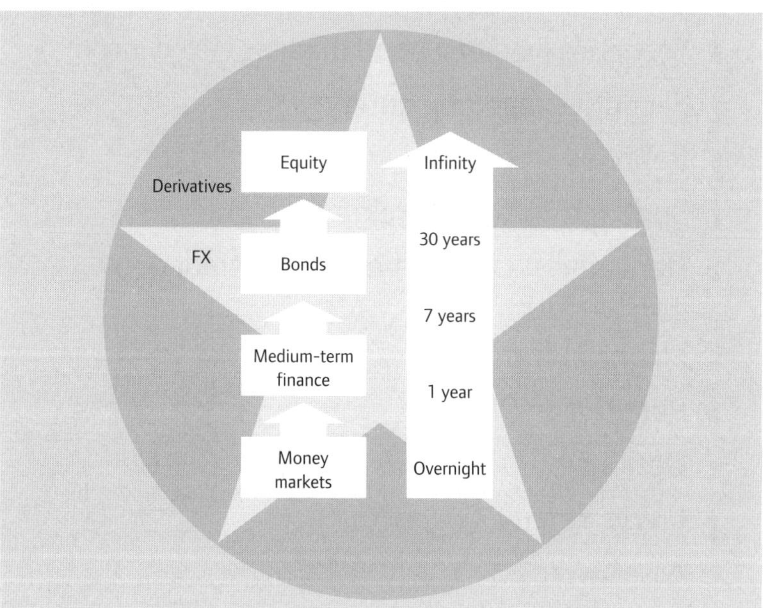

FIGURE 2.1 Market overview

Securities markets: money market transactions

DEFINITION

A money market-transaction is a loan or a deposit with a maturity period of up to twelve months. Interest is calculated on a simple interest basis (not compounded), paid at maturity, and is based on the exact number of days in the transaction period. The lender of the money takes the credit risk (risk of default) and interest rates are often linked to LIBOR

The majority of money market transactions in the one to three month band and will be in the home currency, e.g. pounds in the UK, dollars in the US and euros in 'euroland'. These are often known as 'short' term or 'cash market' transactions. The shortest period available is one day, which is known as 'over-night'. For example, if today is Tuesday and you borrow £5 million over-night, the cash will be in your account today and you will need to repay £5 million plus one day of interest on Wednesday. The longest period available within the money market framework is twelve months. This is because all interest is quoted on an annual basis. Market convention is for interest to be paid at maturity – known as 'in arrears'. If you borrow for three months, you pay in three months, likewise for six or twelve months. But what if you borrow for eighteen months and pay interest at maturity? Then you would need to take account of interest on interest (known as compounding). To avoid the need to do this, ensure money market transactions are twelve months or less. This doesn't mean you can't have a transaction for eighteen months, you could, but you would be paying interest in instalments every six months.

EXAMPLE

On 26 August 2010, a UK company wishes to invest £5 million for three months. It will have one or a group of banks who could quote for this transaction, assume these are the quotes:

- Bank A: 3.35%.
- Bank B: 3.25%.
- Bank C: 3.25%.

Bank A has quoted the most favourable price of 3.35 per cent. As this is an annual rate, because the investment is for three months, the exact number of days in this transaction period has to be established.

TIP

Calculate the number of nights, not number of days – less error prone!

The transaction period is 26 August 2010 to 26 November 2010, and the exact number of days is 92 (5 in Aug, 30 in Sep, 31 in Oct and 26 in Nov = 92). We then need to look at the correct 'day count' for the currency, which is what determines how many days per annum for an interest calculation. As shown in Chapter 1, in the UK it's 365 days (366 for leap years).

$$£5,000,000 \times 3.35\% \times 92/365 = £42,919.18$$

The transaction will be placed on 26 August 2010 and must be repaid with interest on 26 November 2010. Obviously, if the repayment date is a weekend or public holiday, this must be taken account of. You would either go one day forward or back to the Friday, this will therefore affect the number of days in the calculation.

Medium term finance

Figure 2.1 uses the term, medium term finance, which covers transactions that may look like money market deals but are, in fact, longer than twelve months. In this situation, interest is not normally paid at maturity because this could be five years away and constitutes a long-term credit risk on the interest. It is far safer for the lender to have the borrower pay them interest in instalments – usually every three or six months, again based on the number of days in that six-month period. Many of these loans have an interest rate that is re-fixed every time an interest payment is made, giving rise to the term 'variable' or 'floating rate' finance. The interest rate is usually a rate such as LIBOR or EURIBOR.

If the loan amount required by the borrower is substantial it is likely that there will be syndication, leading to the term **syndicated loan**. This means that several banks will share in the lending of the money (and also therefore in the credit risk). For example, a €500m loan may be syndicated between ten banks, each lending €50m and each taking a share of the credit risk.

Securities markets: bond markets (fixed income)

Once the maturity of a transaction stretches beyond about seven years it becomes more cost effective to borrow through the fixed-income or bond markets. Maturities here can range from seven years to thirty years and as far as one hundred years, sometimes to the 'perpetual' markets which are, in effect, infinity!

DEFINITION

A **bond** is a fixed-income security whose future cash flows have been contractually determined in advance. It will be issued at a price appropriate for market conditions and redeemed on a pre-set maturity date at 100 (at 100 per cent of face value), known as **par**. If the bond is linked to a fixed-interest rate it is called a straight, if it is linked to a variable floating rate like LIBOR or EURIBOR, it is known as a – **floating rate note (FRN)**.

The fixed-income or bond markets are largely the province of the big commercial and investment banks who will undertake the design and structuring, the pricing, the marketing and selling and the provision of secondary market trading and prices. Typically, the borrower will need to borrow at least £100 million, $150 million, and need to borrow for longer than seven years for the bond to work optimally. That is not to say you can't have them smaller, shorter or longer.

The borrower must pay a fee to the investment bank for its services, which can be amortised over the life of the bond, so in relative terms the longer the bond, the cheaper the annual cost of the fee. The borrower must also pay an interest cost to the lender of the money.

Terminology is also different:

- **Issuers** (or borrowers) need to raise money to cover short or long-term needs.
- **Investors** (or depositors) seek suitable returns.
- **Intermediaries** put the two main participants together and aim to earn fees and commissions.

Disintermediation

Banks use their extensive networks to find finance for bond market transactions from professional investors such as hedge funds and asset managers – they are not lending their own bank's money. This is known as **disintermediation** and is a key difference between bond transactions and standard bank loans. It affects credit risk because the investment bank is not lending its own money for a bond transaction, whereas a high street bank is lending its own money to one of its clients. The effects will be felt most keenly if there is a default. With a standard loan, the lending bank will take the whole credit risk; with a bond the investment bank does not take this risk – the asset managers or investors take this risk directly. Instead, the bank acting as arranger will take the risk that if the design, structuring or issuance process fails its reputation will be damaged – not its credit risk. This is known as 'brand damage'.

EXAMPLE

A US firm, Company B, wishes to borrow $500 million for ten years, but has never borrowed for this length of time before. First, it will need to choose which investment bank to use. This may well be organised via a **'beauty parade'**, where three or more banks are asked to come up with ideas and quote for the business. Company B will then decide, based on structure, financing and costs, which bank it wants for the bond issue. Up until this point the banks cannot charge a fee for their time and effort, which is often considerable. Once the winning bank is chosen, the mandate is awarded and fees can now start to be charged to Company B.

The investment bank must now sit down with the client and discuss structures, currencies, terms, as well as the potential investor appetite for such factors, with a view to coming up with a working design. This stage could take some months. Eventually, Company B and the bank will agree on structure and timing and usually the last thing the bank does is set the issue price of the bond, often as little as the day before the issue hits the markets.

This is the price that will be paid by the investors; even though the bond will have a face value (principal) of $500 million the minimum transaction size (purchase amount) may well be only $500,000. This allows a range of investors to buy a piece of the bond. A successful bond issue will be oversubscribed with more buyers than required, ensuring a healthy price increase when the bond starts on the trading secondary market, but not too oversubscribed because this would indicate the bond was issued too cheaply.

NOTE

The issue price is only good on the day of issue; subsequently the bond price will fluctuate with market conditions.

What does the borrower (issuer) achieve?

Company B has borrowed money for ten years at competitive rates and will be paying interest once or twice a year to the investors and it must allow for the banking fees to arrive at the total all-in cost.

The all-in costs should still be more competitive than borrowing fixed-rate money for ten years from a bank. At maturity in ten years' time, it will need to repay the investors their money.

What does the investor achieve?

The investor has the choice of investing in a range of bond issues with differing risk and reward profiles. Although a bond may have a ten-year maturity, the investor does not need to hold the investment for ten years; in fact he could buy it today and sell it after a few days. He is guaranteed a fixed-interest rate for the duration, known as a '**coupon**'. These instruments are often known as 'fixed-interest' securities. The yield on the investment will be calculated using a gross redemption yield calculation, which takes into account the purchase price of the bond, the various coupons and when they are paid and the final redemption sum.

If you look at a bond price in a newspaper or on a Reuters/Bloomberg screen, you will see the '**clean**' **price**, which is a reflection of the market supply and demand. This does not show any income streams from the bond. Given that individual investors might have held the bond for different periods, we need to establish how much interest has accrued for them – the gross accrued interest – because interest is accrued daily.

EXAMPLE

On 18 October 2009, a UK **Gilt** is sold for settlement on 19 October 2009 (T+1). The Gilt is the 9 per cent Treasury Stock 2012 and is quoted at £105.53125. The investor has held it since the last coupon date.

- Step 1: find the date of the most recent semi-annual interest coupon payment (check gilt details), it was 6 August 2009, and calculate the number of days between this date and the settlement date (19 October), which is 74 days.
- Step 2: gross accrued interest (GIA) to date = £9.00 × 74/365 = £1.8247 per £100 nominal of stock. This must be added to the price agreed between the buyer and seller to compensate the seller for his accrued interest to date.

Therefore the total price paid by the investor is the current market price (the clean price) plus the GAI, making:

> £105.53125 + £1.8247 = £107.36 (after rounding) per £100 nominal of stock.

The combined clean price + gross accrued interest is called the **dirty price** of the bond.

Securities markets: equity

Referring back to Figure 2.1, equity is at the top of the time line because this method of raising finance is very long-term. Another reason why a borrower may consider issuing equity as opposed to a bond is that he may not want to be legally committed to paying interest.

DEFINITION

Equity is a perpetual security with no redemption date. It gives the holder proportional rights to a share of the company profits via variable dividends. In addition, the **holder** has rights to vote on business policy at company meetings, usually the **annual general meeting (AGM)**, and elect the board of directors.

Equity products have similarities with bonds; there is still an issuer, an investor and an intermediary, and the investment bank still, for a fee, supplies a similar service in terms of sourcing the finance and investors, and facilitating secondary market trading. In addition, if this is the first time a client has issued equity, the initial offering will be known as a market listing, **floatation** or **initial public offering (IPO)**.

NOTE

Equity is known as **shares** in the UK and **stock** in the US.

However, there are fundamental differences between bonds and equity. First, equity has no redemption or maturity date, so if you want your money back and you cannot wait until maturity you will need to sell your shares to someone else using the secondary market. Second, the investor will receive a **dividend** – not a coupon, this will be linked to the company performance, is variable and may indeed be zero. This adds flexibility from the issuer's perspective because if times are hard it can decide not to pay the dividend, whereas with a bond the issuer is legally required to pay the coupon or could be involved in litigation. Third, the equity shareholder owns a share of the company and has rights to vote at company meetings; this is not available to bondholders.

TIP

The owners of a company are the shareholders whereas the controller of the company is the board of directors. This can lead to tension.

Equity investments are regarded as the most risky of all investments because if the company fails the equity owner may end up with nothing.

EXAMPLE

A company wishing to raise money via the stock market will have a number of decisions to make. One of the first decisions will be to appoint a professional adviser. This is usually a commercial or investment bank, which has two 'clients'. First, the bank must abide by the rules and regulations of its country's regulator and stock exchange and, second, it must advise its client on the design and structure of the equity issue. A beauty parade may well be undertaken. Why issue equity? Reasons may include the need to:

- raise large amounts of equity from a wide cross section of the general public;
- sell existing blocks of shares to the public;
- raise a small amount of capital;
- re-distribute existing capital to shareholders, i.e. buybacks;
- obtain a stock exchange listing;
- restructure the company's balance sheet.

The arranging bank will then structure the issue accordingly, seek investors and generally manage the whole process.

What does the borrower (issuer) achieve?

The borrower has arranged financing with costs that are as flexible as possible. It will never have to repay the investors because there is no fixed redemption date, and if the company falls on hard times the dividend does not have to be paid. However, there are now shareholders who may well want a say in how the business is run.

What does the investor achieve?

The investor can put money into a range of companies and share in their profits via capital gain and dividends on the equity. He shares fully in the risks of the business, good and bad.

With both bonds and equity, once a company has external bond or equity holders there needs to be a formal communication programme informing them of anything that affects them. This is usually undertaken by the **investor relations** department.

Repo

As early as 1917 the Federal Reserve (the Fed), the US central bank, was using **repo** as part of its daily market operations. Repos started as a way for dealers to finance their 'long' positions and to cover 'shorts' in the US Treasuries market. We can now repo pretty much any security but government bonds are a favourite.

Estimates of the size of this market vary, but by the end of 2006 the US repo market had exceeded $5.5 **trillion**, ($5,500,000,000,000) and by the end of 2007 the size of the European repo market was €6.4 trillion.

> we can now repo pretty much any security but government bonds are a favourite

Repo participants have two motivations:

- To invest cash – cash-driven.
- To borrow securities – stock-driven.

DEFINITION

A repo is a combined sale and repurchase transaction where one party sells securities to another and at the same time agrees to buy back the same or identical securities at a specified price on a pre-specified date.

The seller delivers securities and receives cash (supplied at a rate known as the repo rate). On maturity, the original seller receives back collateral of equivalent type and quality and returns the cash plus repo interest

Although legal title is transferred, the seller retains economic benefits and the market risk for owning them. If the price of the bond falls it is the seller who will suffer because he has committed to buy them back at a particular price. Should a coupon payment fall within a repo period it is repaid on the same day to the seller (original owner) of the securities, as a 'manufactured' transaction, known as a corporate action. There is a money market leg to the transaction, but repo is described from the securities point of view; e.g. the seller in a repo is selling 'stock' not cash.

How a repo works

A repurchase agreement or repo is a money-market instrument. A bank (collateral seller) might lend bonds that it is holding to a customer (collateral buyer) and simultaneously agree to repurchase them at an agreed date. At maturity, the bank repays the funds borrowed plus the accrued repo interest, and the customer returns the bonds. The customer has therefore invested in a collateralised asset, see Figure 2.2

The reverse transaction where the customer borrows the cash is called a reverse repo. The customer is borrowing short-term funds using securities as collateral. This can lower funding costs significantly, see Figure 2.3.

Parties to a repo transaction do not have to be banks although the majority of them are. The seller in a repo transaction, sells securities and enters into a repo. The buyer in a repo transaction, buys securities and enters into a reverse repo.

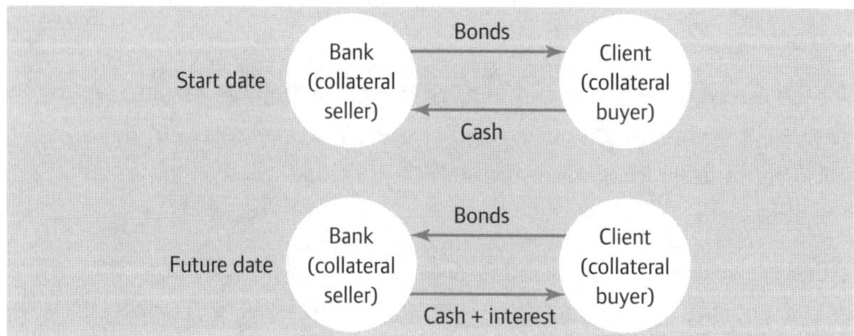

FIGURE 2.2 Repo (repurchase agreement)

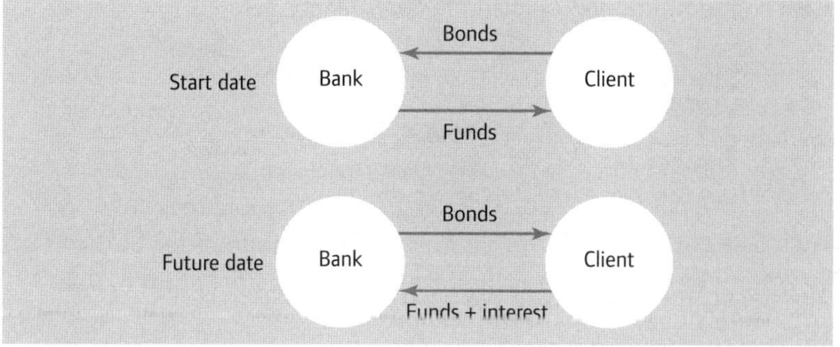

FIGURE 2.3 Reverse repo

If the securities are generic, such as a basket of several stocks, the repo is known as a general collateral trade (GC). If the securities required in a repo are specifically requested the transaction is called a special.

EXAMPLE

In this example the trade date is December 13. Bank A borrows £20m of a UK Gilt 5.5 per cent maturing 25 October 2019, from a customer for value December 14 for 31 days (term):

- Termination date: 14 January.
- Clean price of bond: 104.60.
- Accrued interest on bond: £0.4556.
- Repo rate: 6 per cent.

Cash and securities flows on value date, December 14:

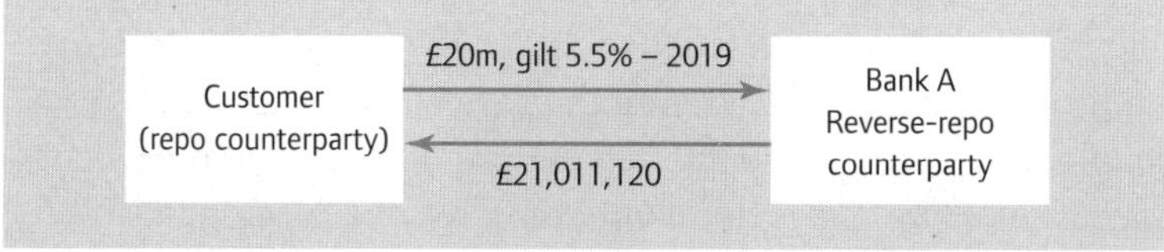

The sterling proceeds have been calculated as:

Par amount x [Market price of the bond + Accrued interest to Dec 14]

20m × [104.60 + 0.4556] = £21,011,120.00

Cash and securities flow on maturity date, January 14:

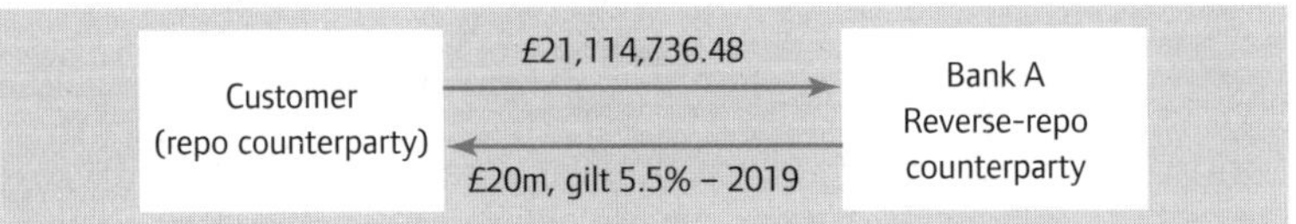

The sterling maturity amount has been calculated as:

Repo interest + Principal amount

Repo interest = Principal × Repo rate × No of days in transaction

= £21,011,120 × 6% × 31/365

= £107,070.37

Total repayment amount at maturity:

= £21,011,120.00 + £107,070.37

= £21,118,190.37

Repos give customers access to funds without having to sell bonds at unattractive market levels and traders can speculate on the market by 'shorting' bonds, by borrowing them to make a delivery.

Haircut

'Repos' and 'reverse repos' are fully collateralised. It is not uncommon for a bank to require a haircut of 1–5 per cent in the nominated or GC securities. This will cover daily fluctuations or even provide added protection in the case of a default. As an example, if a repo trade required a haircut of 5 per cent on collateral of $20m, the seller would only receive $19m from the buyer and repo interest would be calculated on $19m. The haircut would also cover the buyer should the collateral be very risky or very volatile.

Spot and forward foreign exchange

Individuals and companies do not normally buy and sell currencies for their own sake; rather they do so to pay for something else, such as goods and services. In that sense traditional foreign exchange (FX) transactions are fundamentally a part of the payment mechanism. The currency is required by exporters and importers and it is to commercial and investment banks that individuals and companies have turned to convert foreign currency into domestic currency and vice versa.

However, in the past few years the growth in the use of FX by hedge funds and asset managers has been phenomenal, both as they seek additional returns (sometimes referred to as the hunt for **Alpha**) and also to cover any fund risk. This group of market participants are known as financial corporates (see Chapter 3). They are firms whose business is money but they are not banks. Figure 2.4 shows the FX turnover by market centre for the last few BIS triennial surveys and Figure 2.5 shows the rapid growth in the use of FX by financial corporates.

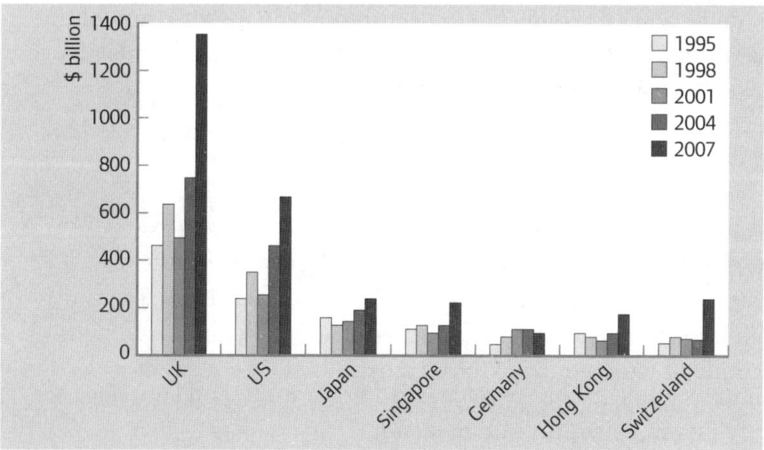

FIGURE 2.4 Average daily volume of foreign exchange. From 2004–2007, volume increased 71% to $3.2 trillion daily.

Source: Author's own work using data sourced from *BIS Triennial Survey 2007* (www.bis.org)

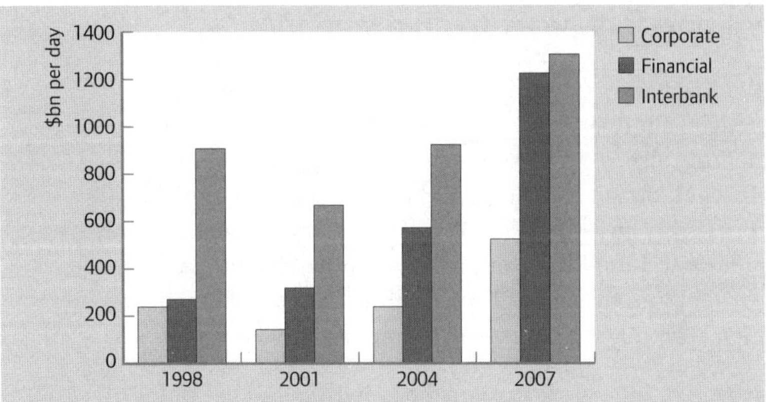

FIGURE 2.5 Growth in FX. In 1998, interbank trading accounted for 64% of the market, by 2007 it was only 43%.

Source: Author's own work using data sourced from *BIS Triennial Survey 2007* (www.bis.org)

Spot foreign exchange

The majority of traded currencies are maintained as bank deposits, so an FX trade involves the selling of a deposit in one currency in exchange for a deposit of another currency. The FX rate is the ratio that determines how much of one currency you get for a unit of the other currency. This is not a cash market – there are no fleets of trucks driving around the world full of bank notes.

DEFINITION

A **spot foreign exchange** transaction is a legal obligation to exchange one currency for another at a pre-set exchange rate for value in two business days' time.

Countries quote exchange rates in different ways, and spot rates are solely driven by supply and demand.

In the UK, dollars are quoted against pounds as £1 = 1.5300, e.g. US dollars per £1.

In the US, the same rate is quoted as $1 = 0.65359 as in how many pence one US dollar will buy. Internationally, in the banking or wholesale market there are market conventions as to how rates are quoted. The base currency which is the pound, euro or dollar needs to be identified and sometimes it is not clear which currency should be the base, e.g. yen against Swiss francs.

It is decided in this order:

1. If one of the currencies is the euro, the euro is the base, e.g. EUR/USD, EUR/GBP.
2. If one of the currencies is not euro but sterling, GBP is the base, e.g. GBP/USD, GBP/JPY.
3. If one of the currencies is not the euro or pound then the US dollar is the base, e.g. USD/CHF, USD/JPY. A notable exception is the Australian dollar, which is quoted AUD/USD.
4. If it is none of the above, the consensus is that it is arranged so that the exchange rate is bigger than 1.00, e.g. CHF/JPY, not JPY/CHF.

Note that the non-base currency is referred to as the 'term' currency.

An FX rate is valid until there is another rate. This can be a fraction of a second or it can be indefinitely and in the market the rates fluctuate constantly. Generally, all spot deals are for value in two business days' time, (unless otherwise specified). This is largely tradition, but we seem to be stuck with a two-day value period. The determination of a spot **value date** can be complicated by world-wide holidays.

EXAMPLE

Friday 27 August 2010: UK Company C, based in Southampton, wishes to sell $1 million and buy pounds. The **trade date** is today and the spot value date would normally be Tuesday 31 August, but the UK August bank holiday is on Monday 30 August 2010, and we need two clear business days. Spot value date will be one day forward on 1 September 2010.

Quoted price: GBP/USD: 1.5350–55

This is quoted with pounds as the base and each £1 is worth about $1.5350.

The left-hand side of the price is known as the bid (1.5350) and the right-hand side is the offer (1.5355) – this is quoted in terms of the bid or offer for the base currency, which is GBP.

On the bid side of the price (left), this is where the bank buys GBP and sells USD.

On the offer side of the price (right), this is where the bank sells GBP and buys USD.

The client, Company C, wants to sell USD and buy GBP. It can buy GBP at the rate the bank sells GBP, which is 1.5355. With $1 million as the transaction amount, this will generate £651,253.66.

EXAMPLE

Thursday 3 September 2009: US Company D, based in Miami, needs to sell $5 million and buy euros. The trade date is today and the spot value date would normally be Monday 7 September, but the US public holiday, Labor day, is on that day, and we need two clear business days. So spot value date will be one day forward on 8 September 2009. This will affect anyone dealing in EUR/USD on 3 September, not just those in the US.

Quoted price: EUR/USD: 1.3680–85

This is quoted with EUR as the base and each euro is worth about $1.3680.

The left-hand side of the price is the bid (1.3680) and the right-hand side is the offer (1.3685). This is quoted in terms of the bid or offer for the base currency, which is EUR.

On the bid side of the price (left), this is where the bank buys EUR and sells USD.

On the offer side of the price (right), this is where the bank sells EUR and buys USD.

The client, Company D, wants to sell dollars and buy euros, and the bank sells EUR at 1.3685. With $5 million as the transaction amount, this will generate €3,653,635.37 delivered into Company D's euro bank account on September 8 2009.

Forward foreign exchange

A **forward foreign exchange contract** is used when the currency exchange is required after more than two business days. Known as a forward foreign exchange contract or an **outright** forward contract, it will guarantee the exchange rate for delivery of the currency on a future date and is commonly used for hedging. Forward FX rates are available for major currencies for up to about ten years and for more minor currencies for one to three years.

DEFINITION

A forward foreign exchange transaction is an agreement to deliver a specified amount of one currency in return for a specified amount of a second currency at some future date. Under normal conditions the forward rate is determined by international interest rate differentials.

EXAMPLE

7 December 2009: A company wishes to sell $1 million and buy sterling three months forward to 9 March 2010. It requests a forward FX rate from its bank; the bank will quote a rate that takes into account the current spot rate and a forward adjustment.

Note that the three-month forward rate must take into account the two-day spot value period, so a forward contract date is not three months from the transaction date, but three months from the spot value date.

Spot GBP/USD	$1.4515
3-month forward points	– 0.0124
Outright rate	1.4391

On 9 March 2010, the company must pay to the bank $1 million and will receive in return, on the same day, £694,878.74. Even if the exchange rate has fluctuated since the inception of the deal – the sterling out-turn is fixed.

The spot rate and forward points together form a compound rate, which is called the outright forward rate. The amount of the adjustment (forward points) will vary depending on the maturity of the transaction and the interest rates of the two currencies.

Currencies that have lower domestic interest rates than the base currency are known as premium currencies, and the forward points in these cases are subtracted from the spot rate, e.g. GBP/USD where the dollar is at a **premium** to pound.

Where the foreign currency has a higher domestic rate than the base currency then the points will be added. These currencies are known as discount currencies, e.g. EUR/GBP where pounds are at a discount to euros.

There are many currencies and it is sometimes necessary to classify them. One widely used method is:

- Major currencies: freely available spot and forward markets, e.g, USD, GBP, CHF, JPY, EUR.
- Minor currencies: freely available, although the spot market may lack liquidity. Restrictions are sometimes imposed on the forward market in terms of maturity, e.g., PLN, AUD, CAD, SGD.
- Emerging market currencies: spot rates are available, but may be restricted with regard to amount or government intervention. Forward market is lacking, intermittent or very expensive, e.g. HUF, ZAR, ROL.

Derivatives: OTC and exchange traded instruments

A derivative product can be either 'exchange traded', where a contract is bought or sold on a recognised exchange, or it can be over the counter (OTC). An OTC instrument is written or created by a bank (or sometimes companies or other financial institutions) and tailored to suit the exact requirements of the client.

An exchange-traded instrument

This is an instrument that is bought or sold directly on an exchange such as Liffe (the derivatives arm of the NYSE Euronext Group, formed in 2007) or the Chicago Mercantile Exchange Group (CME) or InterContinentalExchange (ICE). There are many regulated exchanges worldwide.

Each exchange-traded product has a 'contract specification', which details precisely the characteristics of the '**underlying**', and the obligations of the buyer and seller at maturity. Typical exchange-traded instruments include financial futures and listed options. Trading used to be predominantly transacted via 'open outcry', which used face-to-face contact, hand signals and loud verbal agreements. This style of trading conveys '**price transparency**' and allows every market participant, both big and small, to have equal access to the trade at the same price. In the past decade, with increasingly sophisticated technology available, there has been a shift away from open outcry trading towards electronic screen-based trading of exchange-traded derivatives.

Within the exchange-traded market place there is an entity known as a **clearing house**. This body is responsible for many things, including the 'clearing' of trades. The clearing house also becomes the buyer to everyone who sells, and the seller to everyone who buys and is known as a central counterparty. This is important because it means that, whomever you deal with, your ultimate counterparty will be the clearing house. Whether you deal with a small bank, large bank, French company or US fund, the ultimate counterparty is the clearing house. It is not therefore required to check individual credit lines before dealing, as the exposure will be to the clearing house, not to the firm with whom you transacted, whether via open outcry or screen-based trading.

An over-the-counter (OTC) instrument

An over-the-counter instrument is sold by a bank (usually), to a client and tailored to fit a specific set of requirements. Occasionally, banks will purchase these products from companies or other non-banks, but each buyer and seller must take the credit risk of their counterparty. In the event of a failure, each party to the trade is exposed to the risk that the other party will be unwilling or unable to proceed.

the price of the trade will be agreed upon between the parties

An OTC product allows much greater flexibility in terms of **expiry** date, reference price, amount and underlying commodity, and vast amounts of transactions are executed every day. An OTC instrument can be very simple, in which case it is known as a **vanilla** product, or it can be exceedingly complex. The price of the trade will be agreed upon between the parties, is confidential and will involve many factors.

Financial futures

Financial futures belong to a family of products identified as derivatives and are traded on exchanges such as Liffe, ICE and the CME. Known as exchange-traded derivatives (ETD) they are transacted in terms of number of contracts based on a standardised futures contract specification. All you can do with a future is buy it or sell it, and a vast amount of futures contracts are traded globally, every day.

Futures are the most risky of all derivatives as they may be subject to very rapid and very large price movements; this means that within the institutions that trade futures, rigorous internal controls are paramount to prevent rogue trading and indeed over-trading, and to monitor very closely the risk management of any positions.

DEFINITION

A financial futures contract is a legally binding agreement to make or take delivery of a standard quantity of a specific financial instrument, at a future date, and at a price agreed between the parties through open outcry on the floor of an organised exchange or via electronic trading.

Trading is now largely electronic and the big players are the banks, hedge funds and asset managers. These products are not really designed for the private individual.

NOTE

Discussion of financial futures does not include futures linked to things you can eat, such as coffee, wheat and soya – these are separate and known as 'softs'.

A financial future may be linked to an interest rate, a currency rate, a house price index, equity or even a commodity, such as gold, oil or plastic. The example below shows how an equity index future on the FTSE 100 may be used.

EXAMPLE

September 10: a trader is speculating that the likely performance of the stock market over the next three months is upwards. He wishes to take a position in £100million. With the FTSE trading at 5,500 and the **index multiplier** (the '**tick**') at £10, this would require 1,818 contracts.

To calculate the number of futures contracts, this formula is used:

$$\text{Number of contracts} = \frac{\text{Total value of position}}{\text{FTSE 100 index level} \times \text{Index multiplier}}$$

$$= \frac{£100{,}000{,}000}{5{,}500 \times £10} = 1818.18 \text{ contracts}$$

Figure 2.6 shows the FTSE futures contract traded on Liffe in London.

NOTE

Where does the £10 per tick comes from? In this context, if the index is trading at 5,500 and the tick is £10, it indicates you will need £55,000 to buy all the shares in the FTSE 100 in the correct weightings, with no split shares. This figure, £55,000, is also known as the cash value of the index. It is set by exchange.

The trader will need to buy 1,818 contracts of the December future – this will cover the period up to December, the next three months. Both buyers

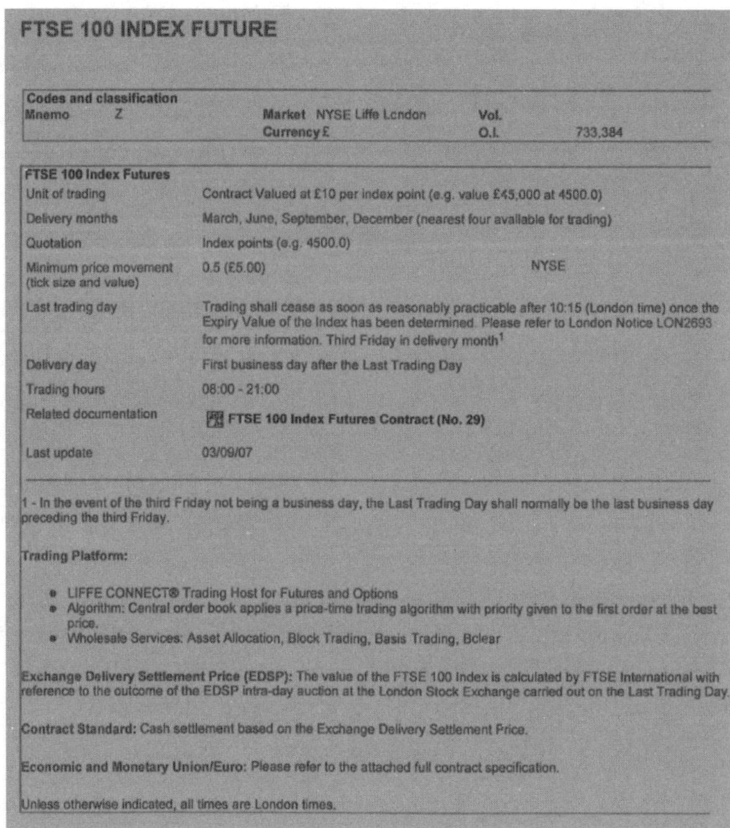

FTSE 100 INDEX FUTURE

Codes and classification			
Mnemo Z	Market NYSE Liffe London	Vol.	
	Currency £	O.I.	733,384

FTSE 100 Index Futures	
Unit of trading	Contract Valued at £10 per index point (e.g. value £45,000 at 4500.0)
Delivery months	March, June, September, December (nearest four available for trading)
Quotation	Index points (e.g. 4500.0)
Minimum price movement (tick size and value)	0.5 (£5.00) NYSE
Last trading day	Trading shall cease as soon as reasonably practicable after 10:15 (London time) once the Expiry Value of the Index has been determined. Please refer to London Notice LON2693 for more information. Third Friday in delivery month[1]
Delivery day	First business day after the Last Trading Day
Trading hours	08:00 - 21:00
Related documentation	FTSE 100 Index Futures Contract (No. 29)
Last update	03/09/07

1 - In the event of the third Friday not being a business day, the Last Trading Day shall normally be the last business day preceding the third Friday.

Trading Platform:

- LIFFE CONNECT® Trading Host for Futures and Options
- Algorithm: Central order book applies a price-time trading algorithm with priority given to the first order at the best price.
- Wholesale Services: Asset Allocation, Block Trading, Basis Trading, Bclear

Exchange Delivery Settlement Price (EDSP): The value of the FTSE 100 Index is calculated by FTSE International with reference to the outcome of the EDSP intra-day auction at the London Stock Exchange carried out on the Last Trading Day.

Contract Standard: Cash settlement based on the Exchange Delivery Settlement Price.

Economic and Monetary Union/Euro: Please refer to the attached full contract specification.

Unless otherwise indicated, all times are London times.

FIGURE 2.6 FTSE 100 index future

Source: Reproduced with kind permission of NYSE Liffe

and sellers of the futures contacts must put up collateral to the clearing house. This is known as the initial margin and is linked to the number of contracts. The initial margin is required to support the trade and all positions will be marked to market daily, by the clearing house at close of business. The marking to market is physical, meaning that if you have lost money on that day you must pay, and if you have made money on that day it will be paid to you. This daily movement is called variation margin.

Note that December future ceases trading in December. It doesn't start trading in December.

In this example – the initial margin for the FTSE 100 is £4,000 per contract, making £7.272 million. This will be returned with interest at maturity – assuming the daily variation margin has been paid in accordance with the rules.

Assume that over the next three months the FTSE rises to 6,000. This represents a 500 tick gain for each contract. Assume also that the contracts close at 6,000 on the last trading day in December, which you can see from the contract specification is the third Friday of the delivery month. This is taken as soon as is practically possible after 10.15am, London time.

Profit = Profit (in ticks) × Number of contracts × Index multiplier:

500 × 1818 × £10 = £9,090,000

In addition, the £7.272 million will be returned. You have made a profit without even needing the money to buy the shares or pay any duty or transaction costs on the purchase.

The real risk in futures is what happens if you get it wrong? In this example, what if the market fell by 500 points? You would lose £9,090,000.

Because of the rapid nature of market movements and as most participants have sizeable futures positions, daily marking to market is essential. This prevents large loss-making positions accumulating because you have to pay your losses daily. This enables a trader to monitor positions very closely and close them out if he is no longer comfortable.

NOTE

Buying a December future does not mean you have to keep in until December, you can trade out of it at any time.

Rate swaps (IRS)

Note that it has become common to drop the word 'interest' from interest rate swaps, although they are still abbreviated to IRS.

(Interest) rate swaps are probably the most popular risk management tool. They belong to the derivatives family of products and can cover interest rate exposures from one week (via overnight swaps) to fifty years and sometimes seventy five years. They are used by banks and companies alike for their own hedging and may be combined with bond issues to achieve favourable funding costs. They can assist a borrower in finding fixed-rate funding if he is unable to access other lending markets. However, swaps are not a method of raising finance, rather they are a way of managing an interest rate risk and possibly transform it from fixed interest rates into floating (LIBOR) interest rates or vice versa.

DEFINITION

An interest rate swap is an agreement to exchange interest-related payments in the same currency from fixed rate into floating rate (or vice versa), or from one type of floating rate to another.

A swap is a legally binding agreement, where an absolute fixed rate of interest is guaranteed. One party agrees to pay the 'fixed rate'; the other, to receive this fixed rate and pay the 'floating rate', usually LIBOR. The underlying loan or investment is untouched, and may well be with another bank. The only movement of funds is a net transfer of interest rate payments between the two parties on specified dates. The interest payments are calculated on an agreed principal amount that is not exchanged.

interest payments are calculated on an agreed principal amount that is not exchanged

Both interest payments are 'netted off' to help minimise credit exposure. Standard documentation is provided by the International Swaps and Derivatives Association (ISDA).

EXAMPLE

A US company, Drax, has decided to refurbish one of its hotels in Florida. Funds of $50 million are required for a period of five years, and the treasurer would ideally prefer to pay a fixed-rate of interest for the period. The only fixed-rate funds available are considered too expensive. The alternative is to borrow the $50 million on a floating rate from the money markets, and roll over the funds every three months. This would, however, leave the company exposed to rising rates. The company has been quoted three-month US LIBOR plus 0.5 per cent for the floating-rate loan.

If the company is uncomfortable with this interest rate risk it can take out an interest rate swap, which would fix the rate of interest and remove the threat of rising rates. It is important for the swap to match the underlying transaction in all respects.

In the example, Drax needs to 'pay the fixed and receive the floating' (rate). The treasurer consults a trading screen to get an indication of current levels in the market (see Figure 2.7)

USDIRS | USD IRS FOCUS | LINKED | DISPLAYS | MONEY

Time	Contributor		IRS Anl Mny/3M	USD LIBOR		USD SB vs 3mn	LIBOR	Contributor	Time
11:49	BROKER	GFX	1.0730	1.0930	1Y				:
11:49	HELABA	FFT	1.3130	1.3430	2Y	1.321	1.361	REUTERS	NYC 11:47
11:49	BROKER	GFX	1.6410	1.6800	3Y	1.660	1.700	REUTERS	NYC 11:46
11:49	BROKER	GFX	1.8680	1.9080	4Y	1.893	1.933	REUTERS	NYC 11:48
11:49	BROKER	GFX	2.0350	2.0750	5Y	2.056	2.096	REUTERS	NYC 11:49
11:49	BROKER	GFX	2.1720	2.2120	6Y	2.199	2.239	REUTERS	NYC 11:48
11:49	HELABA	FFT	2.2990	2.3290	7Y	2.323	2.363	REUTERS	NYC 11:49
11:49	HELABA	FFT	2.3860	2.4160	8Y	2.416	2.455	REUTERS	NYC 11:49
11:49	HELABA	FFT	2.4640	2.4940	9Y	2.494	2.533	REUTERS	NYC 11:48
11:49	HELABA	FFT	2.5330	2.5630	10Y	2.565	2.604	REUTERS	NYC 11:48
:					11Y	2.625	2.664	REUTERS	NYC 11:48
11:49	HELABA	FFT	2.6610	2.6910	12Y	2.697	2.737	REUTERS	NYC 11:45
:					13Y	2.727	2.767	REUTERS	NYC 11:45
:					14Y	2.767	2.807	REUTERS	NYC 11:45
11:49	HELABA	FFT	2.7940	2.8240	15Y	2.823	2.863	REUTERS	NYC 11:45
11:49	HELABA	FFT	2.8370	2.8670	20Y	2.867	2.906	REUTERS	NYC 11:45
11:48	HELABA	FFT	2.8300	2.8600	25Y	2.857	2.897	REUTERS	NYC 11:43
11:49	HELABA	FFT	2.8340	2.8640	30Y	2.861	2.900	REUTERS	NYC 11:43

FIGURE 2.7 USD swap rates

Source: Thomson Reuters

The client wishes to pay fixed, so is on the high side of the price, at or around 2.0750 per cent. This is an inter-bank screen and the client is not a bank. The price for Drax will be higher to allow for the fact that the company's credit rating is not as good as that of the banks. Assume that the swap trader has quoted Drax a rate of 2.10 per cent. This is the rate that will be paid annually; in return Drax will receive three-month LIBOR, which will be reset every three months in line with market rates. The dates on the swap and the underlying loan must be matched, so that the LIBOR payment received under the swap can be paid straight through to the underlying loan. This is represented in Figure 2.8, showing the combined rate is now a fixed rate of 2.60 per cent.

On each of the quarterly rollover dates, which are specified in advance, the LIBOR flow will move and will be available to off-set against the three-month LIBOR + 0.5 per cent required on the loan. The annual fixed rate interest payment will be paid only once a year.

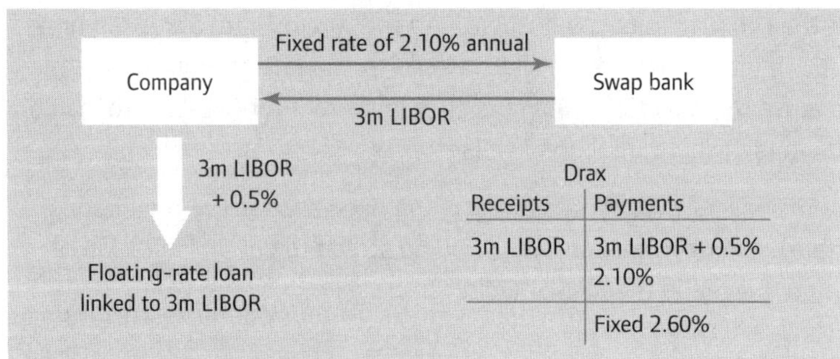

FIGURE 2.8 Swap cash flows for Drax Inc.

The net rate (after hedging) of 2.60 per cent fixed is achieved. This ignores compounding – as the floating rate margin is actually paid quarterly. The client has therefore borrowed floating (or variable) rate money linked to three-month LIBOR, yet after the swap they are now paying interest fixed rate of 2.60 per cent. Note that the example ignores compounding.

Options

Options also belong to the derivative family of products. An option contract is the only instrument that allows the buyer (holder) to 'walk away' from his obligations. This is unique. With most derivatives and forward contracts the client is provided with a guaranteed rate, and there is an obligation to deal at that rate. Forward contracts produce certainty whatever the resulting market conditions. In contrast, option contracts allow the holder the best of both worlds; insurance when things go wrong – you then use the option. When things go right, the ability to walk away from the instrument (or guarantee) and the previously agreed fixed rate, and the ability therefore to deal at a better rate in the market.

Options are available across many asset classes including interest rates/fixed income, currencies, equities and commodities, property and credit. However, unfortunately, options do not come free of charge: a premium is due, usually paid up-front.

Options can be bought or sold on an exchange, in which case they are known as exchange-traded or listed options. Alternatively, they can be tailored to fit the exact circumstances of the client, when

DEFINITION

An option gives the buyer the right, but not the obligation, to buy or sell a pre-set amount of a specific financial instrument at a specific rate on or before a specific future date. A premium is due.

they are known as over the counter or OTC. If the option has a simple structure it is known as 'vanilla', a more complex option may be known as an 'exotic'. Options can be transacted in any one of the underlying **primary markets**, interest rates, currency, equity and commodity. Whatever the underlying commodity, all options are distinguished by the key phrase, 'the right, but not the obligation'. This separates an option from every other instrument. Table 2.1 summarises the main terms.

Table 2.1 Option terminology

Call option:	the right (not the obligation) to buy the underlying.
Put option:	the right (not the obligation) to sell the underlying.
Exercise:	conversion of the option into the underlying transaction.
Strike price:	guaranteed price chosen by the client, which can be described as: at the money (**ATM**); in the money (**ITM**); out of the money (**OTM**).
Expiry date:	last day on which the option may be exercised.
Value date:	the date when the underlying is settled or delivered.
American option:	an option that can be exercised on any business day up to and including the expiry date.
European option:	an option that can be exercised on the expiry date only.
Bermudan option:	an option that can be exercised on selected dates.
Asian option:	an option that is linked to the average rate over a period.
Premium:	the price of the option.
Intrinsic value:	difference between the strike price and the current market rate.

Table 2.1 continued

Time value:	difference between the option premium and the intrinsic value, including time until expiry, volatility and cost of carry.
Fair value:	combination of intrinsic value and time value, as calculated by the option pricing model.
Volatility:	normalised, annualised standard deviation of the underlying reference rate.

EXAMPLE

2 April: a UK dairy firm, Eggzactly, has won an export order to Thailand. Delivery and payment will be in three months' time and will be in US dollars. The treasurer is not sure on which exact day the money will be available in his account, but he is not expecting to be paid weeks in advance. He is worried that the value of the dollar may fall (depreciate) before he receives his invoice amount of $1,250,000. If he does nothing and the value of the dollar falls, he will not realise sufficient sterling from the resulting foreign exchange conversion, but if the value of the dollar increases he will be very happy. He is not sure in which direction the dollar will move, but under his own strict internal treasury guidelines he is not allowed to do nothing and cross his fingers. If he transacts a forward contract with one of his bankers, he must give up any windfall profits, but if he transacts an option, he has insurance if things go wrong and profit opportunities if things go right – but he will then need to pay a premium

On 2 April, the treasurer asks for an indication level on a dollar put, sterling call option, European style, strike = at the money, and an expiry date in three months' time (2 July) for value two business days later. The current financial information is available for GBP/USD: spot rate: 1.8500; outright forward rate: 1.8450.

The strike on the option will be at the money forward (ATMF), at 1.8450. The premium due for this option is 1.15 per cent of the dollar amount. The total premium is 1.15 per cent of $1,250,000, which is $14,375, and must be paid to the bank two business days (value spot) after the deal is struck. The option can now be filed or put in a drawer for three months until the expiry date.

The dollars arrive on time on 2 July. The treasurer will call his bank to check the current level of the spot exchange rate. If the dollar has strengthened (appreciated) to, say, GBP/USD 1.7950, then the option will be worthless and will be abandoned, and the transaction will be effected in the spot market. If the dollar has depreciated to say GBP/USD 1.8950, the client will exercise the option at the agreed rate of $1.8450. The treasurer will need to call the bank and confirm that he wishes to exercise his option, as exercise is not always automatic. Under the option, the treasurer will deliver $1,250,000 and receive sterling at $1.8450, giving a sterling out-turn of £677,506.78. Technically, the option premium should be deducted to work out the breakeven rate (to be absolutely correct, the net present value (NPV) of the premium). This would give a net sterling out-turn of £677,506.78 less the amount of the option premium in sterling (for premium conversion purposes, the spot rate is always used: $14,375,000 divided by GBP/USD 1.8500 = £7,770.27) – a total figure of £669,736.51 making a net rate inclusive of premium of GBP/USD 1.8664.

The option will always be the second-best option in hindsight. If the client knew with total certainty that the dollar was going to depreciate, he would sell forward, a hedging alternative that would cost nothing and allow no profit. But if you are not expecting to profit, you have given up nothing. If the client knew that the dollar would appreciate, he would do nothing and simply sell the dollars at the better rate when they arrived in three months' time. The option allows the client to get the best possible outcome, the 'insured' rate when required, or the profit when the market moves favourably, but a premium is required.

Credit default swaps (CDS)

A **credit default swap** (CDS) is a financial instrument that is similar to insurance, used by financial market participants to manage their investment risk (among other things). Figure 2.9 shows the phenomenal growth of these products from 2001 to 2007, to the extent that they overshadowed the US equity market, the US mortgage securities market and the US Treasuries market *combined*.

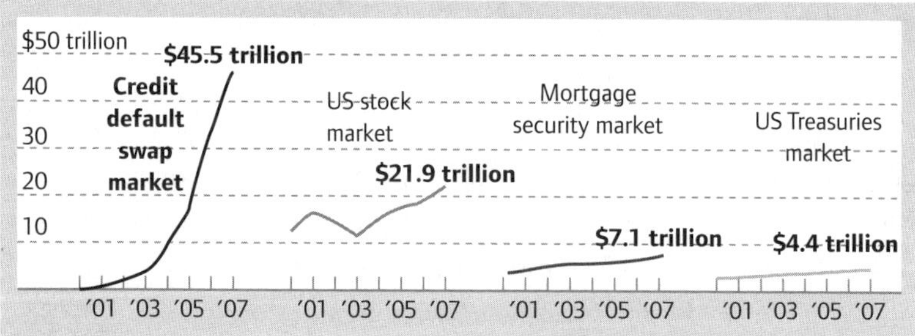

FIGURE 2.9 CDS volumes compared with other securities

Sources: Thomson Proprietary Research; International Swaps and Derivatives Association; © *The New York Times*

As at the end of December 2007, a BIS survey showed that the amount of outstandings in the interest rate swap market was $309 trillion compared with a 'paltry' $58 trillion for CDS. Figures for the middle of January 2009, showed a fall to $29.6 trillion, of CDS outstandings in the most popular products.

DEFINITION

A credit default swap is a bilateral, over-the-counter contract used to transfer the credit risk of a reference entity from one party to another. The protection buyer pays a periodic fee; the protection seller receives the fee and provides protection in the case of a credit event.

A CDS is a product that allows the counterparty to hedge or gain exposure to credit risk. The nature of the default event, the reference asset, and the methods used to calculate the amount payable are specified in the swap contract and can vary depending on the individual transaction in question. The 'underlying asset' may be a single bond, a leveraged loan, an index, or even as **asset-backed security (ABS)**.

NOTE

Most financial derivatives are triggered if there is a move in an exchange rate, an equity or bond price; however credit default swaps have legal triggers. This makes the documentation especially important.

Is this insurance? No!

Although this looks like insurance and resembles it closely, there is a big difference. With insurance, you need to own the asset and prove that you have suffered a loss. This means you have to own the bond in question to benefit from the protection. With a CDS – you do *not* need to own the asset.

EXAMPLE

Last year, a European fund manager purchased €10 million of bonds issued by a Belgian engineering company KTK. It is part of his portfolio and he does not wish to sell the bond because doing so could result in a tax or accounting charge. But let's assume he is becoming concerned about the performance of KTK. He wishes to buy protection and believes that although the bond has ten years remaining, if the company can get through the next five years his investment will be safe. He does not need to cover the whole of the ten year period until maturity – just the period he wishes, be it, one, three or five years. This will be decided at the time of dealing. He decides to cover the full amount of €10 million. This means that if there is an agreed 'credit event' in the next five years he will receive a payment equivalent to the fall in the value of the bonds.

For example, if he paid €10 million and after a credit event the value plummeted to €4 million, he would receive €6 million.

He is buying protection, so he needs to pay a fee, known as the CDS spread. This fee will depend on the perceived risk in the company. Assume he is quoted a fee of 151 basis points per annum from Investor B; this will be paid to Investor B in quarterly amounts for the life of the transaction – based on the number of days in the period. In CDS jargon, the European fund manager is 'paying the fixed rate' on the CDS. Investor B will receive the fixed rate and 'pay the floating rate' on the CDS. The floating rate will only be triggered if there is a credit event, forming the compensating payment paid by the credit protection seller to the buyer, this is illustrated in Figure 2.10.

The credit spread calculation works as follows. For a 92-day quarter the fund manager will pay:

$$€10{,}000{,}000 \times 92/360 \times 1.51\% = €38{,}589$$

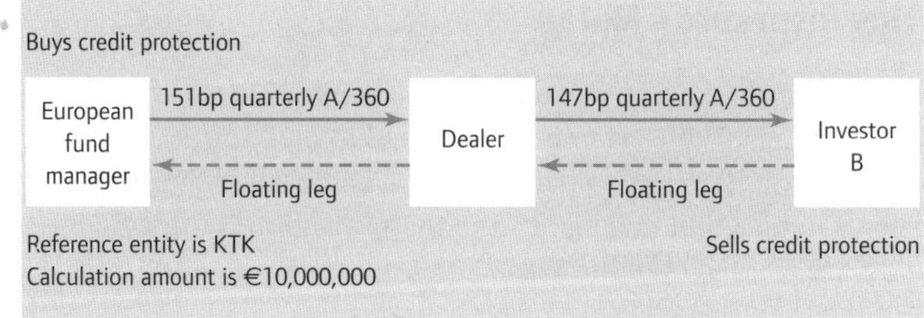

FIGURE 2.10 Cash flows on CDS: Example: 5-year KTK. 147/151 (bid/offer)

Note that 360 days is used as the yearly figure because this transaction is in euros.

Also, note that if there is a credit event, payments cease. So if there is a credit event at month 18, then the CDS will terminate.

What happens next?:

- No credit event: no payout, carry on paying the premium.
- Agreed credit event: the seller of the protection will compensate the buyer of the protection, based on the published ISDA credit event protocol.

In summary, if the European fund manager has bought protection and suffers a credit event on KTK, he will wait for a short time before the recovery amount is calculated by a dealer poll. If this CDS is based on a cash settlement, rather than delivery of the bonds, and the recovery value turns out to be 55 per cent, then he will keep the bonds, but receive a settlement of 45 per cent of €10 million, making €4.5 million. Cash settlement tends to be preferred because there can be problems in obtaining the bonds for delivery and this can distort the cash markets, or trigger tax and accounting charges.

Credit events

There are a finite number of credit events that can trigger the floating-rate payment. The ISDA 2003 credit derivatives definitions note:

- bankruptcy;
- failure to pay;
- restructuring;
- repudiation/moratorium;
- obligation default;
- obligation acceleration.

Each of these have legal definitions. For further details, refer to the ISDA documentation.

Until April 2009, anyone with an interest in a CDS which had suffered a credit event could voluntarily elect to sign up to the relevant ISDA protocol, this brought standardisation to the settlement process. Since April 2009, and in the light of regulatory concerns, ISDA has published the 2009 Credit Derivatives Determinations Committees and Auction Settlement Supplement to the 2003 ISDA Credit Derivatives Definitions (the '2009 Supplement') and the related 2009 ISDA Credit Derivatives Determinations Committees and Auction Settlement CDS Protocol (the 'Protocol'). The 2009 Supplement and Protocol standardises settlement even further.

The Protocol was known as the IDSA '**Big Bang**' and it took effect on April 8, 2009, with over 2000 parties adhering. For more details contact ISDA direct.

The media have latched on to these products – not always fully understanding them – and use them as a way of describing the risk level of a company. If the CDS spread increases (gets numerically larger) the firm has become more risky, if the CDS spread decreases, the company has become more credit worthy and less risky. However, if the CDS spread increases from 151bps to 300bps, does this mean the company is now twice as risky? Possibly, but unlikely, because a major factor will be the traders in the market; if there are more buyers than sellers, they will force the price up.

Many CDS prices are linked to asset swaps. For an explanation of how these work, see below.

Asset swaps

An asset swap could relate to a number of assets and it is no surprise there is an element of confusion here. In its simplest form, an asset swap is simply an interest rate swap where the underlying is an asset, such as a floating rate note (FRN). If an investor is concerned about falling interest rates he may well want to swap 'out of floating and into a fixed' investment rate. Figure 2.11 illustrates how one of these would work.

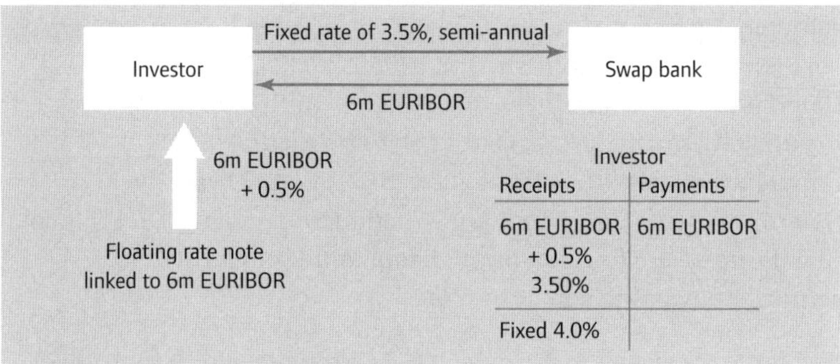

FIGURE 2.11 Asset swap cash flows

EXAMPLE

Consider an investor with a €10m FRN receiving six-month EURIBOR + 0.5 per cent, semi annually. As EURIBOR fluctuates so will the income stream and if this is either too volatile or likely to fall the investor may prefer to continue to hold the asset but swap the interest receipt into a fixed rate, which will not fluctuate.

From the rates shown in Figure 2.11, it can be seen that a potentially unknown floating rate has been converted into a fixed rate of 4 per cent.

EXAMPLE

Pricing on credit default swaps is often said to be linked to asset swaps, although this merely indicates where a CDS should be trading. There is no guarantee that will be the case, because supply and demand are big market drivers.

Assume we are trying to establish the fair price with respect to where the CDS on the Tiger Group should be trading. The numbers in Figure 2.12 relate to these points:

1. Imagine an investor with no money, to whom the bank will make available a funding facility linked to LIBOR. The investor therefore borrows the money, and pays LIBOR interest.
2. The investor uses the money to buy the Tiger Group bond.
3. As the owner of the Tiger Group bond he will receive the fixed coupon from the bond.
4. The investor will pay the fixed coupon from the bond into a vanilla interest rate swap and will receive LIBOR plus *x*bp in return. In the case of Tiger Group, assume this is 55 basis points.

The reason the floating leg on the swap will be LIBOR + 55bp rather than LIBOR flat (+ nothing) is because the coupon that is fed into the swap is higher than current swap rates. Therefore, to preserve the NPV relationship on the swap, the floating leg has to be LIBOR plus something. Under first principles of swap valuation, the NPV of a vanilla interest-rate swap at inception should be zero, i.e. the present values of the fixed and floating legs should net to zero.

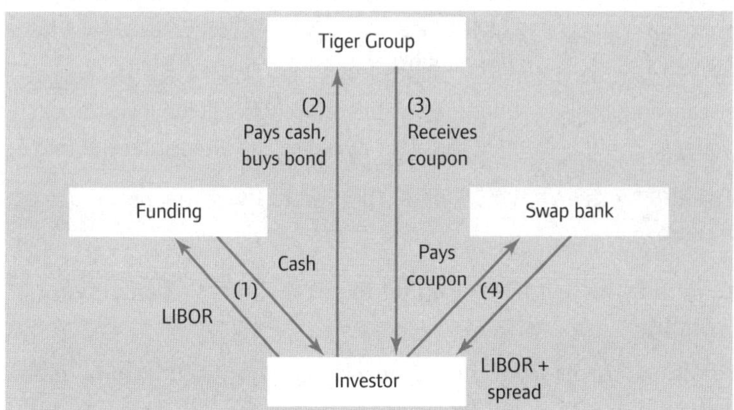

FIGURE 2.12 Pricing CDS via asset swaps

NOTE

This approach to CDS pricing merely indicates where the CDS should be pricing; the difference between what can be calculated and where it actually trades on a particular day is known as the 'basis'.

Collateralised debt obligations (CDOs)

Collateralised debt obligations are one of the financial instruments that have been blamed for the credit crunch that started in 2007. Investors in these assets that have lost large sums of money and the banks and rating agencies that have been involved in the structuring of these products came under criticism relating to the original pricing and subsequent risk valuations on these transactions. Billions of dollars of writedowns ensued and investors holding such assets found it difficult to recover their investments. There is some debate as to whether these are derivatives or structured-finance products, but they are definitely closer to asset-backed securities than anything else. Readers may be familiar with **mortgage-backed securities (MBS)** and collateralised mortgage obligations **(CMOs)**. A **CDO** is similar to this except the assets in the CDO are not just mortgages but also loans.

DEFINITION

A CDO or collateralised debt obligation involves the securitisation of debt instruments, enabling the actual or synthetic transfer of large credit-risky portfolios to investors in the form of bond issues, called tranches, which have differing risk and return characteristics.

From the investment bank's perspective, besides credit risk transfer, the other driving factors that led to the widespread use of CDOs are:

- To reduce the regulatory capital requirements of a bank credit portfolio.
- To offload assets from the balance sheet by outright sale of debt instruments.

- To seek arbitrage opportunities.

From the investor's point of view, the main factors are:

- Exposure to risks that are normally only available to banks.
- Relative value opportunities because of the attractive returns on CDOs.

The CDO market is divided into those structures that don't use credit derivatives – 'cash CDOs' – and those that do – 'synthetic CDOs'. See the reading list at the end of this chapter for more on synthetic CDOs.

EXAMPLE

The earliest CDOs used a cash transfer mechanism to transfer the risk by physically selling debt instruments to a special purpose vehicle (SPV). In cash CDOs, the debt instruments are repackaged by the SPV into tranches of securities and sold to investors. This 'tranching' of assets helps investors to match their specific investment needs. Each tranche was rated by a rating agency and had different risk and return characteristics. The SPV used the funds received from the sale of securities to buy debt instruments. In the case of any defaults, the losses are borne by the investors in bottom-up order, i.e., from equity (first loss) to senior tranche. The investors on their part receive regular interest payments generated from the cash flows from the underlying credits. The riskier the tranche, the higher rate of return to the investor.

Hence, in Figure 2.13, a portfolio of $1 billion of credits (bonds or loans) is bought by an SPV with funding raised by issuing equity,

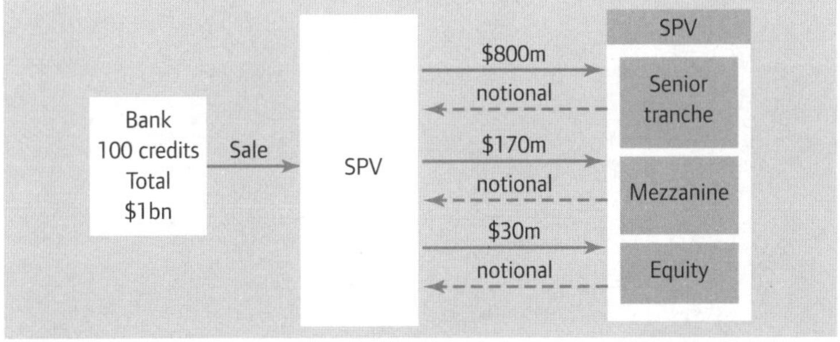

FIGURE 2.13 Basic cash CDO structure

mezzanine and senior tranches of $30 million, $170 million and $800 million respectively. Any losses by the SPV due to defaults by any of the credits are first absorbed by the equity tranche. Should these losses exceed $30 million, then subsequent losses are absorbed by the mezzanine tranche and so on.

The issuer of the CDO, usually an investment bank, earns a commission at the time of issue and earns management fees during the life of the CDO. An investment in a CDO is therefore an investment in the cash flows of the assets, and the promises and mathematical models of this intermediary, rather than a direct investment in the underlying collateral. This differentiates a CDO from a mortgage or a mortgage-backed security (MBS).

Further reading

Mastering Derivatives Markets by Francesca Taylor, Financial Times Prentice Hall, 2007, 3rd ed.

Mastering Foreign Exchange and Currency Options by Francesca Taylor, Financial Times Prentice Hall, 2009, 2nd ed.

DTCC for CDS data, www.dtcc.com.

International Swaps and Derivatives Association, www.isda.org.

3 Key market participants, departments and regulators

...the nature of banks and banking has changed beyond all recognition, notably due to the liquidity and credit crises, plunging commodity prices and the resulting fallout.

- Introduction
- Central banks
- Bank for International Settlements (BIS)
- Commercial and investment banks
- Private banks
- Bank departments: front office, middle office and operations
- Regulators
- Brokers
- Traditional corporates
- Financial corporates
- Hedge funds
- Player motivations
- International Swaps and Derivatives Association (ISDA)
- Exchanges
- Information providers

Introduction

There are market participants within a huge assortment of financial institutions, all of whom have specific roles and responsibilities. Unfortunately, from the outside or to the new entrant this can be bewildering. Dealing rooms especially now are full of screens and information – looking as if you could control a Mars probe from them. How does this market function? Who does what? How do they all fit together?

By far and away the biggest players used to be the banks, but the nature of banks and banking has changed, notably due to the liquidity and credit crises, plunging commodity prices and the resulting fallout. Who would have thought that some of the biggest, oldest and most respected names would no longer be with us?

The changing face of finance also means that there is more governmental influence in financial markets, and how this will develop remains to be seen. Asset managers, not just the hedge funds but also the pension funds, are also very important, not to mention the regulators and financial authorities. This section will establish the behavioural characteristics generally expected from banks, with the caveat that no two banking or financial firms are identical.

Central banks

A central bank is responsible for implementing the monetary policy of a country whereas the government is responsible for implementing the fiscal policy. Most central banks now are 'free' of government intervention and although there are similarities, the operations of central banks vary.

Generally, the roles of a central bank are to be:

- banker to the government;
- banker to the banks;

- lender of last resort;
- responsible for managing the amount of liquidity in the market via open market operations (OMO);
- provider of economic advice to the government;
- regulator for the banking system (in the US, this is done by the Comptroller of the Currency);
- responsible for note issue.

The US Federal Reserve system

The Federal Reserve (the Fed) acts as the US central bank. The system is based on the 12 regional federal reserve banks, which act as regulators for commercial banks in their area (Figure 3.1). The Fed acts as the bankers' bank and the government's bank. It is controlled by a board of governors, which sits in Washington. The Federal Reserve's policymaking body is the federal open market committee, which is made up of regional Fed governors.

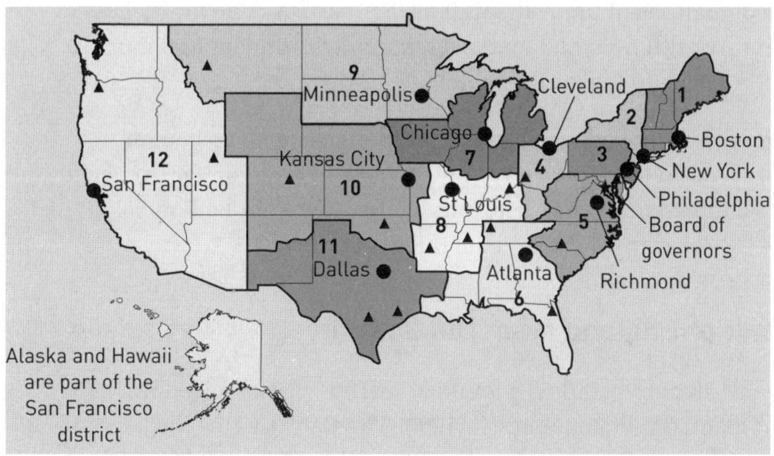

FIGURE 3.1 The US federal system of banks

Source: Federal Reserve Board

The Federal Reserve uses three main tools to implement monetary policy:

- open market operations;
- the discount window;
- reserve requirements.

The most important and dynamic tool is open market operations. The Federal Reserve Bank of New York implements Fed policy by buying and selling US Treasury securities, trading with accredited primary dealers. When the New York Fed buys Treasury securities from dealers, it adds reserves to the banking system and puts downward pressure on the highly sensitive federal funds rate. When it sells Treasury securities, reserves are drained and this tends to increase the federal funds rate.

The discount window extends credit to banks in certain circumstances and sets reserve requirements, which dictate how much banks must hold in reserve accounts. These mechanisms also influence the cost of lending, which, in turn, affects the rate of economic growth and price levels. As the credit crisis unfolded, the operations of the Fed and the US Treasury came under heavy scrutiny with financial markets remaining turbulent and more banks began to look vulnerable.

The New York Fed also carries out foreign exchange market intervention to help achieve policy objectives on dollar exchange rates. Intervention is carried out by the New York Fed on behalf of the US Treasury and the Federal Reserve.

Bank of England (the 'Old Lady')

The Bank of England was founded in 1694, nationalised in 1946 and granted independence in 1997. The Bank (notice the capital letter), sometimes known as the Old Lady of Threadneedle Street, aims to set interest rates to keep inflation low. It also issues banknotes and works to maintain a stable financial system.

The Bank is housed in a three-acre site in the city of London and even has a tube station named after it – Bank station on the Central and Northern line. There is also an excellent museum that is open to the public. It houses many interesting artifacts, including bank notes, furniture, historical records, a gold bar and if I recall correctly, a stuffed cat!

In early 2009 the Bank's website (www.bankofengland.co.uk) stated:

> People need to have confidence that the system is safe and stable, and that it functions properly. It is also important that problems in particular areas do not lead to wider disruption across the financial system. The Bank's role is to contribute to maintaining the stability of the UK financial system. It aims to identify and draw attention to potential vulnerabilities and risks and to assist in efforts to ensure the system remains resilient and risks are reduced.
>
> Substantial work is under way in the light of the recent financial market turmoil to help rebuild confidence in financial institutions, and to reduce the likelihood and impact of a recurrence.

The Bank has a number of tools at its disposal and will, among other things, operate in the UK money markets, set interest rates via the Monetary Policy Committee (MPC), issue Gilts and manage the foreign exchange reserves.

European Central Bank (ECB)

The ECB, based in Brussels, came into being in 1998, and went live in 1999 when the euro was introduced on 1 January. In its own words from its website:

> Since that time, the ECB as the 'captain' of the Eurosystem team – the central banking system of the euro area – has been conducting monetary policy for the countries in the currency union. Its primary objective is price stability over the medium term, because stable prices form the basis for sustainable economic growth and prosperity in Europe.

The ECB is the central bank for Europe's single currency, the euro.

The ECB's main task is to maintain the euro's purchasing power and thus price stability in the euro area. The euro area comprises the 16 European Union countries that have introduced the euro as their currency since 1999 (Figure 3.2).

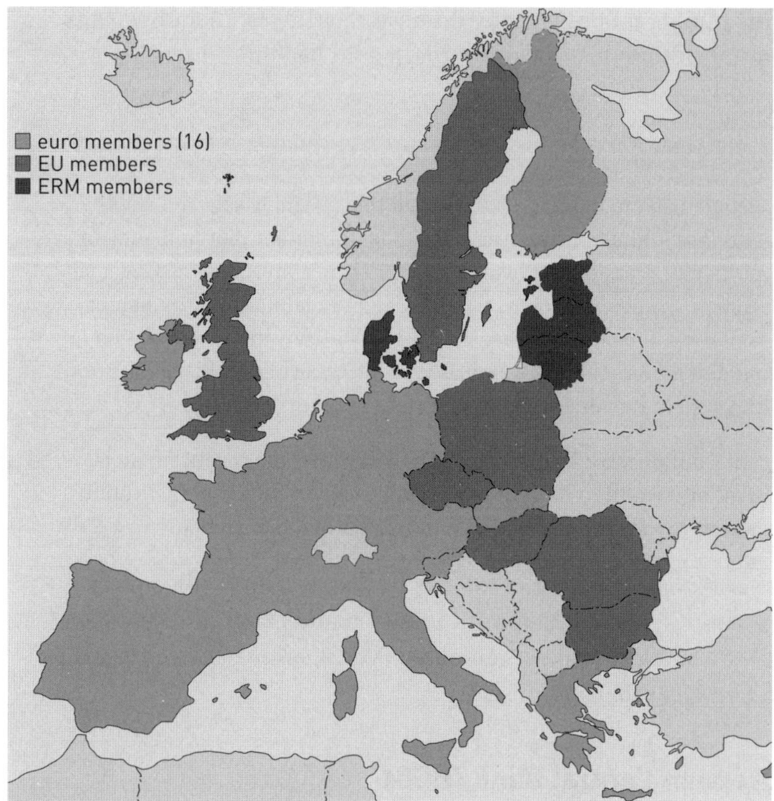

FIGURE 3.2 Map of the euro area (2009) Euro members: Austria, Belgium, Cyprus, Finland, France, Germany, Greece, Ireland, Luxembourg, Malta, The Netherlands, Portugal, Slovakia, Slovenia and Spain

Source: ECB

Each of the nations that has adopted the euro also has a legacy central bank or national central bank (NCB), e.g. Bank of France, National Bank of Belgium, which is responsible for banking supervision.

Central Bank of the United Arab Emirates

The roots of the Central Bank for the United Arab Emirates go back to the UAE Currency Board, established in 1973 with the introduction of the UAE dirham. It was given extra responsibilities and in 1980 became the central bank of the emirates. Its objectives are to direct monetary, credit and banking policy and supervise the implementation in accordance with the state's general policy in such ways as to help support the national economy and stability of the currency. It manages these objectives by:

- managing note issuance;
- supporting the currency, maintaining its stability internally and externally and ensuring its free convertibility into foreign currencies;
- directing credit policy in such ways as to help achieve balanced growth of the national economy;
- organising and promoting banking and supervising the effectiveness of the banking system;
- undertaking the function of the bank of the government within the limits prescribed in the law;
- advising the government on financial and monetary issues;
- maintaining the government's reserves of gold and foreign currencies;
- acting as the bank for banks operating in the country; and
- acting as the state's financial agent at the International Monetary Fund, the International Bank for Reconstruction and Development, and other international and arab funds and institutions and carrying out dealings of the state with such concerns.

Bank for International Settlements (BIS)

The Bank for International Settlements (BIS) is known as the central bankers' central bank. It is based in Basel in Switzerland and is an international organisation that fosters international monetary and financial co-operation. The BIS manages these activities by acting as:

- a forum to promote discussion and policy analysis among central banks and within the international financial community;
- a centre for economic and monetary research;
- a prime counterparty for central banks in their financial transactions, in areas such as foreign exchange and gold;
- agent or trustee in connection with international financial operations.

The BIS also offers products and services to central banks, monetary authorities and financial institutions.

TABLE 3.1 BIS products and services

BIS products and services

Central bank customers have traditionally looked for security, liquidity and return as the three basic features of their placements at the BIS. To ensure liquidity, the Bank stands ready to repurchase its tradable instruments at little cost to its customers and thus respond quickly and flexibly to their needs.

BIS money market instruments

- Sight/notice accounts and fixed and floating-rate deposits in most convertible currencies.
- Fixed-term deposits can also be denominated in and index-linked to a basket of currencies such as the SDR.
- Standard and non-standard amounts and maturities.

BIS tradable instruments

- Issued in major currencies.
- Available in two forms: Fixed Rate Investments at the BIS (FIXBIS) for any maturities between one week and one year and Medium-Term Instruments (MTIs) for quarterly maturities from one year and up to ten years.
- MTIs available also with an embedded call feature (Callable MTIs)

Foreign exchange and gold services

Services offered are:

- spot deals, swaps, outright forwards, options, FX-linked deposits;
- foreign exchange overnight orders;
- safekeeping and settlements facilities available loco London, Berne or New York;
- purchases and sales of gold: spot, outright, swap or options.

Asset management services

Fixed income portfolios are:

- invested in government bonds or high-grade credit securities;
- structured as dedicated portfolio mandates or BIS Investment Pool (open-end funds);
- offered as either single currency or multi-currency mandates in the major world reserve currencies.

Other services

- Short-term advances to central banks, usually on a collateralised basis.
- Trustee for a number of international government loans.
- Collateral agent functions.

Source: www.bis.org/banking/finserv.htm

The BIS head office is in Basel and there are two representative offices, in Hong Kong and in Mexico City. Established on 17 May 1930, the BIS is the world's oldest international finance organisation.

> the BIS is the world's oldest international financial organisation

How might you have come across the BIS? Probably one of the most well known areas where it is involved concerns banking rules and regulations, notably, the Basel II regulations. In addition, it produces financial market statistics, including the BIS triennial survey of foreign exchange and a half yearly survey of turnover in the derivatives markets as well as general banking surveys.

Commercial and investment banks

The 1933 Glass Steagall Act in the US forced a distinction between investment and commercial banks. In 1999, this was effectively repealed by the Gramm-Leach-Bliley Act, which allowed a merging of commercial and investment banking. However, it left open the option for the banks to remain regulated by their 'original' or 'historical' regulator. Put simply, the Fed regulates retail or commercial banks whilst the Securities and Exchange Commission (SEC) regulates investment banks.

An easy way of identifying whether a bank is a commercial bank or an investment bank used to be whether it had branches on the (main) high street. If the answer was yes, it was a commercial bank, like HSBC or Barclays Bank or Citibank (in the US, these are known as BHCs, bank holding companies). If the answer was no, it was an investment bank, such as Goldman Sachs or Merrill Lynch.

Since the credit crunch, this has all changed; investment banks have sought to widen their customer base to provide themselves with more stable business income streams and to help them off-set the affect of some of their credit risky investments.

Commercial banks were licensed to take deposits on the high street whereas investment banks were not. A commercial bank would usually pay a lower interest rate to its depositors, then lend out the funds at a higher rate to companies. In taking on that business model, it took on the credit risk, and indeed the profit opportunity, from buying low and selling high.

To clarify the credit risk aspect; if a commercial bank took in $1 million from local customers then lent the money to a business that subsequently went into bankruptcy, the bank would still need to refund the money it took from the original depositors.

In contrast, an investment bank has no pot of money from depositors, it generates profits from fee income, largely from issuing bonds and equity. These securities issues were often complex, time consuming to put together and large, with $100 million being a small issue. If the fee income was quoted as a percentage of the amount of finance raised (2–4 per cent), a banker didn't need many bond issues to make substantial income streams for his employer.

Another relevant aspect was the way credit risk was treated. Because an investment bank was typically an intermediary arranging finance, taking a fee, but not actually lending its own money, it followed that if a bond issuer went into default, it wasn't the investment banks at risk – it was just the arranger. The risk of loss was suffered by the ultimate investors, the investment managers in the community. Many of these bond issues and other complex structured securities in which they invested required credit ratings from the independent rating agencies, Standard & Poor's, Moody's and Fitch. Some of the more adventurous banks invested in complex mortgage linked securities and collateralised debt obligations (CDOs) and encountered problems with valuation and liquidity because of the credit crunch.

Table 3.2 lists some of the investment banks that are no longer with us.

TABLE 3.2 Some investment banks that are no longer with us

Barings: assets acquired by ING in 1995
Bear Stearns: assets acquired by JPMorgan Chase in 2008
Commerzbank: acquired by Dresdner, 2008
Donaldson, Lufkin and Jenrette: assets acquired by Credit Suisse in 2001
First Boston: merged with Credit Suisse to form Credit Suisse First Boston in 1988
Hambros: acquired by Société Générale
Kleinwort Benson: acquired by Dresdner
Merrill Lynch: acquired by Bank of America, 2008
Morgan Grenfell: acquired by Deutsche Bank, 1990
SG Warburg & Co: now part of UBS
Salomon Brothers: acquired by Travellers Group 1997, was part of Citigroup

In September 2008, the US financial landscape changed when two of the most prominent investment banks, Goldman Sachs and Morgan Stanley, allowed themselves to come under far closer scrutiny from the Federal Reserve, the US regulator. They became full bank holding companies. Figure 3.3 shows the top 20 BHCs by size before Goldman Sachs and Morgan Stanley joined. This decision allowed them to take advantage of the safety net provided by the Fed and to benefit from access to additional liquidity provided. So, it can be argued that there are no remaining true investment banks in the US. Yet this does not mean that investment banking has disappeared. Transactions will simply be executed by banks that offer a range of activities, such as HSBC, Deutsche Bank and Bank of America.

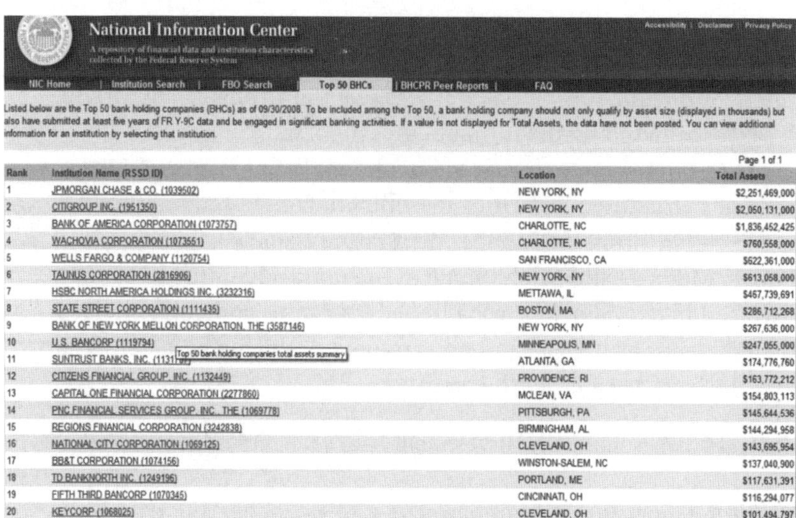

National Information Center
A repository of financial data and institution characteristics collected by the Federal Reserve System

Accessibility | Disclaimer | Privacy Policy

NIC Home | Institution Search | FBO Search | Top 50 BHCs | BHCPR Peer Reports | FAQ

Listed below are the Top 50 bank holding companies (BHCs) as of 09/30/2008. To be included among the Top 50, a bank holding company should not only qualify by asset size (displayed in thousands) but also have submitted at least five years of FR Y-9C data and be engaged in significant banking activities. If a value is not displayed for Total Assets, the data have not been posted. You can view additional information for an institution by selecting that institution.

Page 1 of 1

Rank	Institution Name (RSSD ID)	Location	Total Assets
1	JPMORGAN CHASE & CO. (1039502)	NEW YORK, NY	$2,251,469,000
2	CITIGROUP INC. (1951350)	NEW YORK, NY	$2,050,131,000
3	BANK OF AMERICA CORPORATION (1073757)	CHARLOTTE, NC	$1,836,452,425
4	WACHOVIA CORPORATION (1073551)	CHARLOTTE, NC	$760,558,000
5	WELLS FARGO & COMPANY (1120754)	SAN FRANCISCO, CA	$622,361,000
6	TAUNUS CORPORATION (2816906)	NEW YORK, NY	$613,058,000
7	HSBC NORTH AMERICA HOLDINGS INC. (3232316)	METTAWA, IL	$457,739,691
8	STATE STREET CORPORATION (1111435)	BOSTON, MA	$286,712,268
9	BANK OF NEW YORK MELLON CORPORATION, THE (3587146)	NEW YORK, NY	$267,636,000
10	U.S. BANCORP (1119794)	MINNEAPOLIS, MN	$247,055,000
11	SUNTRUST BANKS, INC. (1131[illegible]	ATLANTA, GA	$174,776,760
12	CITIZENS FINANCIAL GROUP, INC. (1132449)	PROVIDENCE, RI	$163,772,212
13	CAPITAL ONE FINANCIAL CORPORATION (2277860)	MCLEAN, VA	$154,803,113
14	PNC FINANCIAL SERVICES GROUP, INC., THE (1069778)	PITTSBURGH, PA	$145,644,536
15	REGIONS FINANCIAL CORPORATION (3242838)	BIRMINGHAM, AL	$144,294,958
16	NATIONAL CITY CORPORATION (1069125)	CLEVELAND, OH	$143,695,954
17	BB&T CORPORATION (1074156)	WINSTON-SALEM, NC	$137,040,900
18	TD BANKNORTH INC. (1249196)	PORTLAND, ME	$117,631,391
19	FIFTH THIRD BANCORP (1070345)	CINCINNATI, OH	$116,294,077
20	KEYCORP (1068025)	CLEVELAND, OH	$101,494,797

Top 50 bank holding companies total assets summary

FIGURE 3.3 Top 20 US bank holding companies

Source: National Information Center (September 2008)

You may have an image of a dealing room as being full of rows of people sitting at desks, in front of computer screens. These folks might have been screaming or shouting at each other, or looking bored waiting for something to happen. What do all the people do?

Sales

Dedicated sales teams provide the link between the customer and bank traders. Some sales staff may be specialised and speak solely to central banks; others may talk to big companies or other banks. If the bank has a branch network, some staff may speak only to their own branches. The role of the sales team is to generate business for the traders. They will have their own clients and get to know them very well. Customer service is paramount.

> the role of the sales team is to generate business for the traders

A customer may wish to know where, for example, the Standard Chartered share price is trading and ask for indication price from his sales contact. The trader who looks after Stan Chart will make a price, which is then relayed back by the sales person to the customer who may or may not deal; this is known as trade execution.

If the client is happy that he definitely wants to deal he would request the salesperson to buy for him 'at market', but it would be the trader who executes the deal because sales staff generally are not allowed to run positions. This conversation may take place over the phone, but it is increasingly likely now to take place via an electronic network (ECN).

Some firms have a hybrid role which is a 'sales-trader' who can act in both capacities but under strict internal controls.

Traders

A trader is the individual who has to make a price, to buy or to sell. It is irrelevant whether they personally want to buy or sell – they still have to make prices for customers. The professional market will request from each other two-way prices – meaning a bid and an offer, and then deal on the side that suits. This is known as '**market making**' and the trader is expected to keep a two-way price throughout the trading day.

Trade execution is slightly different in the equity market, where you have:

- order-driven markets, where **orders** placed by buyers and sellers are matched electronically;
- quote-driven markets, where prices displayed by market makers allow potential buyers and sellers to trade with knowledge of current quoted prices.

Also in the equity market you have:

- trades that are executed through electronic exchanges. Buyers and sellers are matched electronically; this is known as 'on-exchange' dealing;
- trades executed directly between market participants, these are known as trades over-the-counter (OTC).

Traders across all markets have their own specialities, e.g. USD/JPY, or USD swaps, bonds, or sterling money markets. Throughout the day a trader's position will fluctuate from being long to short or vice versa and at close of business they will calculate (or their systems will) their profit/loss for the day.

Profit and Loss

Profit and loss is known as realised profit/loss, or it may be unrealised, which is in effect a mark-to-market calculation.

EXAMPLE

Earlier in the day, a firm bought gold at $855 an ounce and sold it at $860. This results in a realised profit of $5.

EXAMPLE

The firm bought gold (is long) at $837 (an ounce). At close of business, the trader is still long gold; the price is now quoted at $840–841. On a mark-to-market basis, the trader has made a notional $3 profit – the gold has not yet been sold, but if it was, it would have to be sold at someone else's bid.

There are also sales staff in private banks, but they sell different services and advice to different types of clients.

Private banks

Private banks tend to have a different business model. As well as offering basic banking services, they also offer a complementary range of services for (usually) high net worth (HNW), i.e. rich individuals. These services might include advice on tax planning, including inheritance tax planning, pensions, wealth management, as well as mortgages (large ones) and investment advice. The advice is confidential and is aimed at those who typically have at least $1 million under management, although some firms will target the less affluent with only $250,000 to invest.

Many large banks have private banking divisions. These include UBS, Société Genéralé, Goldman Sachs and HSBC.

TABLE 3.3 Examples of private banks

C Hoare & Co, 37 Fleet Street, London, EC4P 4DQ. Established in 1672 and still owned by the Hoare family.
Coutts & Co. Founded in 1692, but the name first appeared in 1755. The first office was in The Strand in London and it is now owned by Royal Bank of Scotland.
Bank Julius Baer, Zurich, Switzerland. Established in 1890 as Hirschhorn & Grob, but the name first appeared in 1901.

Bank departments: front office, middle office and operations

Most large wholesale banks can be likened to Dr Who's Tardis. On the outside all you see is a door. Once inside the Tardis, the whole thing opens up and there are mysterious gadgets, gizmos and all sorts of other interesting 'stuff'– just like a bank. Although every bank has its own unique identity, they all have similar departments, divided into:

- front office;
- middle office;
- operations (used to be called back office).

Front office

The front office is where the deals are executed and where the traders sit; this is the area that is felt by many to be the power house of the firm. It is here that the traders establish their own prices (market-making) and/or hedge their positions, generate profits (and losses), use the complementary skills of their sales and marketing teams, their quants and structurers. As well as making prices for customers, they will also make prices for the rest of the bank, maybe the brokers, their own relationship managers (account officers), trade finance and anyone else who needs an interest, currency, credit, equity or commodity price. This area also includes anyone who is 'front-facing' to clients, such as sales and sales trading, marketing, economists and origination. This area could also be known as the dealing room, the trading floor, or the treasury department.

Middle office

People in the middle office could come from anywhere that is not front office or operations so it technically includes: risk, accounting, information technology (IT), credit, compliance, product control, human resources, legal and tax. In principle, anyone in one of these departments could prevent a front office deal happening in the first place.

For example, imagine a Turkish lira trade that should not have been executed because there was no currency account or, there was a query over some documentation, or there were incomplete account details, or due diligence and anti-money laundering checks had not been completed. However, the deal was done anyway and now has to be sorted out.

Operations

The operations area in many banks used to be called 'back office', but this term is now largely ignored because to some, it seems derogatory.

It is a banking area that is critical to the success of transactions. With many banking products becoming effectively 'commoditised' (all the same), a range of banks could well quote in competition for a financial product and all offer the same price to a customer. So how does the client choose who to deal with? The answer used to be easy, who took them for the best lunch, who do they get on with personally, where do they feel the greatest rapport? Now it may all come down to who has the most efficient 'ops' department. This will inevitably lead to fewer queries, fewer mistakes, fewer 'where is my money?' type questions.

This department needs to cover activities such as deal capture, validation, confirmations and settlements. For details on what happens after a deal is done, please see Chapters 8 and 9.

It is this department that has borne the brunt of many job losses relating to straight through processing (STP) initiatives as staff are being replaced with complex front-to-back computer systems.

Regulators

Given the problems with global financial markets and the various financial and banking institutions which have suffered, regulators have come under more scrutiny than usual.

Financial Services Authority (FSA)

In 1997, the UK Securities and Investment Board (SIB) was formed from a range of supervisory and regulatory bodies, it was then renamed the Financial Services Authority. Over a period of a few years the roles and responsibilities listed below were transferred to it:

- banking supervision (formerly with the Bank of England);
- Building Societies Commission;
- Friendly Societies Commission;
- Investment Management Regulatory Organisation (IMRO);
- Personal Investment Authority;
- Register of Friendly Societies;
- Securities and Futures Authority;
- mortgage regulation;
- general insurance.

The **FSA** is an independent non-governmental body, given statutory powers by the Financial Services and Markets Act 2000 (FSMA 2000). It is a company limited by guarantee and financed by the financial services industry. The UK Treasury appoints the FSA board, which consists of a chairman, a chief executive, three managing directors, and nine non-executive directors. This board sets the overall policy, but day-to-day decisions and management of the staff are the responsibility of the executive.

Under the FSMA (2000), the FSA has four objectives:

- maintaining confidence in the financial system;
- promoting public awareness and understanding of the financial system;
- securing the appropriate degree of protection for consumers;
- reducing the extent to which it is possible for a business to be used for a purpose connected with financial crime, e.g. fraud and money laundering.

There are also three strategic aims:

- promoting efficient, orderly and fair markets;
- helping retail consumers achieve a fair deal; and
- improving business capability and effectiveness.

Following the run on Northern Rock in 2007, the first run on a UK bank in 140 years, the FSA was forced into the spotlight as it was felt by many at the time that greater support should have been offered. In fact, in the UK there is a 'tripartite' regulator consisting of the UK Treasury (part of the government, in effect, the chancellor and his team), the FSA and the Bank of England. They were all required to agree an approach and it came too late for the Rock. John McFall, chairman of the all-party Commons Treasury Select Committee set up to investigate what happened said:

> The failure of Northern Rock, while primarily a failure of its directors, was also a failure of its regulator.
>
> The FSA appears to have systematically failed in its duty and this failure contributed significantly to the difficulties and risks to the public purse that have followed.

The committee of MPs said the finance ministry was right to have authorised financial support but the tripartite authorities 'did not prepare adequately for that support operation' and should have finalised plans within hours of the decision to help. In February 2008, Northern Rock was taken into state ownership. Ironically, as the credit crisis deepened and investors sought safer havens for their deposits, many tried to deposit with Northern Rock because it was then effectively guaranteed by the UK government. The Rock shut its doors to new investors in some of its accounts in October 2008.

US regulation

In the US, banking is regulated at both the federal and state level. Depending on a banking organisation's charter and organisational structure, it may be subject to numerous federal and state banking regulators. Unlike Japan and the UK, where regulatory authority over the banking, securities and insurance industries is combined into one single financial services agency, the US maintains separate securities, commodities and insurance regulatory agencies (which are separate from the bank regulatory agencies) at the federal and state level as well.

in the US, banking is regulated at both the federal and state level

The main regulators are the Federal Reserve (the Fed) and the Securities and Exchange Commission (SEC).

The Federal Reserve Bank of New York is charged with supervisory and regulatory responsibilities over banks. Those are the full bank holding companies shown in Figure 3.3, though this list is likely to change when the next figures are released.

The SEC, oversees participants in the securities world, including securities exchanges, securities brokers and dealers, investment advisors and mutual funds. Here, the SEC is concerned with promoting the disclosure of important market-related information, maintaining fair dealing, and protecting against fraud. From its website:

- The mission of the US Securities and Exchange Commission is to protect investors, maintain fair, orderly and efficient markets, and facilitate capital formation.

- The laws and rules that govern the securities industry in the United States derive from a simple and straightforward concept: all investors, whether large institutions or private individuals, should have access to certain basic facts about an investment prior to buying it, and so long as they hold it. To achieve this, the SEC requires public companies to disclose meaningful financial and other information to the public. This provides a common pool of knowledge for all investors to use to judge for themselves whether to buy, sell, or hold a particular security. Only through the steady flow of timely, comprehensive, and accurate information can people make sound investment decisions.

It goes without saying that regulation globally is going to be re-examined in the wake of the financial instability suffered from 2007 onwards.

Brokers

Brokers have been an integral part of the financial market place since the first deals were done in the Middle Ages. Traditionally, their role is to act as an intermediary between two counterparties. They are, in effect, acting as an agent to facilitate a transaction; putting in touch willing buyers and willing sellers for a fee, which is known as brokerage ('bro') or commission. They broke all major asset classes, including derivatives, foreign exchange, securities, property and bullion.

Well known brokers are ICAP, Tradition, Tullett Prebon, and Cantor Fitzgerald.

TIP

Within the institutional investor community (financial corporates) where their main instruments are bonds and equity, there is a role known as an agency broker; this is identical to normal broking.

Traditional corporates

These are the companies that make or produce something; it could be machinery, air travel, inks, printing, construction, or computers to name but a few. Generally, the financial remit within their head office is that there will be a treasury department whose business is to manage the financial risks of the business. These will comprise risks relating to funding, currency, interest rates, credit, and liquidity. Some organisations may also act as a bank for the rest of the business and actively take risk, e.g. they might buy yen, not to pay an invoice, but because they think it is going up and they will make a profit. (For more on risks see Chapter 4.)

In terms of treasury organisation and structure, the department will tend to be designated either as a cost centre or a profit centre, but there are many steps in between. This is ultimately determined by the way the board of directors wants financial risk to be managed or mitigated and the resources available to them. As every organisation is different this results in a myriad of structures (Table 3.4).

TABLE 3.4 Treasury department's approach to risk management

Treasury role	Response	Management	Appetite	Performance measure
Advisory	Full hedge	Passive	Averse to risk	Cost centre
Agency (most popular)	Full to selective hedge	A little less passive, more active	Quasi risk-averse	Cost centre to cost-saving centre
In-house bank	Position-taking	Active	Risk-loving	Profit centre

Role of the treasurer

In brief, a treasurer manages the department and its activities based on a treasury policy and procedures manual, which is set by the board of directors. This document will cover areas such as the role of the department, its appetite or aversion to risk, how it manages currency and interest rate risk, who is authorised to deal, which banks should be used and for which activities. One of the objectives relates to minimisation of fraud or losses due to negligence. Segregation of responsibility involves making sure that no single person could instigate a transaction and run with it from start to finish without anyone else being involved, which is very important. Credit risk is also obviously a major concern at present. Many treasury staff are members of the Association of Corporate Treasurers (ACT).

Role of the finance director

Obviously this all depends upon the level of complexity required by the organisation. Essentially, the finance director is the treasury's voice on the board of directors. However, he could also have accounting, financial control, tax and risk reporting to him. He could also have no experience of treasury at all.

A range of treasury structures can be found among companies. In order of complexity, these are:

- Advisory role: sets treasury policy and develops reporting and monitoring systems, becomes a central source of market information, managing head office treasury requirements. But all transactions are executed locally in the subsidiaries.
- Agency role: maintains control of all treasury decisions at a local level, but requires all financial transactions to be conducted through the central treasury department, thereby acting as agent for the rest of the group. Day-to-day management remains with the subsidiaries but treasury executes the deals. Group treasury manages the banking relationships for all subsidiary companies, and because it employs more experienced personnel, better dealing rates should be achieved.
- In-house bank: treasury provides all banking and treasury services for the organisation. For this structure to be adopted, the following are needed:
  - sufficient transaction volumes to make the investment worthwhile;
  - high level of in-house expertise;
  - high credit rating.

The advantages of this approach are:

- improved rates from larger and more frequent deals;
- cash netting/pooling to increase cash management;
- access to disintermediated markets such as commercial paper (**CP**), bonds and euro-currency markets.

On a scale from 1 to 10, with 1 being very averse to risk and very controlled and 10 being an in-house bank, actively taking risk, most corporate treasury departments are somewhere between 2 and 5.

Financial corporates

These are companies whose business is money but they are not banks, e.g. asset managers, insurance companies, pension funds and hedge funds. Sometimes they are known as **institutional investors**. Mostly, they are investors seeking returns in a certain time period: to a pension fund, long term may mean in excess of forty years; to a hedge fund, it may mean months. They may be generating income for themselves or for their clients.

Insurance companies:

- Their objectives are to invest premiums received from customers to ensure there are sufficient funds available to pay claims during the life of a policy (house, contents and car) or on maturity with life policies.
- They will have a mix of asset class exposure, typically though big bond investments and may subcontract management of some funds to specialist asset management houses.

Pension funds:

- They have long-term investment portfolios designed to fund future liabilities of individuals upon retirement.
- They are facing an ageing population, meaning a shrinking workforce funding an older, larger pool of retired people.
- They have an asset mix closely monitored by actuaries and trustees to minimise unnecessary risk and these funds are often subcontracted out to specialist asset management houses.

Specialist asset management houses:

- Offer to manage third-party funds for a fee.
- May have institutional and/or private clients with a discretionary or advisory mandate.
- May manage the funds 'actively' or 'passively', examples are/were Invesco, Aberdeen, New Star and Jupiter.

Generally, these houses will construct portfolios of assets and then manage the portfolio risk-taking into account diversification and correlation. The latter term describes how market events affect the various holdings – will all the securities move up, or will some move up and some down? The term covariance describes how assets move:

- positive covariance (0 to +1): the returns from two securities will tend to move together.
- zero (small) covariance: there is little or no relationship between the two returns.
- negative covariance (0 to –1): the returns from two securities will tend to offset each other.

Each asset manager will have an asset allocation strategy that will need to consider the mix between equity, debt, derivatives and cash. Also, whether they are looking at this from a strategic (long-term outlook – ignores short-term 'noise', aims to hit a benchmark), often used by pension funds, or a tactical standpoint, (more short-term, looking for stocks, picks and anomalies, tries to beat a benchmark). However, as client needs change over time, these will be reviewed regularly.

Hedge funds

Although there is no legal definition of what a hedge fund is, it is reputed that the first hedge fund was started in 1946 by Alfred Winslow Jones who was a stock picker and 'shorted' stocks he didn't like to balance out those he held in his 'long' portfolio.

There are many types of hedge funds, but they tend to have some things in common, notably:

- fees are based on the fund manager's performance;
- the ability to short assets;
- high minimum investment requirements, e.g. $10 million in some funds;
- lock-up periods, which may be as much as three years, during which investors cannot take their money out;
- an emphasis on absolute performance rather than tracking a benchmark;
- the manager's own capital may be invested in the fund and they are typically domiciled offshore, e.g. the Cayman Islands or Guernsey.

Having said that, some investors will not accept any lock-up period.

More than half of all investments in hedge funds come from private individuals, with the balance from institutional investors.

some investors will not accept any lock-up period

The strategy of the fund will be either directional or non-directional. Directional trading may well include the use of derivatives and the long/short equity strategy is by far the most popular – in essence the fund must be long or short, it should not be market-neutral.

A non-directional strategy will involve the use of arbitrage, and are mostly market-neutral.

The typical structure of a hedge fund is shown in Figure 3.4.

Estimates vary as to how many hedge funds there are, but at the end of 2007 there were reckoned to be just under 12,000, of which three-quarters were single-manager funds and the rest were fund of hedge funds – who knows how many are left now?

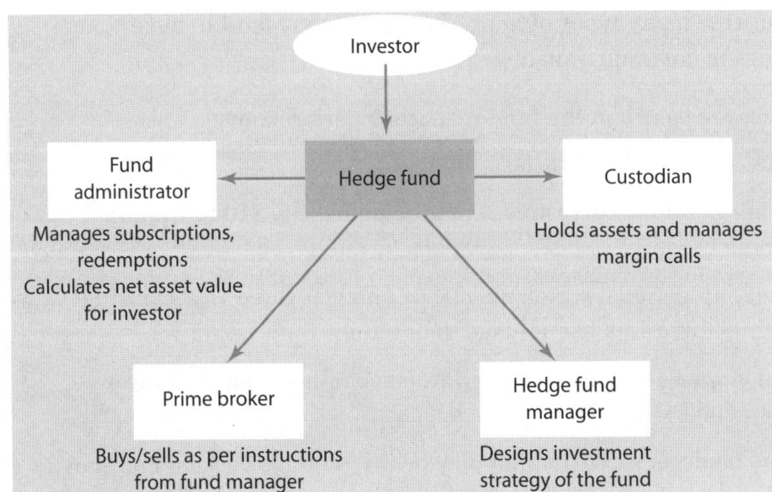

FIGURE 3.4 Typical structure of a hedge fund

Player motivations

Hedgers

A hedger is someone who wants to manage or mitigate their perceived risk. This may be anyone from a small individual with a currency exposure that they wish to protect, to a multinational with a $500m borrowing that needs interest rate protection, or a European fund manager who is worried about the domestic stock market falling. Hedgers generally will 'buy' the insurance or enter into protection. The tools they use are global market instruments that cross borders easily.

Traders

A trader (or speculator) wants to take risk. The banking and hedge fund community dominates here. Most, but not all, traders will make a market in financial instruments, i.e. a bid and an offer. They could be trading supply and demand, or directionally, does the asset go up or down from here? or even volatility – how is the market price going to fluctuate? Their role is to create the asset or derivative, at a price, sell it to the client, run their positions at a profit, and hedge themselves. Traders will also speculate in the interbank market.

Arbitrageurs

Arbitrageurs are individuals or banks that try to identify price discrepancies and profit from them. An example might be someone who can borrow for three months at 4 per cent and simultaneously lend at 4.1 per cent. Obviously, this looks too good to be true, but you would take advantage of it nevertheless. In the derivatives market, you would assume that the physical gold price will move at the same speed as derivatives linked to the gold price. This may not always be the case, therefore there may be profit opportunities from buying one and selling the other.

International Swaps and Derivatives Association (ISDA)

In the OTC derivatives markets, all transactions are executed 'subject to docs'. This means that there is an element of trust between the market participants that the basic legal documentation is agreed and in place. The market standard documentation is known as 'ISDA', after the International Swaps and Derivatives Association.

ISDA Inc. was formed in 1985 with ten members to standardise market practice and address the documentation issues arising from a surge in the volume of OTC derivatives transactions. At that time, each bank and client had their own bank specific documentation.

Picture this: Bank A in the US transacts five swaps in the morning with Bank B in the UK and each sends five full sets of their own documentation to each other (in the post). The same issues are likely to arise every time a trade is executed because the documentation is non-standard and different. The legal teams in each bank must agree any changes for the deal to proceed, which may involve transatlantic phone calls and, in extreme cases, documents sent by air courier. In the afternoon, Bank A transacts ten swaps with Bank C in Germany. The same thing happens again, ten full sets of documentation are dispatched but the queries and amendments will now be different. If a bank transacted with twenty counterparties in twenty four hours, it could receive twenty versions of the documentation.

ISDA was formed to create a market standard document that worked for most counterparties, most of the time. Any variations to the standard document must be negotiated by specialists and are included in a schedule, and every transaction is evidenced by a confirmation.

The practical usage of an ISDA document is discussed in Chapter 9.

Exchanges

The term 'the exchanges' denotes the large institutions that facilitate the trading of exchange-traded derivatives – futures and **traded option** contracts. The majority of the futures and options that concern the readers of this book are settled in cash at maturity – although there are exceptions in the energy and bond markets. This section does not cover exchanges that trade in physical commodities such as grain, coffee or orange juice.

The two largest exchanges are based in Chicago, the Chicago Board of Trade and the Chicago Mercantile Exchange. In 2007, a $9 billion merger was agreed to form the CME Group, and in 2008 the CME Group bought Nymex, the New York Mercantile Exchange. Through their holding in Nymex they also have links with the Dubai Mercantile Exchange and others.

Globally, there are three groups challenging for the top place:

- CME Group (CME, CBOT, Nymex);
- NYSE Euronext (also includes the American Stock Exchange and Liffe) with rumours of a tie-up with the Deutsche Börse;
- ICE (previously bought the UK IPE (International Petroleum Exchange) in 2001, NYBOT (New York Board of Trade) and WCE (Winnipeg Commodity Exchange) in 2007. Now trading as ICE Futures Europe, ICE Futures US and ICE Futures Canada.

Consolidation of such exchanges is expected to continue.

For details on trading with futures see Chapter 2.

Information providers

Financial market participants need good quality and more importantly, real time information. A trip around a bank dealing room will show that most dealers have anywhere from three to six computer screens, displaying prices, charts, pricing models and current positions.

Information is valuable and is not available free of charge. There are a range of subscription services depending on requirements.

After many years of consolidation there are two main independent software vendors. These are Thomson Reuters and Bloomberg. Both provide independent market information and are indispensible to financial market activities.

Further reading

www.bankofengland.co.uk

www.bis.org

www.centralbank.ae

www.cmegroup.com

www.ecb.int

www.federalreserve.gov

www.fsa.gov.uk

www.isda.org

www.liffe.com

www.sec.gov

www.theice.com

www.treasurers.org

4 Key risk management terms

...corporates typically want to hedge or mitigate their risk, whilst banks mostly want to take on risk – although current market conditions are making them quite risk-averse.

Introduction

In writing this book, a number of financial risks came to the forefront of my mind. This chapter aims to explain some of these terms to aid in the comprehension of some of the later chapters. I am not trying to cover every term but the ones that are most relevant in today's markets. I am also making a general assumption that corporates typically want to hedge or mitigate their risk, whilst banks mostly want to take on **risk** – although current market conditions are making them quite risk-averse. This section is divided into generic financial, market and operational risks, followed by some of the more esoteric terms.

Financial risk

When assessing the market risk an organisation faces, the treasurer or risk manager has a range of issues to examine. One of these is to quantify the risk to provide a clear picture of the relative size of the exposure. For example, is it worth worrying about a $25,000 currency risk or might it be too small in the grand scale of things? Could we perhaps 'self-insure'?

Assuming the risk is worth worrying about and the size of the exposure is substantial, then action will be required.

Financial risk can be subdivided into several categories.

Market risk

Interest rate risk

The main approach here is to identify the level of exposure to changes in interest rates. Any controls need to balance the potential loss (both in terms of likelihood and amount) against the cost of insuring against any loss.

EXAMPLE

A company seeking €5 million to finance expansion is offered a facility by a bank linked to a EURIBOR floating interest rate. It is not a bank, so is offered a five-year facility at six-month EURIBOR + 0.5 per cent, to be re-set every six months. Risk arises because it is impossible to know what the rate will be until the fixing is done in six months' time; if the rate increases, the company pays more interest – possibly more than budgeted for – and if the interest rate falls, it pays less interest. Alternatively, if the company took a loan at a fixed rate, it would suffer if interest rates fell; it might be paying interest at a fixed rate of 4 per cent and if rates fell to 3 per cent it would still be paying 4 per cent. This is known as an opportunity loss. Given that no one really knows what is going to happen, hedging instruments have been developed to manage this risk. Popular risk management tools include swaps and options, which are described in Chapter 2. Interest rate risk also includes basis risk and convergence which are described later in this chapter.

Foreign exchange or currency risk

This is the risk that a company would run if, for example, it was based in one country (and one currency) but was either receiving or paying a foreign currency in another.

EXAMPLE

A UK company with sterling as its reporting currency is going to receive $1 million after three months on 10 December. The risk is that the value of both sterling and the dollar could fluctuate, leading to a potential loss or profit when the dollars are converted into pounds. The client has three choices:

- sell forward the dollars at a fixed rate;
- buy an option to sell dollars at a fixed rate;
- wait and do the exchange at the spot rate on 10 December.

The choice is the client's, based on its internal guidelines for hedging currency risk. The rates on September 8 are:

GBP/USD 1.6500 Spot

GBP/USD 1.6300 Forward

The potential outcomes are:

1. Selling forward dollars at 1.6300 will generate a known amount of £613,496.93.
2. Buying an option to sell dollars at 1.6300 will generate at least £613,496.93, but this would require paying an option premium. However, if the exchange rate improves, meaning in this case that the dollar strengthened, the client would make a gain by walking away from the option and dealing at the spot rate. If the dollar weakened, there would be the fall-back position of the rate guaranteed by the option.
3. Doing nothing. Passive risk management means waiting for the exchange rate on the day in December. In the previous twelve months, some currencies have fluctuated by more than 10 per cent in a three-month period, so using this figure, would imply a spot rate of between 1.8150 and 1.4850.

Using the 1.8150 rate, the $1m would only generate £550,964.19, whereas at 1.4850, $1m would generate £673,400.67. On the one hand, the company wins and makes more money than it was expecting, on the other, it might not generate enough sterling to cover its costs. Taking this to a logical conclusion, with no hedging on the currency risk, the company has a 50/50 chance of losing (or making) money.

Note that the approach taken by a company to currency exposures and indeed to risk generally will have been agreed at board level and is evidenced by a document, usually known as the treasury policy and procedures manual (treasury P&P). The treasurer will also need to monitor exposure to changes in exchange rates. For example, can the firm change suppliers to one with a different home currency?

The Association of Corporate Treasurers (ACT) is a professional body that gives information on best practice.

Commodity price risk

How exposed is the company to a change in commodity prices? For example, copper is required for making electricity cables, steel for tin cans, and fuel is a big cost for airlines. Instruments such as options, swaps and forwards can go some way to fixing the price of a commodity, but do you want it fixed if you think the price might fall?

Credit risk

This general term for risk, which has been uppermost in many people's minds in recent years, can be subdivided further.

Credit risk, credit lines and concentration risk

In the financial market, the terms **credit risk** and **counterparty risk** are interchangeable. They describe the risk you run if the other side of your transaction fails, e.g., a client is unable to repay a loan, a prime broker becomes unable to return collateral, the counterparty to a credit default swap (CDS) is unable to make the settlement. This may result in a major default.

Credit lines

Banks will gauge the amount of credit risk they are prepared to take on a client by asking their internal credit department to make an assessment based on data included in such public documents as the client's financial statements and report and accounts; they will also look at independent credit ratings if they are available and past performance. The risk figure they come up with is known as the credit line. It indicates the maximum amount of exposure that the bank is prepared to run with that client at any one time.

> the risk figure they come up with is known as the credit line

EXAMPLE

Assume Client B is a medium-sized company and its credit line has been agreed at £10 million. It has only one outstanding transaction with the bank, a loan of £10 million. The risk weighting of this is likely to be 100 per cent – so the credit line is said to be 'full'. If the client fails the bank would lose the whole £10 million (plus any interest due).

All financial products, including foreign exchange and derivatives, have an individual risk weighting, which won't be 100 per cent but could well be 3 per cent or 5 per cent, either per annum or linked to the nominal principal amount. These amounts collectively must never add up to more than the total on the credit line. Otherwise the bank has exceeded its own risk appetite and we say the credit line has been 'broken'. All financial institutions will monitor the exposures on their credit lines very carefully.

NOTE

Realistically, if a counterparty is going down you can't prevent it happening and you will have very little time in which to react. Therefore utilisation under a credit line needs to be monitored continuously, to assess the exposure should there be a failure.

Banks will grant credit lines not just to clients but also to individual countries and industry sectors. Historically, it has been the case that banks have rated their clients for credit. Since the bank failures and restructurings, it is the clients who are now rating the banks for credit. This leads on to the next related category, concentration risk.

Concentration risk

Concentation risk describes how much exposure someone has to any one particular counterparty. In the context of banking, the term generally denotes the risk arising from an uneven distribution of counterparties in credit or any other banking relationships. It is a sense of how many eggs do I have in a particular basket?

Within the derivatives, securities and foreign exchange markets such risk relates to how many counterparties someone wishes to do business with. Or, given that there are now far fewer banks in the market, how this affects someone's trading and hedging. But, it is not just how many banks someone wants to work with, but how much of their business in total are they prepared to risk by dealing with any single institution.

EXAMPLE

Table 4.1 gives the results of a Euromoney FX Poll, published in May 2008. It shows that the top five banks had 61 per cent of the market, and the top ten banks had 81 per cent. Following the credit crunch, many of these banks became shadows of their former selves. If a client has a lot of FX to manage, very soon it might feel it had more than enough exposure with one bank. The question then arises, would there be enough capacity within the other banks to be able to take up the additional business?

TABLE 4.1 Top banks for foreign exchange by market share (2008)

2008	2007	Bank	Market share (%)
1	1	Deutsche Bank	21.70
2	2	UBS	15.80
3	5	Barclays Capital	9.12
4	3	Citi	7.49
5	4	RBS	7.30
6	9	JPMorgan	4.19
7	7	HSBC	4.10
8	11	Lehman Brothers	3.58
9	8	Goldman Sachs	3.47
10	10	Morgan Stanley	2.56
11	6	Bank of America	2.23
12	18	Dresdner	1.63
13	15	BNP Paribas	1.62
14	17	Credit Suisse	1.51
15	13	Merrill Lynch	1.24
16	12	ABN Amro	1.21
17	14	Calyon	1.04
18	20	Société Générale	0.89
19	19	Royal Bank of Canada	0.72
20	21	SEB	0.62

Source: *Euromoney*, May 2008

Every counterparty that the firm deals with needs to be monitored, including banks, customers and suppliers. The risk is not just that they may default on obligations but also that they may refuse to continue with them.

Settlement risk

Settlement risk is a problem for anyone involved in trading or dealing in securities or currency. For example, it is the risk that one side of a transaction might have paid out the USD on a foreign exchange deal, for example, but did not receive in the CHF against it. This risk is occasionally referred to as **Herstatt risk**, named after the German bank where there was a big settlement failure in 1974. This type of risk has largely been eliminated in the FX market by the introduction in 2002 of **continuous linked settlement (CLS)**. This is a market standard for foreign exchange settlements and is a sophisticated payments vs payments system (**PvP**). There are details at www.cls-holdings.com. The subject of settlement risk in securities is covered comprehensively in Chapter 8.

Liquidity risk

Cash flow risk

Any organisation must ensure it has sufficient cash to pay its bills. This is a function of when payments should be disbursed and also the ability of the accounts receivable department to collect enough funds to meet those liabilities. Surplus cash should be invested in such a way that it can be accessed if and when needed. Companies fail through lack of cash, not depressed profits.

> companies fail through lack of cash, not depressed profits

EXAMPLE

Because of a cash flow problem, there is only a limited amount of cash available to pay the bills below and only one can be paid. Who do you think should be paid?

- staff;
- interest payment to a bank;
- suppliers.

> The correct answer is an interest payment to a bank. Banks, depending on the documentation that has been signed, are very powerful and can in extreme circumstances force the closure of a company; with almost everything else a delay in the payment can be negotiated.

If there is a funding deficit, then money would need to be borrowed and if there are funds which are surplus to requirements, those can be placed on deposit.

Funding risk

To expand, companies need to be able to fund developments whether from external sources or from their own reserves. Companies that need to tap external sources such as bank finance or bond issues will be reliant on there being sufficient liquidity in the market when that injection of cash is needed. After the credit crunch, this area of finance became a concern.

Market liquidity risk

Liquidity in this context refers to the inability to buy or sell something. For example, a bank deposit is illiquid because you cannot sell it to anyone else; whereas a Gilt is very liquid because you can sell it on to anyone. A lack of liquidity is dangerous if you have an asset that you want to sell and can't, rather than if you want to buy an asset and you cannot. If you own an asset and you want to get out of it, if no one is making a price – or you don't like the price – you can't sell it and the price could tumble further.

There is a saying in the market:

> There is a price for buying, a price for selling and a price for selling quickly.

Even this relationship broke down with the some of the mortgage-related debt held by the banks in the latter half of 2008. No one was buying because no one was sure what the assets were worth (see Chapter 1).

Operational risk

As well as a core focus on financial risk, firms also need to identify their operational risks. This does not just mean risks that arise in the operations department but can include a number of areas. The topic is covered in more detail in Chapter 5.

Operations risk

Human resources risk

Risk arises from staffing within any finance or banking department. This ranges from human error, to the level of cover for workers who are on holiday or who are sick, to whether there are enough staff and are they trained in the right disciplines, to whether the right management structure is in place?

Fraud risk

What precautions should be taken to protect against the risk of fraud or money laundering? It is generally recognised that if a party wishes to commit a fraud they will. Accepted practice is that the firm will have procedures in place to detect any fraud or wrong-doing (could be just a mistake) within twenty four hours and hopefully before any money leaves accounts. With respect to money-laundering, there are regulations and the penalties are severe. For more information, see the Financial Services Authority website.

Business continuity (disaster recovery)

This is the risk that the finance and treasury function cannot continue to operate. There are two aspects to this:

- Will the treasury be able to continue to operate within its own location or at a back-up site?
- Will the treasury be able to communicate sufficiently and securely with external providers, such as banks, fund managers, clients and any outsourced service providers?

Following the 2001 terrorist attacks in the US when a number of firms needed to use their recovery sites simultaneously, infrastructure services were put under pressure, notably transport, communications and the provision of food and catering.

In the UK, following the London bombs in July 2005, when the public transport system was shut down, what good was a recovery site if you couldn't get to it?

Best practice now is that the recovery site is in another centre, with efficient road, rail and air links.

Systems and operations risk

As part of an assessment of operational risk, a firm needs to measure the risks that arise from their systems and how they link to other systems in use both elsewhere and externally, to banks, counterparties, prime brokers, custodians, clearing houses and exchanges. This will also include how trades are confirmed and settled. Third party providers have developed technology for this, notably, DTCC, DTCC Deriv/Serv, Markitwire, Omgeo and Thunderhead. Their roles are explained more fully in the Trade Lifecycle chapters.

Global regulators have become concerned about trade confirmations several times and have asked the financial community to improve their processes.

Reliability, capacity and longevity

Another area of concern relates to the tasks that systems are required to perform. Are they reliable? Can they expand to cope with new tasks in the future? What is the lifespan of these systems? When will they need an upgrade?

Data integrity

Firms also need to ensure that the data captured by and held on these systems is secure. Do the systems have sufficient protection against hackers and viruses? Do they only allow authorised persons access to the stored data? Do you believe the data on the systems?

Alpha

Alpha means 'value added' or additional return, over and above the benchmark return relevant for a passively managed portfolio of that specific asset class. Assume a UK fund manager has a dollar portfolio that increases in value by 15 per cent in a year. If only 10 per cent is directly related to stock price movements, other things being equal, the remaining 5 per cent may well come from the additional currency risk that the fund is exposed to.

Alpha comes from the capital asset pricing model (CAPM) which describes the pricing of an actual portfolio, related to its risk, hence:

Return of the portfolio = $\alpha + \beta$ (market return) + ε

Where:

α = excess return

β = elasticity of the portfolio

ε = random error

Using currency risk as an example, Alpha comes about as investors seek to generate additional gains from FX as an asset class within a more structured portfolio. It may appear in the small print of any documentation as 'alternative investments', where the objective is to gain additional returns that are uncorrelated to the underlying portfolio.

Another related term is currency overlay. By investing in foreign securities you inevitably take on currency risk, which may drag down the portfolio valuation or enhance it.

Looking at portfolio management generally, Alpha may also describe the relationship between a fund's historical performance and its current performance. If a fund has an Alpha of zero it just means it did as well as last year, or as well as expected, given the current Beta. Alpha can be positive, negative or zero.

Because a fund's return and its risk are both contributory to its Alpha, two funds with the same returns could have a different Alpha. Lastly, it is impossible to judge whether Alpha reflects managerial skill or luck. Is that high-Alpha manager a genius, or did he just stumble upon a few hot stocks?

Basis risk and convergence

Basis risk indicates there is a potential mismatch somewhere, often due to a differing structure or underlying maturity. Using a non-financial metaphor, it is like hedging apples with pears – they are both green, both fruit, but they are different.

The term is most commonly used in the futures markets and describes the gap between where the future is trading (for a future delivery date) versus where the underlying asset is trading today. In effect, one is trading at a current price, the other at a forward price. At the expiry date of the futures contract, the forward price and the current price in the cash market should be the same. The process whereby the cash market and futures markets come together at expiry is known as convergence; at that point the basis should be zero. If there is incomplete convergence, typically before expiry on the futures contracts, you have a basis risk, but also an arbitrage opportunity.

DEFINITION

Basis = Current price of the asset – Future price of the asset

EXAMPLE

Three-month euro cash is trading at 2.45 per cent, while the nearest futures contract is trading at 2.35 per cent (implied by a futures price of 97.65).

Basis = 2.45% – 2.35% = 0.10%

In other words, 10 basis points.

Note that basis as illustrated here is negative.

This is when the interest rate implied by the future is lower than the cash price (Figure 4.1a). Figure 4.1b illustrates the opposite occurrence.

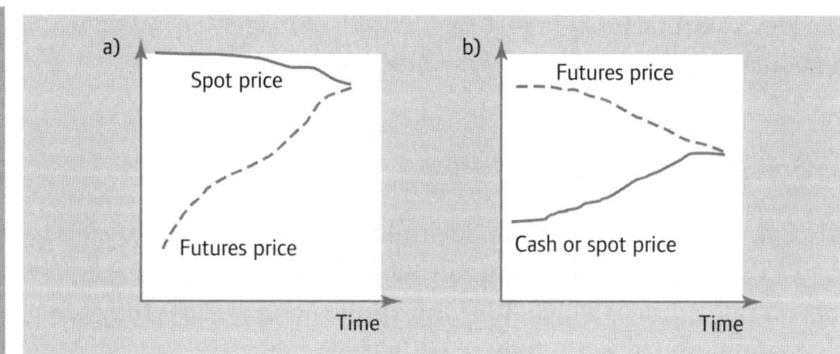

FIGURE 4.1 Convergence

'Black Swan'

The term Black Swan comes from the book, *The Black Swan: The impact of the highly improbable* by Nassim Nicholas Taleb. It describes the risk of being totally unprepared.

It shows how limited people are when it comes to learning from experience. If they haven't experienced something, they can't learn from it. This is especially true in the financial markets. When Northern Rock in the UK ran into trouble, the regulators were unprepared for what was in essence a run on the bank as depositors sought to remove their money. The regulators were very prepared for a hedge fund failure, but that's not what happened. A Black Swan is typically an event with three attributes:

- It lies outside the realm of regular expectations.
- It has extreme impact.
- Human nature tries to rationalise it after the event, making it 'explainable and predictable'.

Here are some recognised Black Swan events:

- The 11 September 2001 terrorist attacks in the US.
- US authorities rejecting the original $750 billion bail-out package for the financial system in September 2008.

- The credit crunch (although there is some debate about whether this could have been foreseen).
- Fall of Pompeii.

Risk and its management are obviously very important in a financial market place and formal procedures need to be in place for its management.

Further reading

The Black Swan: The impact of the highly improbable, Nassim Nicholas Taleb, Penguin, 2008.

Currency Overlay, Neil Record, Wiley, 2003.

Association of Corporate Treasurers (ACT), www.treasurers.org

Financial Services Authority, www.fsa.gov.uk

5 Key strategies for managing operational risk

Tony Blunden

The six main operational risk processes are fundamentally entwined.

- Introduction
- Operational risk governance
- Risk and control assessment
- Indicators
- Events
- Scenarios and modelling
- Reporting

Introduction

Financial regulators first started talking about 'other risks' in the 1990s after events such as Barings, BCCI and Sumitomo highlighted the fact that financial securities institutions were subject to risks other than market risk and credit risk. After several years of debate (sometimes passionate and sometimes irrelevant), the industry settled, at first uneasily, on a definition of operational risk: 'The risk of [direct or indirect] loss resulting from inadequate or failed internal processes, people and systems or from external events.'

The reference to 'direct or indirect' loss survived for only a short time before being dropped. That it crept into the definition at all was testimony to the early efforts of operational risk managers to identify operational risk through a focus on loss events. It was also unfortunate that there was an early over-emphasis by the regulators on losses.

Today, the identification, measurement, monitoring and management of operational risk is recognised as comprising of six processes:

- Governance: encompasses the direction and review by senior management of operational risk within the institution.
- Risk and control assessment: identification and subjective measurement of operational risks and their mitigators.
- Events: the identification, capture and analysis of both internal and external events arising from the occurrence of operational risks.
- Indicators: identification, capture and analysis of measures of risks (and controls).
- Scenarios and modelling: analysis of the effects of extreme but plausible operational risks on an organisation, including mathematical analysis.
- Reporting: allows the immediate four processes above to be brought together in a coherent manner for use by all levels of management to supervise and control operational risk.

The six main operational risk management processes are fundamentally entwined with each other.

Governance summary

The first step in operational risk management is to ensure that governance structures are in place and understood by all staff. A board-approved operational risk policy together with terms of reference for the relevant bodies is essential. These ensure that the board of directors and all staff have a clear view of their responsibilities and of the board's strategy. As such, they are also useful documents from a perspective of managing regulatory relationships as they can be used as a reference for the documentation of senior management responsibilities around operational risk.

A framework is also often developed during this initial period of operational risk management. There are many frameworks but they all have in common a description (whether pictorial or in words) of how the identification, measurement, monitoring and management of operational risk will occur within the organisation.

An example of an operational risk management framework is given in Figure 5.1.

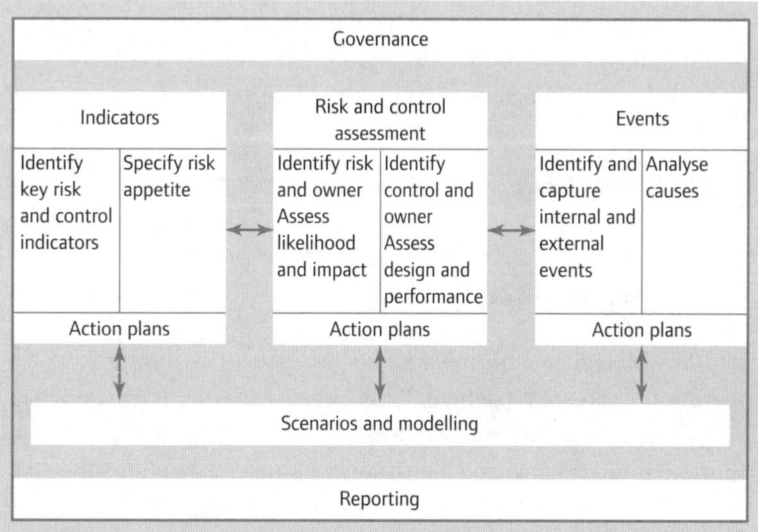

FIGURE 5.1 Generic operational risk management framework

Source: Courtesy of Chase Cooper.

A timeline that indicates the intermediate milestones for the progression of each of the processes is also often drawn up during the governance phase of operational risk management. This, of course, allows senior management to manage and review the development of operational risk processes within the organisation and to set and influence the speed of the development.

It is interesting that the FSA noted (in its Operational risk management practices paper, February 2005) with regard to governance in firms '... this activity was sometimes inhibited by the lack of clear direction on risk strategy from the Board of Directors'.

Risk and control assessment summary

This is often the first process of operational risk management carried out by an organisation. Most firms have performed some form of risk assessment or control assessment, although many have not yet taken it to a state where business benefit can be derived from it. Although a first risk and control assessment is almost always subjective, it can be of value to a business if it is linked to strategic objectives. As risk assessments progress and the links between losses and key indicators are established, the assessments become more influenced by objective data. However, a continued focus on the business objectives will help to ensure its use at the most senior levels of management.

Indicators summary

> there is scepticism around the advantages of the use of indicators

There is scepticism around the advantages of the use of indicators for operational risk management. This appears to stem from a wish by many in the financial industry to start the identification of appropriate indicators with a blank sheet of paper and with little or no reference to previous work from other operational risk processes. Those who are making headway in the use of indicators have invariably linked their metric identification process to the risks and controls identified by the firm in previous risk assessments. This automatically enables a focus on the main risks (as identified by the risk and control assessment) and provides clear assistance in easily recognising predictive indicators. Given a link of risks to the business objectives, risk indicators allow senior management to assess the likelihood (or otherwise) of meeting its own strategic plan. Such devices are excellent for embedding operational risk management within a firm.

Events summary

Much has already been written (by regulators and other commentators) of the use of events and losses in operational risk management. Regrettably, a great deal of this writing has focused on the modelling of operational risk using losses. Much less attention has been paid to the benefits from understanding the causes of the events and to linking the causes to the strategic risks already identified by the firm in its risk and control assessment. Both internal and external events and losses can be used by firms in causal analysis, although inevitably the external analysis will be more difficult as the control environment that failed will be less understood. The use of this analysis of objective data to challenge the subjective nature of the risk and control assessment is vital to coherent and comprehensive operational risk management.

Scenarios and modelling summary

As noted above, too much focus has been placed (until recently) on the use of losses in operational risk modelling. It is very helpful that Basel (in its paper 'International convergence on capital measurement and capital standards', June 2004) and the FSA (in its CP05/3, January 2005 and subsequent papers and rules) finally acknowledged that the internal control environment of a firm and scenario analysis are both valuable components of an operational risk model. (For the sake of completeness, the other two components of a comprehensive model are internal losses and external losses.)

Both risk and control assessments and indicators can be used in modelling operational risk and can add to the business benefits that can be derived from such modelling. As well as a capital figure that can be used for capital allocation to business lines, a model that uses risk and control assessments can assist in a cost-benefit analysis of the controls used by a firm. Challenges can be made to the effectiveness of the controls, given the size of a particular risk, and to the allocation of resources for each control. A detailed analysis of operational risk modelling is beyond the scope of this book.

Reporting summary

Many organisations have increased the amount of operational risk reporting carried out in the past few years. Unfortunately, often this increased reporting has simply resulted in a greater amount of paper containing ever more detailed analysis. In practice, reporting must be tailored to the needs of the receiver. The board of directors is generally interested in operational risk reports that address its interests, i.e. strategic risks (and controls) and exceptions to lower levels of risk across the entire organisation. Department heads, on the other hand, are relatively focused on their own risks but often require considerable detail on those risks.

Much reporting often also focuses on the risks, without thought for the linked controls and action plans that can demonstrate a firm's commitment to using operational risk management to enhance the firm's business decisions.

Operational risk governance

Good risk governance as required by the FSA (through its principles for business) and the European Union (through its Capital Requirements Directive) requires robust governance arrangements in relation to the risk management of financial firms. There are also many other governance requirements around the world that apply to the risk management of many types of institutions, such as listed companies. Operational risk governance, in common with other forms of corporate governance, is about enabling senior managers to direct operational risk strategy and to review its effectiveness. From a practical perspective, this will encompass a policy document approved by the most senior executive body of the firm; a framework showing the identification, measurement, monitoring and management of operational risk; terms of reference for relevant bodies; and a timeline for tracking and reviewing the development of operational risk processes within the firm.

Operational risk policy

A documented operational risk policy allows senior managers to communicate to all staff the approach of the firm to operational risk management. As such, the policy should be approved by the board of directors. Alternatively, in some firms, the executive or management committee may approve the policy document or at a minimum, review and comment on it before board approval.

The contents of an operational risk policy depend on a company's culture. However, it generally contains:

- A definition of operational risk. This is typically the Basel II definition, although some firms still include a reference to indirect losses as well as to direct losses. Strategic business and reputational risks are often explicitly included by firms even though Basel excludes them. However, it is more unusual for the boundaries between operational risk, market risk and credit risk to be clearly identified, although definitions of the other types of risk are often included.
- A statement of risk appetite. This is often a high-level initial statement that will be broadened and deepened as the firm gains knowledge of the operations of risk management processes and how these are used.
- An overview of the risk management processes. Although this is necessarily high level, it helps in making clear that the board and senior managers have considered how operational risk management will be carried out. A short description of each process is common with the links and reinforcements between each process often stated to show a holistic approach to operational risk management.
- A statement of the roles and responsibilities of people and departments. The board must manage any potential conflicts of interest that exist between operational risk, internal audit and

compliance. This point is particularly applicable to any firms where operational risk management was carried out by either internal **audit** or compliance. Clear roles for these three areas must be documented. In smaller organisations, the functions overlap and the policy must be consistent with the size, nature and complexity of the organisation.

- A glossary of terms so that all staff have a clear explanation of the terms used.

Policies also often have references to categories and sub-categories of risk, to the role that central risk plays (compared with risk management units in the businesses) and to the risk reporting flows of information.

Operational risk framework

It is rare for two frameworks to look the same. However, many organisations seek to manage operational risk using the same processes and, therefore, such frameworks are inevitably similar in concept, if not in detail (as shown in Figure 5.1 on p. 123).

> it is rare for two frameworks to look the same

The FSA's PS142_2 published in July 2003 comments that a framework contains 'governance structures and the tools to identify, assess and monitor' operational risk.

Terms of reference

Given the broad and subjective nature of operational risk, it is essential that the various governance bodies in a firm understand their duties and authorities with respect to its management. Although the board of directors is ultimately responsible for organising and controlling the firm's affairs, the board relies on other bodies, such as a risk committee, to assist it in carrying out its responsibilities. The duties and authorities of each body dealing with operational risk should be clearly laid out in the terms of reference of that body. Additionally, the level of risk reporting to each body should be clearly identified.

Timeline

Given the number of interlinking processes in operational risk management, a timeline to identify when each process is expected to be operational is important in introducing operational risk management. In addition, at some stage, the company will probably want to use software to capture and handle the data being captured and created. The timeline will also aid management and review of risk management. Senior managers and the board will find that they can more easily understand the implications of changing the speed of the development of operational risk.

Benefits of operational risk governance

Benefits from implementing operational risk governance include:

- increased comfort for the board and senior managers that risks are being managed effectively;
- a structured approach to implementing an effective and consistent risk management framework;
- clarified risk ownership reducing duplication and overlap;
- assurance that operations are aligned with the board's risk appetite.

Risk and control assessment

Operational risk and control assessments are often the first process that a company uses to conduct operational risk management. Frequently, the assessment is carried out without a framework in place and without much thought being given to corporate governance around operational risk management.

Objective

The objective of a risk and control assessment is to identify and monitor the operational risks and controls to which a firm is subject. Unfortunately, this apparently simple objective is fraught with possibilities for invalid and mistaken identification of risks. Improper recognition of risks rapidly leads to a loss of confidence in the process and to a potential discrediting of the operational risk staff and sometimes risk management in general.

Performing an assessment

Options for carrying out an operational risk assessment include:

- Third party review, typically by a consultant or external auditors;
- Facilitated assessment by a consultancy with internal risk management and business managers. This uses the business's understanding of it's objectives to identify and agree the business risks. The effectiveness of internal controls is also documented and action plans are agreed where necessary.
- Self assessment by business managers. This uses the detailed knowledge of people in the business to identify the business risks and to agree on their monitoring.

These methods of operational risk assessment have an increasing level of business benefit although these benefits are balanced by an increasing level of process sophistication. In particular, self assessment gives the best platform for cultural change.

Any of the methods above can be used for risk assessment, control assessment or risk and control assessment. Commonly, firms start with an assessment of risk (initially evaluating the risk after allowing for the mitigating effect of the controls). Both standalone assessment methods give some value, although neither gives the value that can be derived from a combined risk and control assessment. For example, there is generally little shared assessment in control self assessments, even when the business reviews the process for the assessment of control effectiveness. By contrast, in risk and control assessments carried out by the business there is usually a natural element of co-assessment to ensure consistency.

Possible methodologies

Practices that can be used to carry out any of the three assessment methods include:

- Workshops, which can be effective and efficient for staff who are open to discussion and challenge. However, the drawback is that a first risk and control assessment generally takes a full working day.
- Interviews, which work well in companies that are used to one-to-one discussion of issues. Interviews are relatively inefficient because iteration is necessary to obtain agreement on the risks and controls. They are nevertheless effective when an entire cadre of staff cannot be spared for a full day workshop.
- Questionnaires, can be easy and quick although these need strong management and communication skills to achieve cohesiveness in the results. Good design of the questions is fundamental to obtaining an outcome that has business benefits. This is often harder than it may appear as risks, control failures and indicators can easily become confused in the mind of the person answering the questionnaire.

Why do assessments go wrong?

Reasons why risk and control assessments go wrong include cultural issues, administrative hurdles and value perception.

Cultural issues

As noted earlier a common language is important for a consistent approach to operational risk management. It is impossible to aggregate risks, compare risk exposures or analyse control profiles without an agreed view of common terms. All three actions are typical uses of a risk and control assessment. An inconsistent quality of identification can also be a result of a lack of understanding of risk terms or it can result from not applying an audit to the risk and control assessment results.

Another common cultural issue is the lack of support from senior managers for the process. This is often characterised by a lack of attendance by senior management at risk and control assessment workshops or by sudden departures. Also appraisal or review mechanisms may not take into account good (or bad) risk management by employees.

Finally, operational risk management is sometimes used to reduce risk rather than manage it appropriately. Some companies aim for a perceived level of best practice, whereas operational risk management should focus on managing risk at a level suitable to the firm's size and substance.

Administrative hurdles

Risk and control assessments are often unnecessarily paper-intensive. Implementation is difficult across regions of the world and particularly across cultures. It is also burdensome to maintain and can be orientated towards a policing role, looking for a fault and assigning blame rather than forward looking and proactive.

risk and control assessments are often unnecessarily paper-intensive

Value perception

Sufficient thought must be given to the reporting of risks and controls so they can be monitored. Inadequate reporting provides limited business value and the results from the risk and control assessment should be linked to other users of the information. There is also a much greater perception of the value from a risk and control assessment when the action plans generated (either to enhance controls or add new controls) can be seen to be followed up. The greatest value to be obtained from operational risk and control assessments is from linking them to losses, key indicators and mathematical models.

Carrying out assessments

Level

The level at which an assessment is to be carried out should first be decided. Many organisations first look at the main processes undertaken and assess the risk and controls over these. Other organisations leave such process risks until the strategic risks and controls have been assessed. This second practice has the advantage that the processes can then be placed into the context of the business objectives and their risks and controls, rather than trying to fit the process risks into the strategic level at a later date. The other advantage of starting with business objectives as the risk drivers is that there is rapid buy-in from senior managers.

Approach

Risk and control assessments can be carried out using two assessment approaches, which can also be combined. The most common starting point is to assess the risk after the controls (i.e. after taking into account the mitigating effect of the controls). This is known as net or residual risk assessment. However, losses generally occur when controls fail and therefore net risk assessment by definition does not give any values for the likely unexpected loss that the firm will suffer when the 'after control failure' risk event occurs. Only values for 'expected' losses are measured in net risk assessment. This problem can be overcome with the use of gross risk assessment followed by an assessment of the controls. The risk is assessed before taking into account the effect of any controls imposed by the firm, as these will have failed when the risk occurs.

Enhanced approaches

Some risk and control assessments combine the above two approaches by assessing risks at a gross and net level as well as assessing the mitigating controls. Often an assessment of the risk at a 'target' level (i.e. after any remedial action) is also made. In any of the approaches, the action plans for enhancing the perceived defective controls are also identified. The owner of each action plan is identified together with a brief description of the plan, its expected completion date and any cost involved.

Owners

As well as risks and controls being assessed, the owner of each risk is generally identified, as is the owner of each control. It is common in a first pass through of the owners of the risks in a strategic risk assessment that the managing director is the owner of the majority of the risks. However, once the board has been challenged, the MD normally owns a significant minority (but not the majority) of the risks to the business objectives.

Scoring

Following identification of the risks and their owners, the risks are usually scored. Using two dimensions – likelihood and impact. Controls are also often scored in two dimensions (design and performance) rather than simply by effectiveness. The scores of the risks and of the controls are usually arranged on a scale of 1, 2 and 3, or low, medium and high. Some use up to ten levels. It is useful to use an even number of levels so that there can be no sitting on the fence by using the middle level for most risks and controls. Probably the most common number of levels is four or six, with four levels being high, medium high, medium low and low.

The scale for likelihood is linked to the likely rate of occurrence of the risk and that for design and performance is linked to the likely failure of the control. However, the impact scale requires some thought because different companies use different impact criteria such as the impact to annual revenues, three-year plan profits or the share value.

Cause, event and effect

Another consideration is to isolate the risk events (i.e. what you want to capture) from the risk causes, the risk effects and the control failures. Most methodologies for risk assessment (see above) will produce a combination of all four risk types unless some guidance is given. It is the risk event that is required in an assessment because risk causes and effects change over time. If controls are applied to changing circumstances, the controls may become less effective because of the shifting conditions rather than the efficiency of the control itself.

Control assessment

This can be carried out either on the cluster of controls that mitigate a risk or on each control within the cluster. The greatest business benefit is derived from assessing each control as a control may operate on several risks and its varying effects can therefore be judged. Additionally, controls are often identified as either preventative or detective controls to aid the design of action plans over the further mitigation of a risk and to aid the identification of leading indicators.

Monitoring assessments

Assessments are monitored in various ways and also for varying reasons, such as: identifying the highest risks and the poorest controls; the effectiveness of controls to the degree of over and under control of the risk. The scoring used in the assessment is also used in the monitoring. Typically, the likelihood and impact scores are linked together to give a composite value that can be used for comparing one risk with another.

> a risk can be categorised as a major risk even when it is calculated as a minor risk

There are varying levels of sophistication in risk monitoring. The 'heat map' of Figure 5.2 shows the drawbacks in using fixed values for the boundaries of the impact and likelihood. A risk can be categorised as a major risk (because it falls within that square) even when it is calculated as a minor risk (and therefore requires less attention).

More flexible representations, such as Figure 5.3, allow both a basic categorisation of the risk at four levels of impact and likelihood with a less rigid approach to the boundaries and therefore a more practical approach to prioritising risk.

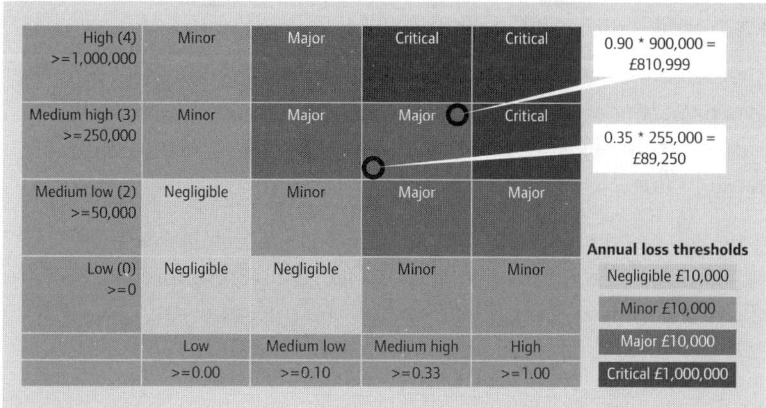

FIGURE 5.2 'Heat map' of fixed boundaries with four levels of impact and likelihood

Source: Courtesy of Chase Cooper.

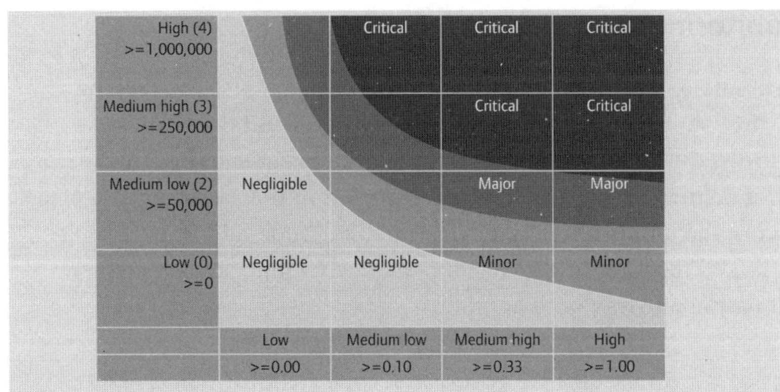

FIGURE 5.3 More flexible heat map with varying boundaries

Source: Courtesy of Chase Cooper.

Software

No commentary on risk and control assessment would be complete without reference to software for capturing risk and control assessment data:

- Dedicated software that focuses on risk and control assessments using any methodology (sometimes together with process mapping and action plans).
- Questionnaire-based products.
- Analytical tools based on mathematical algorithms.
- Integrated operational risk products that capture risk and control data as part of an overall approach to operational risk involving indicators, losses and modelling as well as risk, controls and action plans.

The choice of software will depend on how comprehensive an approach is required. However, it is easier to buy a comprehensive tool and grow into it than it is to change the software later. Points to consider when implementing operational risk software include:

- Fit with company culture: select software that works in the same way as the firm, e.g. if workshops and brainstorming are used, do not select a questionnaire-based tool.

- Fit with the IT culture.
- Fit with the risk culture: software that focuses on controls is not going to work well if the firm is committed to a combined risk and control assessment.

Indicators

Indicators are fundamental to an operational risk management framework and yet the financial services industry seems to continue to be puzzled and confused by them. In particular, the term key risk indicator (KRI) appears to cause difficulty. Many firms that have identified their indicators have ended up with several hundred of them, calling into question whether there can ever be that number of *key* indicators. Others have striven for a very small number of indicators that will tell them about the well-being of the firm overall. This approach brings to mind a doctor trying to assess the complete state of a patient's health by only taking blood pressure, pulse and listening to the heart. Clearly a good place to start, but definitely not to finish.

Before considering how to work with KRIs, it is a good idea to consider how they fit into the overall picture. The identification, measurement, monitoring and managing of relevant indicators of key risks is one of the three fundamental activities of operational risk management.

When using KRIs, it is important to deal with such factors as ownership and accountability, reporting, training and record retention as well as the more usual points of how to carry out KRI work (at a high level).

- KRIs are useful for challenging the subjective data in risk and control assessments (RCAs). An indicator of likelihood that is showing deterioration (and therefore an increasing likelihood of the risk happening) enables the operational risk team to challenge and confirm the current qualitative scoring of a risk's likelihood as well as advise the risk and control owners that corrective action should be taken.

- KRIs should also be differentiated from indicators of controls and from performance indicators. Key control indicators are themselves important and should be analysed and addressed separately (and linked to relevant KRIs). Performance indicators tell you about the state of the business rather than the state of the risks or the controls.
- KRIs can be financial or non-financial and can be simple measures. Many KRIs are simple business metrics such as the measurement of staff turnover.
- KRIs can make risk appetite accessible to a broad range of staff. It is easy to understand threshold levels that are linked directly to metrics already used in the business and often the data required for KRI management is already used by the business.

There are three approaches to identifying KRIs:

- starting from nothing;
- using existing management information;
- using existing RCAs.

Starting with a blank sheet of paper has the advantage of not being influenced by previous work. However, it can appear to be isolated from other operational risk initiatives.

Using existing management information means relatively little additional work is required from managers.

The quickest way to identify key risks is to start with the RCA. Some risks will be clearly more severe. These are the key risks. Indicators of these key risks will be metrics (either financial or non-financial) that tell you about how the likelihood or the impact of the risk is changing. Additionally, using the RCA provides controls to mitigate the key risks and helps to identify metrics that relate to the controls. The distinction between KRIs and control indicators is important because it facilitates the identification of predictive indicators. Furthermore, it helps identify which controls each mitigate a number of risks. These too can be considered key controls and therefore worthy of indicators.

By now, there will be many indicators. The ones on which to focus can be identified by using the indicator's thresholds. For any metric there will be a range or value at which management is comfortable, which can be called the green zone. As the metric moves towards or beyond the boundaries of this comfort zone, managers will become less comfortable and at some point will become concerned (amber zone). At an even greater level of divergence from the comfort zone, there will be the red zone signifying that immediate and sustained action is required. The green/amber and amber/red boundaries are ways of stating the appetite of the firm for movements in the parameters of that particular risk or control. It is likely that many of the indicators identified will be in the green zone. Managers, of course, should focus on the indicators in the amber and red zones.

This is commonly achieved through 'dashboards'. These will commonly show a traffic light for each indicator, how it is moving (up, down or stable) and recent values as well as possibly the green/amber and amber/red values.

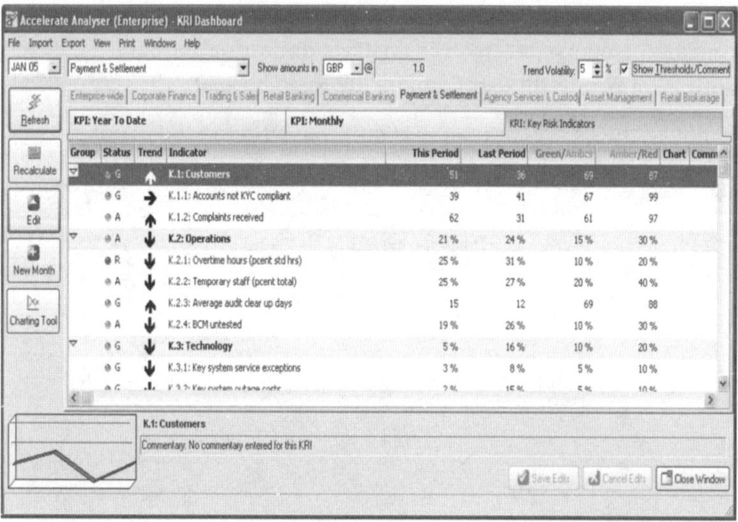

FIGURE 5.4 Key risk indicator 'dashboard'

Source: Courtesy of Chase Cooper.

Figure 5.4 on p.139 shows an example of a KRI dashboard.

In summary, a workable set of indicators can be attained using KRIs. This is a straightforward operational risk activity that can bring consistency and completeness to operational risk management.

Events

As noted earlier, there has been a great deal of focus on financial losses. Yet, these form only a subset of the events that can happen (Figure 5.5). As well as losses, a company can make gains from errors and a risk occurrence can lead to no financial effect at all. However, the common thread is the failure of one or more controls. The capture of that failure and subsequent analysis is a vital part of operational risk management.

Data that needs to be captured

Many types of data are captured in trying to analyse events. However, almost all firms record the following:

- Loss event category (often an industry standard, although sometimes a firm will also have its own categories).
- Relevant business line or business unit that suffered the event (sometimes also the business line in which the event was detected).

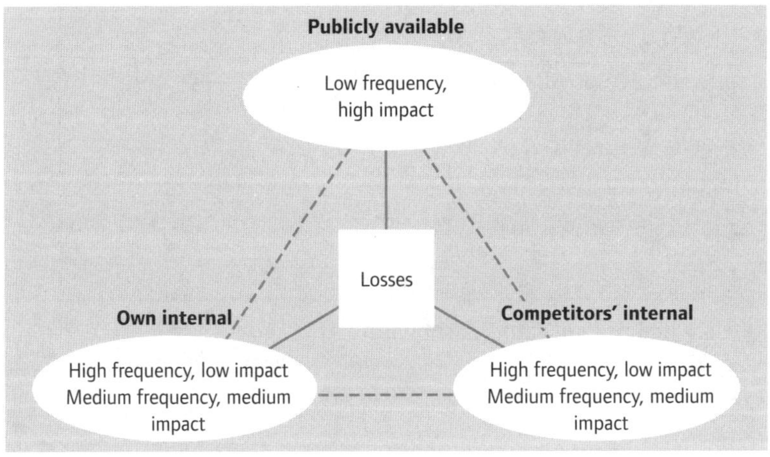

FIGURE 5.5 Types of losses

Source: Courtesy of Chase Cooper.

- Geographic region in which the event occurred.
- Date of start of event, discovery date and end date.
- Control(s) involved and management actions taken.
- Loss value and recovery values such as insurance (where applicable).

Most commentators differentiate between two types of events: internal and external. However, external events themselves split into two areas with widely differing characteristics and uses. It is therefore important to identify these two types of external events.

Many firms are members of consortia that share data. Each of these collects the internal events recorded by each member, anonymises the data and distributes the result to all consortium members. This allows each member to gain an insight into the control failures of peers, without identifying the peer itself. The insight gained enables each member to assess the relative state of its own controls compared with its peers' controls and to learn lessons about which controls may be under pressure in the industry. Advance notice of likely control pressure is invaluable because it gives time to strengthen controls before the event occurs. However, the competitors' internal event data (typically high frequency and low to medium impact) is of a similar type to a firm's own internal event data. A peer's events may be more extreme in terms of losses but nevertheless generally will be of a similar size.

advance notice of likely control pressure is invaluable

Operational risk management is also concerned with infrequent and high value events as these can pose dangers to a firm. Such events are very often in the public domain. An analysis of these events will also yield valuable data for a firm. If, for example, a large loss has been suffered by a peer who is not a member of the consortium to which the firm belongs, an examination of the firm's risk and controls relevant to the loss may prevent the firm from suffering the same type of loss.

Scenarios and modelling

Operational risk scenario analysis enables a company to investigate its operational risk sensitivities. The point of the evaluation should be to gauge potential vulnerability to exceptional but plausible events. These identified (and often artificially constructed) events must have a low probability of occurrence and should be realistic.

Before considering scenario analysis, it is important to differentiate between stress testing and scenario analysis. Used as a narrowly defined term, stress testing typically refers to changing a single operational risk parameter (often by multiples of the standard deviation or by a fixed percentage) and assessing the change in a firm's operational risk profile. By contrast, scenario analysis simultaneously moves a number of operational risk parameters each usually by different amounts (based on a combination of statistical results, expert knowledge and/or historically observed events).

By gaining a better understanding of operational risks, controls, indicators and potential losses, scenario analysis helps managers clarify the interactions and causal relationships between risks. It also helps compensate for the subjective nature of operational risk and control assessments, incomplete coverage and interpretational difficulties associated with operational risk indicators and the lack of data in recorded operational risk losses.

The first point to consider when developing scenarios is to do so alongside other techniques, such as forecasting. Many businesses undertake routine business forecasting when developing rolling three-year plans and these will yield operational risk data that will, by definition, match senior management's thinking. By taking account of the broader business environment, the chance of an improbable operational scenario (or improbable derived event) is reduced. If this technique is followed by a review with senior management of the draft scenarios, a rational set of data is more likely to emerge.

The data used in the scenarios is, of course, paramount to deriving valid results. These data can be obtained from applying the developed scenarios to the firm's existing operational risk register, indicators and loss database. For example, by considering how the identified risks and controls will change in a given scenario a new stressed risk register is produced for that particular scenario. Consideration of the operational risk indicators and existing losses for the same scenario will yield a complete set of initial operational risk data for that test. Repeating this process for each identified scenario will produce full data for all the developed operational risk scenarios. Having achieved a complete set of data, it is important to check internal consistency within each scenario and comparability over the full set. Although the operational risk scenarios are likely to be widely varying in detail, there will still be comparisons that can be drawn and the data must be checked for coherence.

The mathematical models used for generating scenario results can be the same as the models used for capital calculations, assuming that these models already comply with the regulatory needs of allowing consideration to be given to internal losses, external losses and the internal control environment. Data developed in the scenarios will take these three elements into account and therefore an operational risk scenario analysis model may already exist in the firm. Figure 5.6 shows the scenario analysis screen of a typical model.

By running each scenario through the model, values will be produced that will give an insight to the sensitivities of the firm to extreme operational risk events. Mathematical modelling is only a starting point but it will enable questions to be raised in a logical and consistent fashion, which will improve management discussion.

In summary, it is possible to develop a range of data for operational risk scenarios that are consistent with business forecasts and that give valuable data to senior managers to improve understanding of the firm's operational risk profile. Given a perceived increase in the risk of disruption from global pandemics, terrorist attacks or natural disasters, companies should carry out scenarios involving operational risks as well as financial risks.

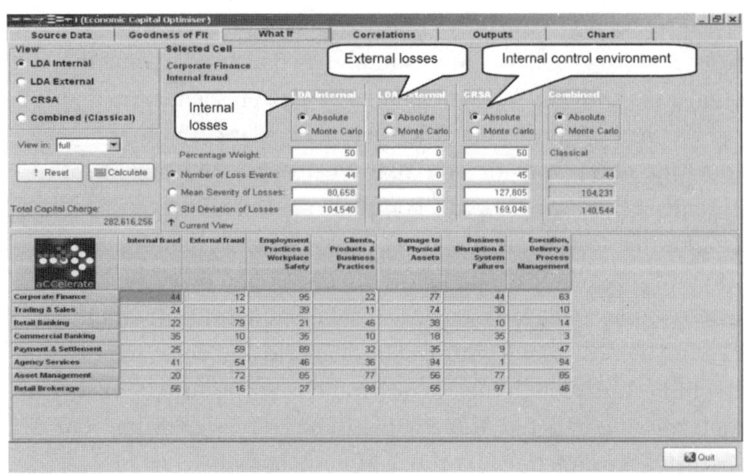

FIGURE 5.6 Scenario analysis screen

Source: Courtesy of Chase Cooper.

Reporting

The effective management of operation risk depends on comprehensive, focused reports. These should be presented in a timely manner and must reference both the detail (such as actions being taken to enhance controls) and the overview (such as the business objectives to which the risks and controls attach).

Report definition

Before a report is designed, it is important to define what is required from the report. A report definition is usually a single sheet of paper that typically contains:

- the name of the report;
- its objective(s);
- to whom it is going;
- names of data fields to be used;
- any calculations required on the fields (by the coding before the report is printed);

- manual actions to be performed on the fields (to obtain the final report);
- how to use the final report (including typical actions).

A report definition does not contain a draft design or a prototype report.

One of the advantages of a report definition is that it makes the designing of the report very much easier as the needs are clearly stated. If the report is to be coded, it also considerably reduces coding time as, again, it is easy to see what is required.

Principles of reports

Presenting complex risk information is a significant task and different audiences require different information. For example, a board report typically will contain mainly exception information whereas a report for a head of department is likely to contain all the information about that department's risks, controls, actions, indicators and events (but only for that department). It is important that risk reports enable people to take ownership of the information. This empowers the owner to take decisions and manage risks and controls. It should also be borne in mind that managers may not understand the language being used and some awareness sessions may be required. Finally, information requirements are dynamic and reporting is therefore an evolving process.

6 Key acronyms and market jargon

During my time in the financial markets it has become apparent that many people use language as a disguise and market jargon as a weapon.

- Introduction
- 'Everything is in the price'
- Market-makers, price-takers and bid-offer spreads
- Mine/yours and long/short
- Rollover
- Market slang and sayings
- Bips, pips and ticks
- Non-deliverable forwards (NDFs)
- Volatility ('vol')
- The Greeks: Delta, Gamma, Vega, Theta
- Straight through processing (STP)

Introduction

During my time in the financial markets it has become apparent that many people use language as a disguise and market jargon as a weapon. There is an element of territory about this – if you don't know what I am talking about, you can't see how really simple it is, so I can tell you it's all very complicated and you are very impressed with how clever I am! Just remember, everyone who works in these markets is human and can make mistakes. I hope this chapter will give the reader the background and confidence to challenge anything said that seems unclear or needs clarification. This section includes terms and jargon and market sayings which, given time and exposure, anyone would pick up; I just hope I can provide a fast track for you.

'Everything is in the price'

This means that every asset that a bank, asset manager or commodity house trades in (loans, deposits, derivatives, FX, credit, energy) will have a price; this needs to take into account all current available data. For example, a foreign exchange rate or derivative price will need to include all of these elements:

- Energy: prices and worries about oil price and its by-products, including jet fuel, diesel, petrol, gas, bunker, and supply/demand/availability. Ditto for electricity.
- Weather: this could include considerations on temperature, rainfall and hurricanes, which affect oil production, farming, energy, food consumption and transport.
- Terrorism: certain parts of the world become no-go areas, affecting population movements, tourism, spending, cost and supply and/or demand of foodstuffs, oil production and/or its transportation.
- Politics: certain political parties are more liberal in terms of spending, on arms, defence and health service. Elections can also have a big effect.
- Economics and statistics: data releases for areas such as inflation, producer prices, trade figures, employment, growth, housing starts can all affect the 'view' on an economy or currency.

- Commodity prices: prices of raw materials for industry, including gold, food and energy.

Likewise, any asset class will be affected in the same way, including energy (oil, gas, coal and electricity), metals (precious and base metals), commodities (wheat, soya, tea, orange juice) plastics and their derivatives. Some of these will have prices offered by banks, others by physical producers such as BP. If everything is in the price, why do rates move? As data comes in on say economic performance or trade figures or unemployment, prices need to reflect these changes and the banks will move their prices, making their assets cheaper or more expensive.

If everything is in the price, why do rates move?

Every week, on Monday in the *Financial Times* there is a section on the back page relating to market data releases for that week, titled Informa Global Markets economic calendar. I have always found this helpful (Figure 6.1).

Informa Global Markets economic calendar

Country	Economic Statistic	Median Forecast	Previous Actual
MON			
US	Sep industrial production	−0.2%	−2.8%
US	Sep capacity utilisation	76.4%	76.4%
TUES			
UK	Sep consumer price index*	0.1%	0.5%
UK	Sep consumer price index**	4.9%	5.2%
US	Sep producer price index*	−1.8%	−0.4%
US	Sep producer prices**	6.2%	8.7%
WEDS			
US	Oct consumer price index*	−0.8%	0%
US	Oct consumer price index**	4.1%	4.9%
US	Oct housing starts, annual rate	780,000	817,000
US	Oct building permits, annual rate	775,000	805,000
THURS			
UK	Oct retail sales*	−0.8%	−0.4%
UK	Oct retail sales**	1.5%	1.8%
UK	Oct PSNCR	−£2.8bn	£12.6bn
UK	Oct cumulative PSNCR	£18.5bn	£21.3bn
FRI			
Emu	Nov flash PMI SA	40.5	41.1

*month on month ** year on year *** quarter on quarter SA seasonally adjusted

FIGURE 6.1 Monday's market data schedule in the *Financial Times*

Source: *Financial Times*

This notes data releases for the week ahead, the country, the last figure (previous actual) and, more importantly, what the market 'expects' the next figure to be (median forecast). This is a consensus of market sentiment. For example, if the consensus is that European inflation will increase from 2.5 per cent to 2.6 per cent, that figure will inevitably be factored in to most prices. Should the actual release also be at 2.6 per cent, prices will probably not move. However if the figure is very different, say higher at 3.0 per cent there is often a knee-jerk reaction. In that situation, the immediate short-term move would be to sell the euro; but in the longer-term investors may think the authorities might well increase interest rates to combat inflation, so they will get a better deposit rate.

Almost instantaneous dispersal of information is achieved via the group of independent vendors such as Bloomberg and Thomson Reuters.

Market-makers, price takers and bid-offer spreads

Financial firms will make 'two way-prices' in the assets in which they trade; a price where they will buy and a price where they will sell. This is known as 'making a market' and they therefore become 'market-makers'. The larger firms will make markets in most asset classes but not necessarily in all.

Professional clients with larger amounts to transact will not ask for a price at which to buy or sell as the bank making the price will invariably quote a price which reflects this. This means that if I ask for a price at which to buy the asset, the price will probably be marked up, and if I ask for a price to sell the asset, the price will probably be marked down. So, instead, a market professional will request prices for both transactions, for example:

> Request: 'Make me a price in Spot Cable, in 5 (million pounds)'
>
> Answer: GBP/USD: 1.5085/95
>
> Written in full, this is GBP/USD 1.5085–1.5095. Most likely, the quote from the bank to another professional would simply be '85/95'.

The bid is on the left (the smallest number); the offer is on the right (the larger number).

The bank will have to make the price without knowing whether the customer is a buyer or seller. Using this approach, the customer can see both sides of the price and can choose whether to deal or not. This also minimises the potential profit for the bank – the bid-offer spread.

Any customer who is only interested in one side of the price is a price-taker.

EXAMPLE

Consider an exporter who has received $10 million as payment for work in the US. He now wants to convert it into sterling. Using the data above, he would be dealing at 1.5095, generating £6,624,710.17.

Banks will generate trading income by trading the difference between the buy and the sell price, known as the bid-offer spread. The intention being that the bank will buy at the cheaper price, sell at the more expensive price and make the difference, using the data above, the bid-offer spread is 10 'pips'.

If the transaction amount was £5 million, the profit to the market maker would be:

$$5{,}000{,}000 \times 0.0010 = \$5{,}000.$$

NOTE

Market makers in FX quote in the base currency, for example when buying and selling a specific sum of pounds, but the profit and loss calculations are quoted in the term (non-base) currency – which here is US dollars.

Mine/yours and long/short

There is a market convention among traders that rather than say at the end of a conversation, 'I confirm that I have bought...', they just say '**mine**', and alternatively, you would say '**yours**' to indicate that you had sold.

If you have bought the asset and had said 'mine', you are now said to be **long**. If you had sold the asset you are now **short**. These terms on their own need to take into account any existing positions. Throughout the day a trader may well go from being net long to net short. If you are net long, you have bought more than you have sold, if you are net short, you have sold more than you have bought.

Short selling was in the press a lot in 2008 and 2009 as speculators 'shorted' bank and other financial shares. This means they sold shares they didn't own in the hope that the price would fall and they could buy back the shares later, but at a cheaper price. They seemed to achieve their objectives!

Rollover

The term rollover is used predominantly in the currency markets where companies have entered into forward foreign exchange transactions and are unable to fulfil their commitments. The rollover is executed to close out the forward and to then re-sell or re-buy forward again.

Many corporates sell (or buy) forward their foreign exchange receipts (or payables) to fix the exchange rate and guarantee for themselves a fixed amount of their home currency. Unfortunately, in many cases the actual date when the currency arrives in the company bank account can vary. But whether the currency is a day late or a week or a month, it will be too late to fulfil the terms of the foreign exchange forward contract, which will have quoted a specific date. The two following examples will illustrate how this works with both a receivable and a payable.

EXAMPLE

Company A is a UK exporter and is expecting to receive a $1 million payment in six months' time on 7 July. The firm is concerned about volatility in the currency markets and wishes to lock in the exchange rate for the conversion into sterling. The company contacts its bank and requests a six-month outright forward rate. It deals at GBP/USD 1.4970, with delivery of the dollars to the bank on 7 July as part of the contract.

In early July, their US client informs them of a delay on the contract and on 5 July they are told the currency is going to be delayed by a minimum of one month. However, the original FX forward deal still needs to be honoured. It is impossible to 'walk away' from this commitment – however, you could if this receipt had been hedged with an option.

5 July

Company A needs to close out the forward transaction at GBP/USD 1.4970, where it was supposed to deliver dollars. But it has no dollars, so it will need to buy them in the foreign exchange markets via a spot transaction, based on the spot rate at the time of dealing and maturing on 7 July. Assume sterling has weakened and the rate is GBP/USD 1.4125.

Original forward sale of dollars maturing on 7 July will generate:

$1,000,000.00 @ 1.4970 = £668,002.67

To honour the forward deal, Company A must purchase the USD spot.

Spot deal maturing on 7 July, will cost:

$1,000,000.00 @ 1.4125 = £707,964.60

Overall, the cost of the close-out is:

£39,961.93

So far, all that has happened is that the forward FX deal has been honoured. Now, the dollars have to be sold forward again to the new (expected) date in one month's time. This will be achieved by another forward transaction – for one month. This will be executed *on the same day* as the close out SPOT deal. Assume the new forward rate is GBP/USD 1.4130. This will now generate for Company A, £707,714.08, a better rate than the first forward deal – if the dollars arrive as expected, but this must be offset against the cost of the close-out.

The two transactions combined – the close out spot deal and the new forward deal, comprise the rollover. Every time a forward deal is rolled there is an effect on cash-flow, either for you or against you, as well as the impact of paying away two bid-offer spreads.

EXAMPLE

Euro payable example: 26 June

Corporation C is a US importer and needs to purchase €5 million with US dollars in three months' time, to pay an invoice. It is concerned about the weakness of the dollar and wishes to hedge the exchange rate for the currency conversion. Corporation C contacts a bank and requests a three-month outright forward rate. If today's date is 26 June, the three-month forward date for delivery of the US dollars will need to be 28 September (this takes into account the spot value date). It agrees to deal at EUR/USD 1.4036, with delivery of $7,018,000.00 to the bank on 28 September, the same day it will receive the €5 million as part of the contract.

In mid-September, Corporation C finds a defect in one of the supplied goods and decides to withhold payment for one month. The original FX forward deal must be honoured.

26 September

Corporation C needs to close out the forward transaction at EUR/USD 1.4036. It must take delivery of the euros, value spot, sell them straight away, and then buy them forward again.

Assume the dollar has weakened and the spot rate is EUR/USD 1.4250.

Original forward deal maturing on 28 September will cost:

€5,000,000.00 × 1.4036 = $7,018,000.00

To honour the forward deal, Corporation C must sell the euro spot:

spot deal maturing on 28 September, will yield:

€5,000,000.00 × 1.4250 = $7,125,000.00

Overall, the benefit of the close-out is:

$107,000

Note because the euro had strengthened, there was a gain on the close-out.

So far, all that has happened is the forward FX deal has been honoured. Now, the euros have to be bought forward again to the new date in one month's time. This will be achieved by another forward transaction – for one month. This will be executed *on the same day* as the close-out spot deal, let us assume the new forward rate is EUR/USD 1.4200. This will cost Corporation C $7,100,000.00, a worse rate than the first forward deal, but this can be off-set by the net rollover gain of $25,000.00.

NOTE

While working in a UK corporate treasury, I had experience of many of these types of transactions. For one particular Middle East export contract there were monthly forwards going out for twelve to eighteen months and the cash started to flow from the client more than three years late. Every single deal had to be 'rolled over' every month. There is a form of insurance cover under the UK governments, export credits guarantee department (ECGD) scheme which is *very* helpful in such circumstances.

Market slang and sayings

Some readers may be familiar with UK cockney rhyming slang for example, 'trouble and strife' = wife, 'apples and pears' = stairs. In financial markets there are equivalent terms – not for everything and it is dying out, and not all of it rhymes. It's probably safe to say that the origins of some of this are lost in the mists of time, but here are examples of some of the more popular terms.

'Cable' is used for the GBP/USD foreign exchange rate. As an example assume the forex rate when the question asked is GBP/USD 1.5650–1.5655.

Question: 'What's cable?'

Answer: '50/55'

Question: 'What's the big figure?'

Answer: '6'

The origins of the term go back to the transatlantic cable, that went into service in 1866 between the US and UK. This allowed consistent messaging between the two centres and for many years, well into the 1960s, this was the sole method of getting a price in GBP/USD.

This led to another piece of slang: 'What's the Betty?' (Betty Grable = cable). Some of this goes back a long, long time!

'What's the Rembrandt?' means what is the big picture? (Rembrandt painted really big pictures.) What is generally going on in the market?

'Yards of yen, or yards of euro, or yards of...' I once asked a colleague on the spot FX desk in a bank, the question, 'Why do we use this term for billions.' Instead of saying 10 billion euros worth of something, we say 10 **yards**. There was a pause while he thought; then I got the riposte, 'That's how long the f***ing bit of paper has to be to write all the noughts on!'

There is the likelihood that on a noisy trading floor, millions and billions could be mis-heard and the incorrect amount might be dealt.

There are also potential French origins here as 'milliard' was the word for one billion.

'Pound sterling' is rumoured to be from the Old French term for strong, durable, immovable, 'esterling', going back to the 1150s.

Also in the late 1150s the Hanseatic League was formed. This was principally made up of Baltic traders, who then had power over the English kings who were always looking to borrow money. They were given certain rights and privileges to trade and became known as the Easterling, which became shortened to sterling.

Believe whichever one you think plausible – I wasn't around at the time!

Specific foreign exchange market slang

Here are just a few terms for amounts. They are used in the sense of 'Make me a price in a...'

'Carpet' means, make me a price in 3 million of the **base currency** (BC) . Reputed origin – UK prison system, if you are imprisoned for three years you get a carpet in your cell. 'Double carpet' means, make me a price in 33 million (BC).

'Cable in a lady' means make me a price in 5 million (BC). The origin is in UK folklore combined with rhyming slang, Lady Godiva = fiver.

'Desmond' means make me a price in 4 million (BC). Origin: Desmond Tutu (2+2).

'Dave Allen' means me a price in 4.5 million (BC). Origin: the Irish comedian Dave Allen who died in 2005. He had lost part of the index finger of his left hand.

> 'Dave Allen' means make me a price in 4.5 million

Bips, pips and ticks

Financial markets involve large sums of money, with exchange and interest rates quoted to many figures after the decimal point. This is how to subdivide into even smaller increments.

Basis point (bp)

Each 1 per cent is subdivided into 100bp. If you could borrow at 3.2 per cent and invest at 3.3 per cent you would have made a 10bp profit. If the principal amount had been $1 million you have generated a profit of $1000.

Pips

This is the smallest denomination of a currency rate. If you had been quoted a spot foreign exchange rate of GBP/USD 1.5010–20, this would be a price with a 10 pip bid-offer spread.

Ticks (and half ticks)

These are the smallest denominations of a futures price movement.

In the Eurodollar STIR (short-term interest rate) futures, if you could have bought ten contracts at 98.20 and sold them five days later at 98.50, you would have made a total profit of 30 ticks. In this contract, each tick is $25 (half tick is $12.50), therefore making you a profit of:

30 ticks × $25 × 10 contracts = $7500.00

For details on the instruments mentioned above, see Chapter 1.

Non-deliverable forwards (NDFs)

Non-deliverable forwards (NDFs) are forward foreign exchange contracts (typically up to two years) in currencies with restricted convertibility – often from the emerging markets.

The contracts are essentially contracts for differences (**CFDs**) where the difference between the contracted forward amount and the spot reference rate at maturity is net settled, usually in dollars, allowing the emerging market currency to remain in situ.

EXAMPLE

A US importer has bought some goods worth $4.8 million from South Korea and has agreed to be invoiced by the supplier in Korean won. Payment is due in six months' time, by which time the USD/KRW exchange rate might have moved against him and require him to pay more dollars for the won. Assume normal foreign exchange forward contracts are unavailable.

The strategy used is for the importer to buy forward for six months using an NDF, KRW 6 billion at a forward rate of 1250 to the USD. Assume, that at maturity in six months' time, the dollar has weakened and the current spot rate is then USD/KRW: 1175, this becomes the settlement rate.

To calculate the settlement amount:

$$\frac{(1250 - 1175) \times 4{,}800{,}000}{1175} = \$306{,}382.98$$

The settlement amount may be positive as shown here, in which case the forward seller of the dollars (buyer of the KRW) receives the settlement. If the settlement amount is negative, the forward seller of the dollars (buyer of the KRW) makes the payment. The $306,382.98 will go to offset the additional costs that the importer now faces as a consequence of the weaker dollar.

Note that this does not provide the Korean won for the client; it simply protects an exchange rate. The importer now needs to execute a physical spot foreign exchange deal at a rate as close as possible to the settlement rate.

Volatility ('vol')

Volatility is a term used in the financial markets to describe how 'overheated' a market is. If things are very quiet this demonstrates low volatility, if things are crazy with prices fluctuating wildly, this would be highly volatile.

A volatility input is required for option pricing because of underlying assumptions in pricing models. The 'grandfather' option pricing model was written by **Black and Scholes** in 1972 and has been much revised since. The model assumes that with the underlying asset, for example a commodity such as gold, the price behaves in a similar fashion to a log-normal distribution. For more background on this see Chapter 2.

Normal distributions are typically found in nature, for example, the height of trees, the weight of children and the length of snakes. The volatility input into the option pricing model generates a prediction of how a particular price or rate will move in the future. It will not necessarily predict what the price will be on a specific date, but just how the price will behave; will there be a large degree of scatter around a theoretical average, with prices all over the place, or will there be little movement as the commodity price stays within a narrow range? The best way to explain this is by using an example from nature.

EXAMPLE

You have been given the job of statistically sampling a penguin population in Antarctica. Height data is being collected from a sample representation of Emperor penguins. One hundred penguins will be measured and the data analysed. From the data the average height of the penguins – known as the mean – can be calculated.

In the late eighteenth century the German scientist and mathematician Gauss undertook research. He showed that if you sampled data from any population with a normal distribution, once you had calculated the mean you could determine certain 'confidence limits' by evaluating the standard deviation of the population; this in turn indicated the amount of dispersion – the difference of numbers from their expected value – of each data point from the mean.

He calculated that if you took the mean (which you have already calculated) plus or minus one standard deviation you could ensure that 66 per cent of all the data readings would fall between these limits. He then predicted that if you took the mean plus or minus two standard deviations you could then guarantee that 95 per cent of all the data would fall within these wider limits. This is more statistically significant.

Let's assume the Emperor penguins have been measured, the mean has been calculated at 1 metre, and the standard deviation computed from the data, and is 10 per cent. This would give us a normal distribution (Figure 6.2).

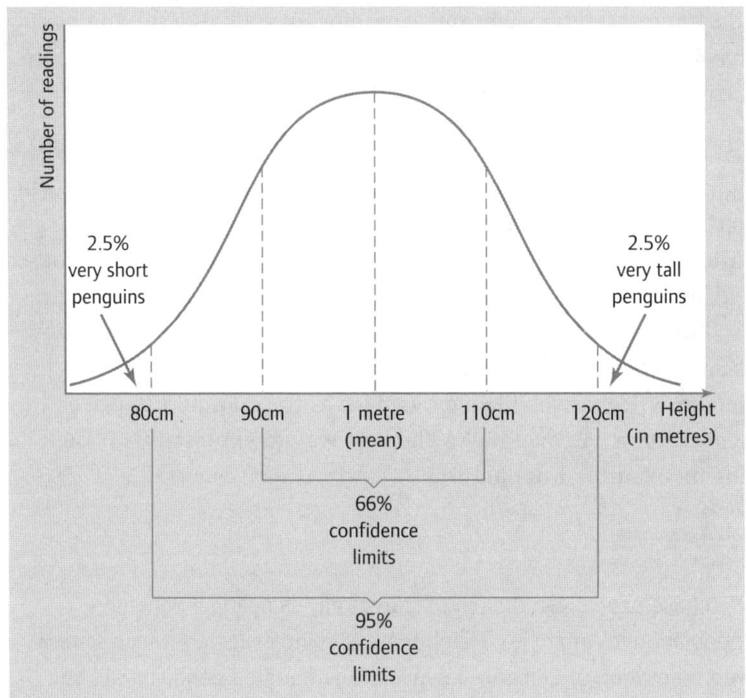

FIGURE 6.2 The projected analysis of the height of Emperor penguins

Source: *Mastering Derivatives Markets* by Francesca Taylor, Pearson Education, 2007.

Once the data has been collected it is not too difficult to carry out the calculations – anyone who has studied statistics will recognise the shape of the normal distribution, the bell curve. But how does all this fit in with options and option pricing? Well, standard deviation and volatility are the same thing.

The statistical definition of volatility is 'the normalised, annualised standard deviation of the returns of the underlying commodity'. The biggest problem in using volatility is trying to establish what the level of volatility will be in the future, before there is any data to back it up.

Consider a trader trying to price a currency option in three-month USD/JPY. He has to guess the shape of the normal curve: will it be steep with low volatility, and most readings about the mean, or will it be very flat, with high volatility and many readings widely scattered? In fact, the trader is trying to guess how volatile the exchange rate will be in advance. Not an easy thing to do. Figure 6.3 shows the shape of the distribution when volatility is low, at 5 per cent and Figure 6.4 shows high volatility at 15 per cent.

the trader is trying to guess how volatile the exchange rate will be

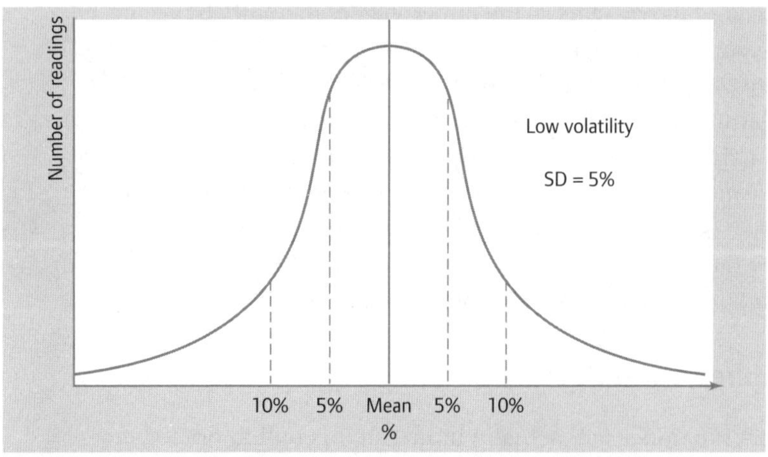

FIGURE 6.3 The effect of low volatility on the shape of the normal curve

Source: *Mastering Derivatives Markets* by Francesca Taylor, Pearson Education, 2007.

There are two types of volatility: historic and implied.

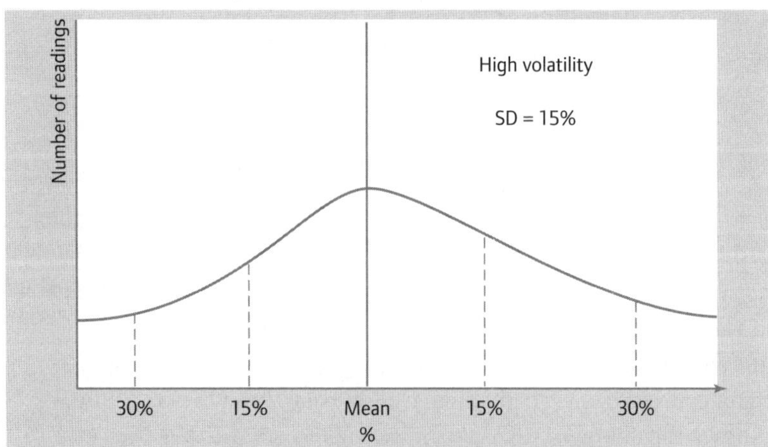

FIGURE 6.4 The effect of high volatility on the shape of the normal cuve

Source: *Mastering Derivatives Markets* by Francesca Taylor, Pearson Education, 2007.

Historic volatility

Data can be collected historically; it is possible to analyse the spread of movements of the underlying commodity by recording, for example, the daily closing prices of USD/JPY. If these prices were plotted on a graph, a type of scatter pattern would emerge. Volatility is, in effect, the definition of this scatter. Whilst this type of analysis allows historical data to be examined, it can only ever *indicate* future prices. It will not be able to predict prices but, rather, give an idea of where they might be, taking into account how the commodity has moved in the past. This is, of course, assuming you believe that history repeats itself.

Implied volatility

What the trader will actually input into his option pricing model is **implied volatility**. This is the current volatility level implicit in today's option prices.

Volatility itself has a spread. It is quoted as an annual percentage. For example, it might be quoted as 10.1–10.3 per cent. If the client wants to buy the option, use 10.3 per cent; if he is trying to sell it to you, use 10.1 per cent.

For more details on option pricing see Chapter 2.

The Greeks: Delta, Gamma, Vega, Theta

With an option, once the trade is transacted, only the strike (exercise) price will remain fixed; all the other variables such as the number of days to expiry, intrinsic value, volatility, cost of carry, will change with the market or with the passage of time. Each variable changes the value (premium) of the option in a distinct way. These changes are described as the 'option Greeks.' The most important Greeks are:

- delta;
- gamma;
- vega;
- theta.

Delta

The definition of delta is: 'The change in the option premium for a unit change in the underlying exchange rate or price.' This is an important measure because it shows how the price of the option will change as the underlying market moves. The value of delta can range from zero to one, i.e. as it moves in and out of the money, and the intrinsic value of the option fluctuates. It is also known as the 'hedge ratio'.

Gamma

This is the only option Greek that does not measure the sensitivity of the option price. Instead, gamma measures how the option's delta changes when the underlying asset moves. The definition of gamma is: 'The rate of change of delta for a unit change in the underlying exchange rate.' The more frequently an option portfolio needs to be re-hedged then the higher will be the gamma of the portfolio for a given movement in the underlying asset.

Vega

Vega is: 'The change in the option premium for a one per cent change in volatility.' This is a straight-line relationship. As volatility increases so does uncertainty and so does the premium. An option with a high volatility gives the holder a greater chance of more profitable exercise than an option with low volatility.

Theta

The definition of theta is: 'The change in the option premium for a given change in the period to expiry (usually the passage of a day).'

The time value component of the option expresses the risk premium in the option. To the option **writer** this risk premium is highest when the option is at the money, because at this point there is the greatest uncertainty over whether the option will expire worthless or have some value at maturity.

If the option moves into the money, the writer can be more sure the option will be exercised; if it moves out of the money the opposite applies. The more deeply in or out of the money the option moves, the greater the confidence of the option writer in the final outcome: will it or won't it be exercised?

For more information on options, see *Mastering Foreign Exchange and Currency Options* by Francesca Taylor.

Straight through processing (STP)

For a number of years, banks and financial institutions have been trying to cut their costs. Traditionally, many people have been employed in operations departments, the bulk of whom were engaged in largely clerical work. It is upon these staff that the reduction in headcount has been felt most keenly.

STP is the way that the banks have been seeking to automate post-trade processes, which can be affected more quickly, by computer systems, at less cost and with fewer errors.

There are still people employed in these departments but they tend to become involved when things either are too complicated to be input into a system – notably the more exotic products, or there has been a 'fail', perhaps because of incomplete or inaccurate data. This is known as either 'exception management' or 'fails management'.

I had a conversation in 2008 with colleagues from DTCC in New York whose firm handles all the purchases and sales of bonds and equities in the US. They estimated that their automated processes had streamlined the system and 'displaced' upwards of 750,000 jobs over fifteen years. Ironically, these computer systems are not cheap, but over the longer term costs savings can be seen.

Chapter 8 from Mike Simmons and Chapter 9 from Bill Hodgson both explore what happens after the deal is done and will give examples of how STP works.

7

Key trading principles for the front office

Richard Moore

There are no rules or principles however diligently followed that will guarantee success. Only by aligning personality, hard work and discipline can the probability of long-term success be improved.

- Introduction and market background
- What is a trader?
- Your only objective is to make money
- Money management
- Psychology
- Thoughts on how to be a trader
- Success factors for trading
- Conclusion

Introduction and market background

Wednesday, 16 September 1992 is etched on the memories of the currency traders of that era. The day is still referred to by commentators, strategists and traders as a seminal lesson in economic mismanagement, or proof that you cannot buck the market.

It was the day George Soros is alleged to have made a billion pounds betting that the UK government would be unable to sustain the sterling/deutschemark rate necessary for the UK to remain as part of the Exchange Rate Mechanism (ERM). It was also an excellent opportunity to observe good, bad and indifferent traders and how they dealt with extreme and exceptional market movements and circumstances.

If there was one lesson from that occasion, and time and again afterwards, it is that there are no rules or actions, however diligently followed, that can guarantee trading success. That is not to say that certain types of behaviour or trading styles do not make success more or less likely but it is only the unique combination of these behavioural characteristics combined with the innate and unteachable individual qualities of every trader that determines ultimate success or failure. It is this combination that will be discussed in the next few pages.

> 'To thine own self be true'
>
> William Shakespeare

You will not read this quote in any book or commentary of trading rules but it is one of the most important rules, if not the only rule of trading. There are numerous strategies for making money in the markets, a fundamental approach, a technical analysis approach, a trend following approach, a mean reversion – the list is almost endless. What is often confusing is that no approach is inherently wrong and no approach is inherently right and every approach could work and every approach could fail.

What singles out the more successful traders is that that they have married an approach to their personal psyche and they stick to it no matter what. Exactly what the approach is doesn't matter, but it will always match their trading personality and they stick to it automatically and unquestioningly.

Sterling's departure from the ERM dominated the economic headlines for many months post that fateful September day. Typically wise after the event, commentators and journalists – often the same ones who heralded the UK's entry into the ERM as a masterstroke – busily distanced themselves from that viewpoint to attack a humbled Conservative government.

For the first time the name George Soros started to appear in mainstream newspapers and organisations known as hedge funds were referred to. Amazing as this seems today, the world before 16 September 1992 had not heard of George Soros, let alone hedge funds. Trading rooms and traders around the world devoured every piece of information they could on Soros, sterling and hedge funds. The effect in trading rooms was in many ways no different to the emergence of a pop star or sporting hero to teenagers or children.

the effect in trading rooms was in many ways no different to the emergence of a pop star

Many traders became macro hedge fund managers and adjusted their style accordingly. The day trader who had never run an overnight position was taking risk based on three-month views. The efficient manager of small ticket deal flow was now regurgitating *Financial Times* editorial as a basis for their long-term views and, in short, much of the market became 'wanna be' George Soros or hedge fund managers. The equilibrium of many trading rooms was altered and profitability began to suffer because so many traders broke the rule, 'to thine own self be true'.

It is not to say that learning as much as possible about the Soros trading style is wrong or a waste of time. Much could and would be learned from listening to and reading about George Soros, the mistake is to believe that it is in any way possible to align Soros's trading rules, behaviour and habits with any other human being and expect good long-term results.

The day trader should be a day trader, the technical trader the technical trader and so on. US investor Warren Buffett regularly talks about operating within your own 'circle of competence' and that it almost doesn't matter how big the circle is. Much more important is that you know precisely where its boundaries are and you have the discipline to operate within them. This simple rule, above all others, is the one that is most frequently ignored and this is the one that you should consider above all other trading rules and the rule that should be uppermost in your mind when you read this chapter.

What is a trader?

Traders come in all shapes, styles and sizes. What does that mean? To begin, let's look at some of the differences that can exist among traders.

First, there are traders who sell and buy many asset classes, such as equities, rates, credit and foreign exchange. Within those asset classes there may be sub-classes. For example, in equities you may have those who specialise in healthcare or technology. In FX you may have those who specialise in emerging market currencies. You also have traders who trade across asset classes.

Second, there are many styles of trading:

- directional traders who bet on whether an asset or instrument is going up or down;
- relative-value traders who seek to profit by speculating that one asset is cheap or expensive relative to another asset;
- macro-direction traders who look for broad global trends;
- micro-direction traders tend to focus on micro events such as a single company's earning releases;
- technical analyst traders rely solely on technical analysis;
- fundamentals traders base everything on company fundamentals;
- those who combine both technical and fundamental trading.

Then factor in that you also have traders who:

- are successful in developing purely systematic trading strategies;
- don't use any quantitative analysis in their trading;
- trade options and try and earn 'time decay' by selling 'insurance';
- only use options to buy 'insurance';
- only use options;
- never use options;
- will hold positions for weeks and months;
- are 'day traders' and will flatten out all positions at the end of the day;
- will not hold a position for more than a few seconds.

Then there are those who only want to be market-makers and those who only want to be market-takers.

One could survey the landscape of the trading community and potentially find all the styles mentioned above and others, all mixed into all the asset classes mentioned above to produce an almost infinite set of permutations and combinations of individual trading styles. The sole unifying objective in each asset class, in each style with every trader is simply to make money.

While one would think this is obvious, it is not. A combination of ego, intellectualism, rationalisation and other psychological factors often causes traders to 'lose their way' and focus on something other than 'making money'. This cannot be emphasised enough; to be successful, a trader must remember at all times, he or she is working to a singular goal. It is not to be a 'big swinging dick', it is not to ride a long trend. It is not to catch the turn of the market, *it is to make money.*

Your only objective is to make money

Early in my trading career I worked closely with two very different senior traders.

Trader A researched every aspect of a trade and could articulate the fundamental economic argument in support of every trading position undertaken. He was incredibly bright with a stellar academic pedigree and a mind that was used to identifying and solving problems, and I often found myself in awe when I listened to him discuss his market position and views. His opinions were long in the making and he tended to keep his positions for extended periods of time and would feel slighted when the market refused to behave as his analysis suggested it should.

Trader B was a very different character. He had a low boredom threshold, allied to a capability to assess quickly the core of the issue, making him a much more instinctive trader. His views on the markets were, by comparison, superficial and capable of change in an instant.

It made him less interesting to listen to as you came to learn that a passionate argument about why sterling must head higher would readily turn into a short sterling position later in the day when something had changed his mind.

Yet, during the early years, it was the instinctive trader, with superficial market views who delivered outstanding trading results each year, with the more researched and academic individual delivering far less impressive results, often with significant losses.

The lesson here is not that one approach is better than the other, although it was probably true that the trading approach and personality of the instinctive trader was better calibrated in the instinctive trader. The lesson is that as a trader your only objective is making money. Erudite discussions about markets, perfectly formed technical trading patterns buying at the bottom or selling at the top are incidental to the absolute requirement to make money every month and every quarter. Great trading ideas and being right about the market matter little if you cannot find a trading strategy that makes money.

In a modern trading environment with Bloomberg terminals, constant news and technical software, it is easy to lose sight of the fact that only two things can happen to a market; it can go up or it can go down, and you can only be long or short and the outcomes will be a profit or a loss. You should never lose sight of the fact that as a trader you only have the one goal – to make money and be profitable.

> only two things can happen it can go up or it can go down

Money management

In any discussion or paper on trading there will always be a discussion of 'money management'. To repeat, the goal of a trader is to make money.

The best trading strategy in the world, even if profitable, won't help if your capital is wiped out before the gains kick in.

Money management is key. What this means is to ensure that any trade or strategy has an appropriate trigger for getting out of the position. This is to ensure that the trade does not consume more capital than the trader intends to put into that strategy. Many have hard and fast rules about money management and these will be discussed in this chapter. However, differing trading styles will warrant different money management rules – such 'discipline' is an essential ingredient in successful trading.

Psychology

Trading is primarily a game of psychology. Traders are constantly battling with themselves, their history, and their own personal demons in attempting to 'beat the market'. This chapter will attempt to shatter many common myths. Being successful in the market is understanding that there are no 'rules'. You need an edge in the market to be successful and only you can figure out what your edge is. You need to develop your own style, understand what works for you and slay your demons. If you can do that, if you can slay your personal demons, keep the focus on your objective and develop a real passion for the markets, you can be successful, no matter what your style is.

Thoughts on how to be a trader

A question of asset classes

One of the first decisions a trader needs to make is what to trade.

To 'beat the market' a trader needs to take into consideration the following:

- access;
- transaction costs;
- liquidity and transparency of the market;
- capital requirements;
- information advantage.

Access

Not all markets are available to every trader. There are regulatory regimes and requirements, different ways of being short or long and different methods of accessing the market. For example, there are many currencies that are restricted in terms of who can buy or sell them and thus a 'non-deliverable market' has developed. Many exchanges have restricted 'shorting' of equities. While most developed countries' FX and equities can be traded online, this is not true of all fixed income instruments. There is also a big difference between:

- streaming quote internet access;
- the ability to 'make markets' on the web;
- a request for quote-only access.

Many markets require you to make a phone call and access the market through third parties. Understanding the access you have to a market is critical in deciding whether to trade it.

Transaction costs

An underappreciated, but massively important factor in trading is transaction costs. For example, there is no point in developing a 'high frequency' trading strategy to earn an average of 3 cents a trade if you can't trade for much less than what you plan to earn. Many market-takers fail to appreciate the true cost of the bid/offer spread. Some market participants have developed complex algorithms to understand the market microstructure so they can embed the true cost of transactions into their overall strategy before implementing it.

Transaction costs include bid/offer spreads, commissions/brokerage, financing and margin costs. Commissions tend to be fixed but other charges can change with market structure and volatility. When thinking about and developing trading strategies, it is imperative to incorporate transaction costs.

Liquidity and transparency of the market

Do not underestimate the importance of knowing the value of your portfolio at all times. While some markets are transparent, say G10 FX, others are less so. Even in a transparent market, there may be a lack of liquidity. Many thinly traded small-cap equities will give the illusion of transparency, but try and buy or sell a decent-sized position and you will find that transparency is an illusion. Again, remember that the goal of trading is to make money. Paper profits are worthless if they can't be turned into money because the market traded doesn't have the liquidity to provide the trader with the ability to take profits. Similarly, all the efforts put into developing money management techniques are a waste of time if once again the liquidity or transparency of the market means that the mark-to-market levels are not reflective of the position size, relative to the ability to exit.

> even in a transparent market, there may be a lack of liquidity

Capital requirements

There are markets where you can leverage your capital twenty to one or greater. There are markets where you get no leverage. Even on the liquid US exchanges, some equities can be leveraged while others cannot. Every trader has limited capital. Part of your success in 'making money' will be in understanding how to use your capital to achieve the maximum return. The understanding and use of leverage in all aspects of trading is key to capital management. When you are right, leverage will magnify your returns and when you are wrong leverage can quickly wipe out your capital. Consider the effect of leverage on a simple stock trade where a trader has $100,000 of capital levered four times allowing him to purchase $400,000 of stock. A 25 per cent move up in the stock will generate a 100 per cent return on invested capital; a similar size move down will destroy the trader's capital. Understanding your capital, your leverage and market volatility will be vital to long-term trading success.

Information advantage and trading edge

There is an unquantifiable number of traders taking a position in any particular asset at any point in time. When deciding what asset class you will trade you need to think about what your edge will be. You are competing against tens of thousands, if not millions of traders around the world who all have the same goal as you, but by definition cannot all be successful. The edge may be based on information, quantitative analysis, technical analysis, correlation and relative value, the moon phase, gut feel or anything else traders use. Figure out what your style and edge will be and taking into account the liquidity, transaction costs, transparency, access and capital requirements, make your choice.

What's your trading style?

Systematic

The style of trading varies greatly with personality type. To begin with there are traders who develop, monitor and continually renew systems that are purely quantitatively based. These 'black box' systems spit out trades that are executed electronically or manually depending on the asset class. Probably the most successful trader of our time, James Simons who runs a hedge fund call Renaissance Technologies, trades only systematic strategies. Such strategies can be long-term investments, have shorter-term horizons or can be 'high frequency' trades that have one to three second horizons or even millisecond horizons. Typically, individuals with a maths background, often people with doctorates in astronomy or physics, design these systems.

The most dangerous pitfall for the lay person to fall into is known as optimisation. This happens when someone decides to be a systematic trader and develops a system which optimises the result based on history and back-testing. Typically, this will result in the 'perfect' system for the time horizon tested, but often will not succeed in the future. While systematic trading can be, and is a very profitable style of trading, designing systems is a different skill from discretionary trading and this chapter will focus on discretionary trading.

Discretionary

Discretionary traders all make decisions that are not systematic, but based on varying inputs. The following is a range of those inputs and styles:

- traders who go with their 'gut feel';
- people who trade based on underlying economic or company fundamentals;
- technical traders who use chart patterns;
- traders who buy and sell based on an analysis of flow and go with the 'momentum of the market';
- event traders who focus on data releases and make their bets based on a forecast or the outcome of those events;
- relative value traders who bet on a widening or narrowing of the value of one asset against another.

Define your market

As I wrote earlier, traders must develop a style that fits their personality. However, even though you've developed that style, you must realise that markets are dynamic and not every market will suit your style. Between 2004 and 2006, G10 currency volatility was typically between 6 per cent – 8 per cent, markets were 'range-bound', seemingly going nowhere, and 'carry strategies', which are typically suited to quieter markets, were successful. A carry trade in its basic form is owning a low interest rate currency and lending a high interest rate currency and not expecting the currency rate to move to compensate the lender of the low interest rate currency. A typical carry trade before the credit crunch involved the Japanese yen. In the UK and certain other European countries it became popular to swap your sterling mortgage interest rate of say 5 per cent, with a yen mortgage interest rate of say 1.5 per cent. Over the course of a year, this strategy would save 3.5 per cent in interest costs and provided sterling did not weaken by more than 3.5 per cent, would be successful. In quiet, range-bound markets this was a successful strategy for much of the five years up to 2008. Then, it was catastrophic because the GBP/JPY rate fell from 200 yen to the pound to 125. In simple terms, although you might have saved 3.5 per cent in interest costs when you converted your mortgage back to sterling you would have found the outstanding mortgage had grown by more than 35 per cent.

You must begin every trading day defining what type of market you are in, and adjusting your style to suit that market. If you are a trend trader, be careful when the market falls into ranges and adjust your trading style. The first thing to do is cut your position size as you look for the trend to begin. If you are a range trader, be careful of markets that are trending as they can trend longer than you think they can and when they reverse, they will reverse harder than expected. Find ways to help you define when the range market has returned. Studies have shown implied volatilities can be a good signal for this.

Then there are markets that are prone to overshoot and retrace. I know a firm whose traders are day traders, many of whom like to wait for these moments. These strategies worked well in 2005 and 2006, but in 2007 management noticed that the markets tended to trend for most of the day and only retraced at the end of the day and in the early part of the Asian market. They told those traders who employed that strategy to sleep in and only come to work at 11am. All of a sudden those strategies started to work again because the managers and traders defined the market, realised it didn't suit their style and made adjustments to compensate.

Understand market drivers

No matter what your style is and no matter what asset class you trade, always remember that the drivers of markets are important and dynamic. There are times when equities drive credit markets and times when credit markets drive equities. At times, the Canadian dollar can be driven by moves in gold, at times it can be driven by moves in oil and at times it can be driven by moves in London. Certain technical levels are important to watch even if you are not a technical trader. There are times when fundamentals and data releases are important and times when they aren't. Even economic data releases vary in importance. In the spring of 2008, the market was fearful of inflation and the CPI releases drove the markets. In the autumn of 2008 it was consumption data that drove the markets as the inflation fear was gone and the CPI release had become irrelevant.

It is also vital to understand market positioning and expectations. Often, the best information on market positioning occurs when data comes out that is not what was expected and the market reacts in the opposite way to how it should. In 2008, US employment figures for May that were released in June were much worse than expected, but the interest rate markets couldn't rally much after the release and at the end of the day had sold off significantly. Clearly the market was 'long'. Over the next week, the market sold off 50 basis points. No data was able to turn the trend.

Money management revisited

There are as many techniques for setting stop losses and take profit levels, as there are trading strategies. Here are a few factors to include in any money management strategy:

- Entry discipline is important. The market goads you to get into positions at bad levels. Keep your discipline.
- Always have an idea of where you will get out. As irrational as a traded price is, it could become more irrational before it returns to sanity and you could be bankrupt. For example, Fed funds finished 2008 below 25 basis points, the lowest rate in history. In

the spring of 2008 you could have put on a position in the Fed fund futures markets that would only have lost money if the fed had *raised* rates by December by more than 25 basis points to 2.25 per cent. One could easily have argued that was irrational, but the implied rate soared 75bp by mid-summer before the ultimate collapse of over 250bp.

- Take profits. Again, many traders define discipline as good money management by having stop loss orders in the markets. However, without a corresponding discipline around taking profits, one will typically watch profits appear, disappear and have the stops kick in.
- Set stops. For those riding a trend, trailing stops may be most appropriate where the stop loss is regularly adjusted so that some profits from a winning position are protected. For example, a popular and successful currency trade throughout 2008 was to run a short sterling, long dollar position (short cable). If this position were established at say GBP/USD 2.00 a trailing stop loss today, with the spot rate at $1.42, might have been adjusted down to $1.50, a profit on the overall trade but characterised as a stop loss, because in practice it protects a profit.
- For those playing momentum, it is best to add to winners; in the cable trade that would involve increasing the size of the position at say $1.90 and again at $1.80. For those trying to pick bottoms, it may be best to add to losers within a defined loss strategy. Money-management discipline is important, but should vary with both trading style and the market environment.

Trading success trends

Most traders go through times when they are profitable and times when they are not. Money management is critical in the difficult times. It is important to remember that if you have an edge and stick to your strategy, you will become profitable. While at times the best thing a trader can do is 'clear the decks' and square all positions, it is generally poor practice to stop trading. The message I gave to traders was: 'You're a trader, trade.' Taking time out of the market usually doesn't improve performance. An occasional break is not a bad idea, but probably makes the most sense as a good run comes to an end, not as a bad run is coming to an end. During a difficult period, a trader should cut down their position size, rethink their inputs, define the markets and keep trading.

Success factors for trading

While there are many styles of trading, successful traders all share some traits.

Commitment and work ethic.

The markets move five days a week, often twenty four hours a day. When the market is not active, there is time to read, prepare, back-test, analyse, read again and network. Understanding what others are looking at adds value, figuring out positioning adds value, preparing and thinking about what events may trigger moves, adds value. One must be committed to trading and willing to work extraordinarily hard to beat the markets as there are millions vying for the same outcome.

one must be committed to trading and willing to work extraordinarily hard

Be passionate about markets and trading

It is without doubt a truth that without an innate curiosity about markets allied to a passion for trading, a career in trading is not possible. Probably the most talented individual that worked for me had what can almost be described as a religious zeal for market knowledge and information. He was at his most content, alone researching a trading idea or strategy and this thirst for market knowledge did not confine itself to the working day or office hours. In many ways it was sad to learn that much of his recreation time was spent doing what for others was characterised as work – reading and researching the markets. Within twenty four months of joining our company and in only his second year of trading he had recorded the best performance in the history of the department and this was a record he went on to beat more than once. You walked away from every discussion about his market view a little more knowledgeable about a particular market and confident that he could discuss any market with a specialist or expert and give more than he would take from the conversation.

Although this individual was exceptional, a passion for markets and a passion for trading is present in all good traders. This was not based on a necessity to do a job and make money – it was something that would stay with them long after they had finished their trading careers and I came to believe it was not something that could be learnt, taught or adopted over the long-term.

Numeracy

Markets are about numbers, probabilities, statistics and psychology. Being comfortable with numbers and maths helps drive success.

Be flexible and dynamic

Those who are stubborn won't succeed in the long-term. The market tells you when you're right and when you're wrong. Losing money is OK; losing money is a regular part of a successful trader's commercial life and accepting that reality is essential for long-term trading success. More importantly, it is the management of the relationship between the size and frequency of losing and winning trades that is critical. Part of the discipline of a trader is being open to being wrong and it is accepting that the unexpected tail event may, and frequently does, occur. The year 2008 is littered with examples of this.

The owners of Lehman Brothers shares in the US or Royal Bank of Scotland stock in the UK would have never have imagined at the beginning of 2008 that their stock would be worthless in the case of Lehman's and trading for pennies in the case of RBS by the end of the year.

Success as a trader is about knowing when history is relevant and when it isn't. Be dynamic; what worked last year will not work this year – this is almost true in every market in every year and a failure to realise this can be the ruin of many a trader.

Sterling's exit from the ERM in 1992 spawned a generation of traders who would perennially run short sterling positions as they re-lived the move from DM2.75 to DM2.20. Sadly, having touched a low of DM2.20 in 1993, sterling then spent much of the next few years regaining its losses and a short sterling position was generally a losing position.

Then, in the late 1990s, there was a two-day period where dollar against the yen fell 19 per cent and within that a three-hour period when it fell 12 per cent. This spawned a generation of traders who would sit short dollar yen hoping for a repeat performance and quick profits.

Conclusion

All markets are in a constant state of change. Sometimes this change is fast and sometimes it is slow, but it is never static. Markets are dynamic, correlations are dynamic and volatility is dynamic; accordingly it follows that traders need to be dynamic. In practice, success in trading requires a trader to evaluate and change their strategies and approach continuously.

8 Key stages in the lifecycle of a securities trade

Michael Simmons

No business can be bottom-line profitable without efficiency in its operations department.

- Introduction
- The trade lifecycle: an overview
- Straight through processing and static data
- Trade execution
- Trade capture
- Trade enrichment
- Trade agreement
- Settlement instructions
- Pre-settlement statuses
- Failed trade management
- Trade settlement
- Updating internal records
- Reconciliation
- Summary

Introduction

A trade that has been **executed** (by the traders in the front office), whether to buy or to sell **securities**, is only the starting point of a series of steps known as the trade lifecycle, which culminates in **settlement** of that trade.

In the case of securities (i.e. equity and bond) trades, 'settlement' relates to the exchange of securities and cash between buyer and seller. Theoretically, for every trade executed, settlement should occur on the scheduled date of settlement; in reality, in many (not all) securities markets some trades will not settle on their due date, because of the seller's inability to deliver the securities or the buyer's inability to pay. Such trades are commonly known as **failed trades**, meaning that settlement will be delayed (not cancelled), and such fails may have adverse financial implications for sellers and buyers.

For an individual trade, the trade lifecycle is designed to remove obstacles to timely and efficient settlement so that trading profits are retained. Besides retention of profits, another important focus for some firms (e.g. investment banks) is the efficient servicing of its institutional clients (e.g. hedge funds); efficient trade processing is crucial in retaining clients and winning new clients.

OTC securities trades involve the risk of the buying party recording and processing trade details that are different from those recorded by the selling party; if such discrepancies are not resolved in a timely fashion, the trade may fail to settle on its due date. Such risks do not apply to trades executed on-exchange, as the exchange itself is the trade's point of origin, and there can be no doubt over any of the trade components. For these reasons, this chapter describes the primary steps involved in the safe and secure processing of OTC securities trades, following trade execution up to the point at which the trade is settled.

The trade lifecycle: an overview

This section will focus on the trade lifecycle from the perspective of one trading organisation, Firm F, that:

- buys, holds and sells securities;
- trades in equities domiciled in various locations and in **international bonds**;
- trades with counterparties that are both market professionals (**sell-side** firms), and institutional investors (**buy-side** firms);
- has an account with Custodian C, who, on Firm F's behalf, settles trades and maintains a securities account and a cash account.

Note that it is normal practice for securities trades to be settled in the natural location of the individual security. In fact, the ultimate location of securities within most established financial centres is the country's **central securities depository (CSD)**, which holds securities in safekeeping on behalf of the CSD's participants (or account holders), and facilitates the movement of securities and cash between buyers and sellers. For example, Qantas shares are held electronically within the Australian securities depository (known as CHESS), and to settle a purchase of Qantas shares, a buyer will need to maintain an account at CHESS, or to use the services of a **custodian** who is a member of CHESS. The same concept applies in all the main financial centres, including US securities, where equities are held and settled in the Depository Trust & Clearing Corporation (DTCC), and in the UK where Euroclear UK & Ireland (formerly **CREST**) is used. Consequently, a firm that buys, holds and sells securities globally may well use the services of several custodians in a variety of locations. An option is to set up an arrangement with a **global custodian**, which provides a single point of contact for the account holder.

From the perspective of a trading firm that buys and sells securities, the efficient processing of a trade involves both internal and external management. Internal management of a trade involves, for example, the passing of trade details between internal systems, which if processed correctly will enable subsequent important actions. External management of a trade involves, for example, taking corrective action (at the custodian) when it is discovered that a counterparty has trade details that differ from the trading firm's own details.

Figure 8.1 shows the main steps in the trade lifecycle. Each of these steps will now be explained.

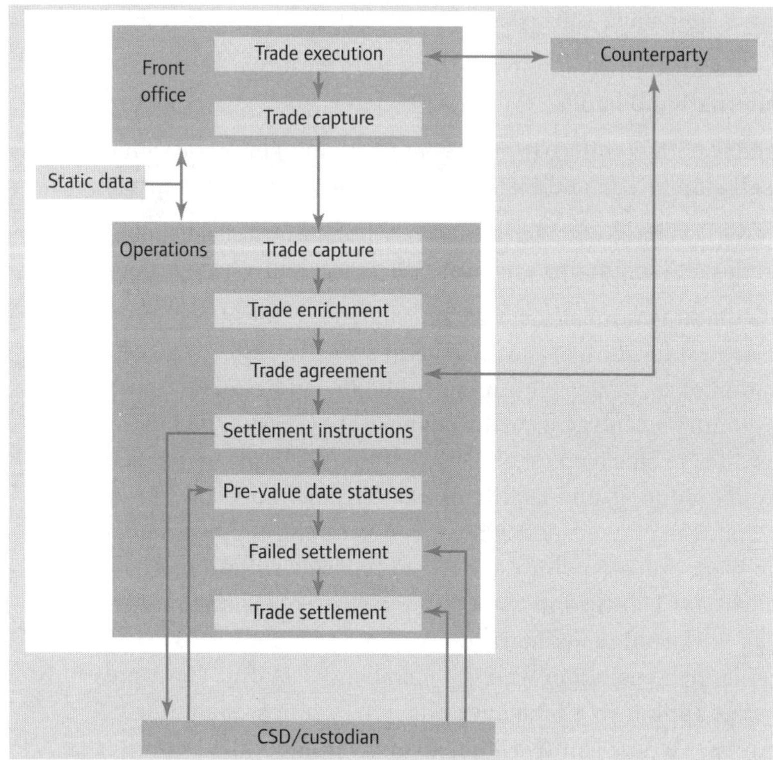

FIGURE 8.1 The trade lifecycle

Source: *Securities Operations: A guide to trade and position management* by Michael Simmons, John Wiley, 2002.

Straight through processing and static data

Within any financial services firm, straight through processing (STP) is of paramount importance. STP can be defined as the objective of processing trades fully automatically (following input of trade details), throughout all stages of the trade lifecycle, including internal/external and outgoing/incoming information. In this day and age, the sheer volume of trading (in larger firms running into tens of thousands of trades a day) would require armies of operations personnel to manage trade processing. Instead, there is a heavy reliance on IT systems to automate such processing, wherever possible. Static data (explained below) play a big role in achieving STP.

Most firms that trade in securities wish to settle their purchases and sales over their specific account number at their relevant custodian; this is true of Firm F and of their counterparties. Such details (e.g. Firm F settles its trades in Australian equity via Custodian C, account number ABC0017769) are known as **standing settlement instructions (SSIs)**. Occasionally, a firm may decide to change its custodian within a particular financial centre, but this is far from a daily occurrence; this may occur with the type of frequency that an individual changes his personal bank.

Furthermore, individal securities have unique and publicly available identifiers (e.g. **ISIN** codes). These may change only under specific circumstances. (Although the intention is to create unique identifiers, this is not always achieved as occasionally the same ISIN may be found for two securities.)

individual securities have unique and publicly available identifiers

STP is achievable if, internally within a securities trading firm, such details as SSIs and ISIN codes are stored within a database of accessible information; this database is commonly known as **static** data or reference data. Then, once a trade has been executed and the basic trade details have been captured, the firm's internal systems are programmed to access static data and to locate the appropriate and additional information necessary for complete operational processing; this process is known as **trade enrichment**. For each trade, STP enables automation of follow-on tasks such as issuance of **trade confirmations** to counterparties and issuance of **settlement instructions** to custodians.

TIP

To avoid confusion between standing settlement instructions and settlement instructions:

- an SSI is issued by a party to its counterparty at the start of their relationship, stating the account details of where that party wishes to settle all their trades in a specific market (e.g. Firm F settles all its trades in Australian equity via Custodian C, account number ABC0017769);

- a settlement instruction is issued by a trading party to its custodian, and contains details of an individual trade that the trading party requires the custodian to settle on the trading party's behalf.

Conversely, if any of the essential information is missing (e.g. Firm F is not holding counterparty G's SSIs for Canadian equity), internal systems are programmed to halt processing until such time as the missing information is discovered, inserted into static data and the trade resubmitted for the relevant information to be attached. This particular trade has been subject to exception management and STP has not therefore been achieved (for this trade).

In an ideal world, static data should be present before trade execution, so that STP can be achieved.

In summary, the more focus that can be given to the gathering and insertion of accurate and timely information to static data, the higher the achievable rate of STP. STP makes full use of automation with minimal reliance on manpower, whereas exception management requires manpower to discover the information before trade processing can be completed.

In describing the following steps within the trade lifecycle, it should be assumed that static data is present.

Trade execution

Trade execution is the act of agreeing to undertake a securities trade, on specifically agreed terms, between buyer and seller. It is a contractual agreement between buyer and seller and the contractual commitment of each party (the seller must deliver the securities, the buyer must pay) must be fulfilled. (The only exception to this would occur if both parties agree to cancel the trade).

Trade capture

Trade capture is the act of recording details of individual trades internally, within the trading firm's own systems. This stage is regarded as the 'foundation on which the house is built'; if the trade is captured accurately, there is every chance that the trade will settle on its due date. If not captured accurately it may still be possible to settle on time, but the chances are reduced. This aspect must be considered in conjunction with the number of days between trade date and the due date of settlement; this topic will be discussed later in this chapter.

Such recording should ideally occur immediately (by the trader) upon trade execution, because if not done so, the trader may forget the details, resulting in incorrect details or a failure to record the details at all. This trader must adopt a disciplined approach to this.

ANECDOTE

In very busy times, I've seen a trader holding several phone conversations as he executes trades every few seconds; yet the trader makes no attempt to record (even to scribble) any details as a reminder. Once the panic has subsided thirty minutes later the trader could not recall correctly all the details of all the trades. This caused a lot of work.

The minimum details that must be captured by the trader are show in Table 8.1.

TABLE 8.1 Minimum trade details

Trade component	Description	Example
Trade date	The date the trade was executed. This is important to record correctly because it could affect the value date and entitlement to equity corporate actions	15 March YYYY
Trade time	The hour and minute of execution; expressed as hh/mm. Recording of trade time is a regulatory requirement	08:13
Value date (see note below table)	The due/intended date of settlement. Also known as contractual settlement date.	18 March YYYY
Operation (buy/sell)	Whether the firm is buying or selling securities	Buy

Table 8.1 continued

Trade component	Description	Example
Trading book	The discrete trading function within the trading department that owns this trade	Book XYZ
Quantity	The number of shares or the quantity of bonds bought or sold	Equity: 600,000 (shares) Bond: $12,000,000 (face value)
Security	The specific security bought or sold. Great care must be taken as many bonds have very similar titles. Note that in an automated environment, a coding system (such as ISIN) is normally used to identify the security.	Equity: IBM Corp common stock Bond: IBRD 5.25 per cent 1 February 2030
Price	The specific price at which the securities were bought or sold. Equity is expressed as a 'unit' price (price per share), whereas bonds are expressed as percentages	Equity: $72.34 Bond: 99.15%
Counterparty	The specific counterparty from whom securities were bought or to whom securities have been sold, including their location	Counterparty T, Hong Kong

It is important to note that the information captured by the trader is the basic (skeleton) information only; to enable full operational processing, information will need adding during the trade enrichment stage.

Regarding value date, in every market there is a standard/default number of days between trade date and value date; this is known as the **settlement cycle** and is commonly expressed as T+1, T+2, etc., meaning that value date is trade date plus one day or plus two days, etc. In early 2009, the following settlement cycles apply:

- US treasury bond market and UK government bond ('gilt') market: T+1;
- US equity market and UK equity market: T+3.

It is important to note that these are defaults; under normal circumstances, traders do not mention value date when negotiating a trade as it is assumed to be the default for the particular market. However, if, for example, a buyer has funds available in five days' time, the buyer can request the seller to make the value date T+5 for that particular trade, which the selling trader may or may not agree to. If the trader agrees to a special value date, it is essential that such details are captured accordingly.

Within the securities division of many firms, traders use dedicated trading systems that are separate from the main processing system used by operations personnel. This is necessary because traders require specific information and very fast response times from their systems, whereas the operations department require a broad array of functions and volume-based processing capability. Under the circumstances where a firm has separate trading system(s) and processing system, there is a need for an interface between front office (trading) and back office (operations) to facilitate the passing of trade details electronically. Note that the intention is to pass exactly the same details from the trading system to the processing system (following which further details will be added within the processing system via the trade enrichment process).

Trade capture within any system requires the specific security and the specific counterparty to be present within static data. If not present, trade capture cannot occur and the firm's exposure cannot be recorded, until the data is firstly discovered, then set up. This is true of both trading systems and processing systems. It is also essential to ensure that trading systems and processing systems contain precisely the same details at the same time to avoid such situations as the processing system missing a trade, which could lead to monetary loss particularly in a T+1 market. Reconciliations are typically conducted daily to ensure the systems are aligned. Everyday occurrences regarding trade capture within financial services include the following:

- Trades executed but not captured in trading systems because of missing securities or counterparty static data. Note that failure to capture a trade in a trading system will guarantee the trade is not captured within the processing system.
- Trades executed and captured within trading systems, but not captured within the processing system because of missing securities or counterparty static data.

Accurate and timely static data remains a major focus area for all financial services firms.

Trade enrichment

Trade enrichment is the process of adding essential information (within the operations processing system) to the skeleton details received from the trading system. Its purpose is to develop the details to the point where all stages within the trade lifecycle can be processed.

Enrichment can be achieved automatically as part of STP, providing that all required information is present within the firm's static data.

Trade details received from the trading system are shown in Table 8.2.

TABLE 8.2 Details received from the trading system

Trade component	Example
Trade date	15th March YYYY
Trade time	08:13
Value date	18th March YYYY
Operation	Buy
Quantity	600,000
Security	IBM Corp common stock
Price	USD 72.34
Counterparty	Counterparty T, Hong Kong

Additional trade details enriched by the processing system (defaulted from static data) are shown in Table 8.3.

TABLE 8.3 Enriched data from the processing system

Trade Component	Description	Example
Trade reference	An unique number given to a trade to identify it from any other trade	Prin501677
'Our' SSI	The specific custodian and account number (belonging to us) over which we wish to settle the trade	Custodian C, account ABC0017769

Counterparty SSI	The custodian and account number (belonging to the counterparty) over which we believe the counterparty wishes to settle	Custodian F, account 992MM005
ISIN code	The unique external identification code of the particular security traded	US123456789
Trade charges	Mandatory additional amounts to be added or subtracted	SEC fee
Counterparty confirmation preferences	The method by which the counterparty wishes to receive formal advice of trade details	SWIFT
Net Cash Value	The final cash amount to be paid to or received from the counterparty	USD 43,404,000.00

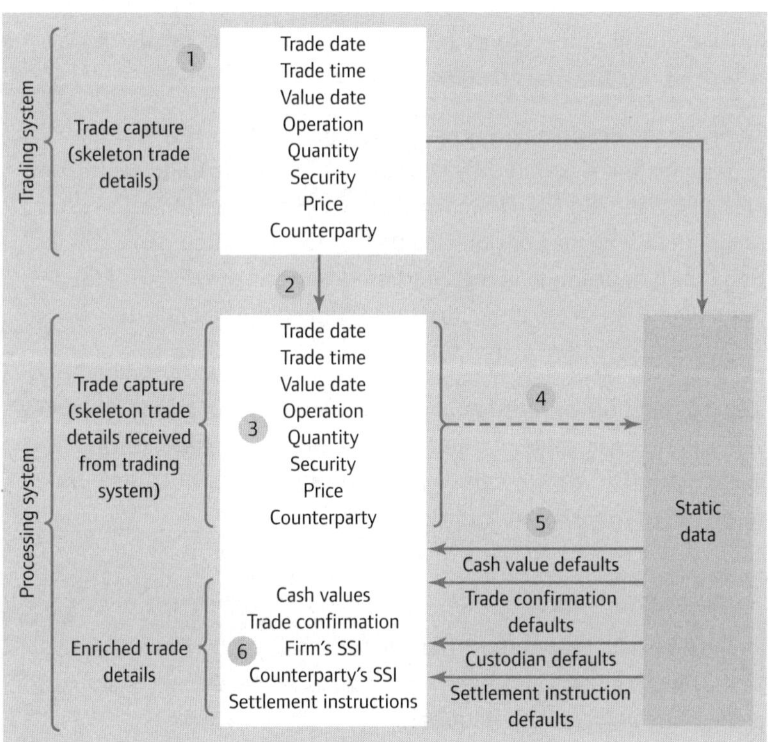

FIGURE 8.2 The data enrichment process

Source: *Securities Operations: A guide to trade and position management* by Michael Simmons, John Wiley, 2002.

The enrichment process is summarised in Figure 8.2 on the previous page. The main stages in the process::

1. Basic details are captured within the trading system.
2. These details are passed to the processing system via an interface.
3. The basic details are captured within the processing system.
4. The basic details are used as the basis for locating additional data.
5. Additional data is located and passed to processing system.
6. The basic trade details are enriched with the additional data.

At completion of step 6, the trade has all required details to enable full operational processing to commence.

Trade agreement

Trade agreement is the process of ensuring that trade details, as captured by a firm, are agreed by the counterparty.

Although trade details were agreed at the time of trade execution, there remains the risk that differences exist following trade capture. Trade agreement is designed to identify whether the counterparty has the same details as 'us', or not. Details that do not match place timely settlement of trades in jeopardy, and, as described previously, failed trades can and do cause monetary loss. Therefore, if details do not agree, urgent corrective action must be taken.

To provide an idea of the size of the problem, within a high-volume environment, error rates of 5 per cent may be acceptable to the management. (Error rates can be defined as a trade requiring some form of amendment, or outright cancellation.)

ANECDOTE

In one particular organisation, the error rate was greater than 35 per cent. Underlying reasons were due to a combination of trader inaccuracy and missing or inaccurate static data.

It is possible for any trade component to be different from the counterparty's details, as in Table 8.4.

TABLE 8.4 Errors can occur in any trade component

Trade component	Example errors
Value date	As this is the intended date of settlement (when securities and cash are due to be exchanged) it is essential that this date is agreed by the counterparty
Operation	Sometimes both parties state that they are buying, or both parties state they are selling
Quantity	One party has 3,000,000, the other has 300,000
Security	The incorrect security can be stated, particularly in the case of bonds where issuers such as the World Bank have many bonds in issue with very similar details
Price	One party has a price of €15.15 while the other party has a price of €15.16
Counterparty	Sometimes the correct entity is stated, but in the wrong location. Sometimes the captured counterparty is completely wrong.

The following are example methods of communicating trade details to counterparties:

- contract notes: the traditional paper method;
- e-mail trade confirmations: a current, electronic method;
- **SWIFT** trade confirmations: one of the most popular methods because of its highly structured message format, facilitating automated generation and transmission. Requires subscription by sender and receiver.
- **OASYS**: an electronic mechanism allowing subscribers to communicate trade detail to one another with the ability for the recipient to affirm (or deny) their agreement. Designed for use between institutional investors and their brokers.
- **TRAX**: an electronic system in which seller and buyer are obliged to input trade details which TRAX attempts to match and publishes a matching status (matched, unmatched). Designed for use between market professionals.

Institutional investors typically are only receivers (rather than issuers) of trade confirmations; one of the primary indicators of a broker's performance is the speed of issuance of and accuracy of information contained within trade confirmations. Brokers are typically issuers of trade confirmations, but may also receive trade confirmations from other market professionals.

Some firms dedicate personnel to the checking of incoming confirmations against their own records; other firms choose not to. Yet choosing not to check incoming confirmations is a risky strategy, because in the event of a discrepancy coming to light such a firm would be in a weak position if a loss were incurred by the counterparty, and if the counterparty can prove that the firm failed to highlight the discrepancy earlier in the trade lifecycle.

By whichever method trade agreement is undertaken, it is essential that once a discrepancy is identified it is investigated and resolved immediately. It is anticipated that in the coming years settlement cycles will reduce (e.g. markets that currently operate on a T+3 basis may move to T+2 or T+1), meaning that the available time to resolve discrepancies before value date will reduce, necessitating firms to become ultra-efficient in the identification and resolution of trade discrepancies.

Settlement instructions

Issuance of a settlement instruction is the mechanism by which a buyer or seller communicates the need to settle a securities trade, to its custodian.

As mentioned earlier in this chapter, custodians are appointed by securities trading firms to settle securities trades, and to hold securities and cash on behalf of such firms. From the custodian's perspective the securities trading firm is the account holder.

> from the custodian's perspective the securities trading firm is the account holder

It is important to note that before receipt of a settlement instruction, the custodian will be unaware that a trade has been executed (by its account holder). Upon receipt of a settlement instruction, the custodian is required to:

- confirm receipt of the instruction to the account holder;
- attempt to match the details of the instruction, with the counterparty's instruction;
- update the instruction with its matching status (i.e. matched, unmatched);
- advise the account holder of the current matching status;
- settle the trade on (or after) the value date;
- advise the account holder once settlement has occurred;
- update securities holdings and cash balances as a result of settlement;
- issue statements of securities holdings and cash balances to the account holder.

Note that even where a trading firm has completed the steps in the trade lifecycle, including achieving trade agreement with the counterparty, settlement will not occur without issuance of a settlement instruction.

All custodians state deadlines for the receipt (from their account holders) of settlement instructions, relative to value date. For example, for its trading in Japanese securities, a New York-based firm uses the services of a Tokyo-based custodian; let's assume that the custodian imposes a deadline of 20:00 Tokyo time on value date -1. The New York firm must remain aware of the time zone difference between New York and Tokyo and issue settlement instructions so as to be received by the custodian's deadline, requiring the firm to issue instructions before 06:00 on value date –1 New York time, because Tokyo is fourteen hours ahead of New York in one period each year (time zone differences can vary during the year). See Figure 8.3.

If custodians' deadlines are missed, it may be impossible for settlement to occur on value date, and the trade will become a failed trade.

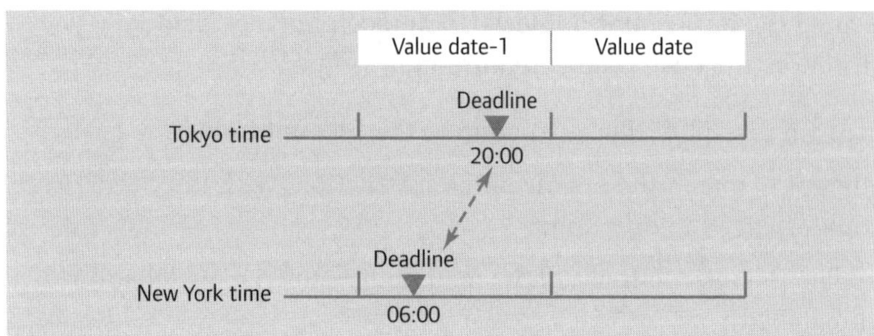

FIGURE 8.3 Settlement instruction deadlines and time zone differences

Risks associated with the settlement of securities trades include:

- when buying securities, making payment to the seller before receipt of securities;
- when selling securities, delivering securities to the buyer before receipt of cash.

The only way of overcoming such risk from the perspective of both buyer and seller is to exchange the securities for the agreed cash amount simultaneously. Within the world of securities, simultaneous exchange is known as **delivery versus payment (DvP)** settlement. When an account holder issues a settlement instruction to a custodian it is the account holder's responsibility to tell the custodian how it wishes the custodian to settle the trade. DvP settlement is represented in Figure 8.4.

DvP is the preferred method because it mitigates the previously stated risks. However, in some firms it is also an everyday occurrence for a minority of securities trades to be settled

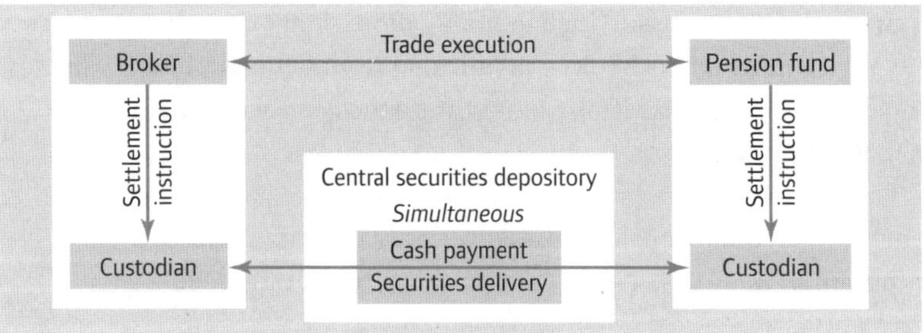

FIGURE 8.4 Delivery versus payment settlement

non-simultaneously; in such firms this is less than 1 per cent of all settlements. Non-simultaneous settlement is commonly known as **free of payment (FoP)** settlement. The following is an example of why, for an individual trade, FoP is used and why DvP is not used; the example is known as 'cross-currency settlement'. Following receipt of an order from an institutional client, when a broker sells securities to an institutional investor, under normal circumstances the broker wants to receive the 'natural' currency of the security; if the broker sells to a client a US Treasury bond, the broker would normally want to receive US dollars. Let's assume the broker's counterparty is a UK-based pension fund, that wishes to settle all its trades in pounds regardless of the natural currency of the security. Under these circumstances, it is common practice for the broker to calculate the sterling equivalent of the dollar purchase cost, and request the client to make payment of the sterling amount to the broker's UK bankers, on value date. Let's assume the pension fund made the sterling payment on value date; therefore the cash side of the trade has been settled. Meanwhile, also on value date, the broker must deliver the securities to the pension fund's custodian account, on an FoP basis; therefore once delivery has occurred the securities side of the trade has been settled. The trade has now been completely settled, but in a non-simultaneous way. This particular example of FoP settlement is represented in Figure 8.5.

As this trade is settling non-DvP, from each party's perspective there is no guarantee that their counterparty will either make the payment on value date, or deliver the securities on value date. For example, at the close of value date, the broker could be in a position where it has neither securities or cash, if the client failed to make payment. From the broker's perspective, although it is recognised there is risk involved in settling non-DvP, if its client requests FoP settlement the broker normally complies, from a client service standpoint (although the broker is likely to agree to FoP settlement for trustworthy clients only). Note that the broker would normally undertake a foreign exchange trade and sell the GBP to raise the USD it originally wished to receive.

On an individual trade, the method of communicating the settlement basis (whether DvP or FoP) to the custodian is a component of the settlement instruction.

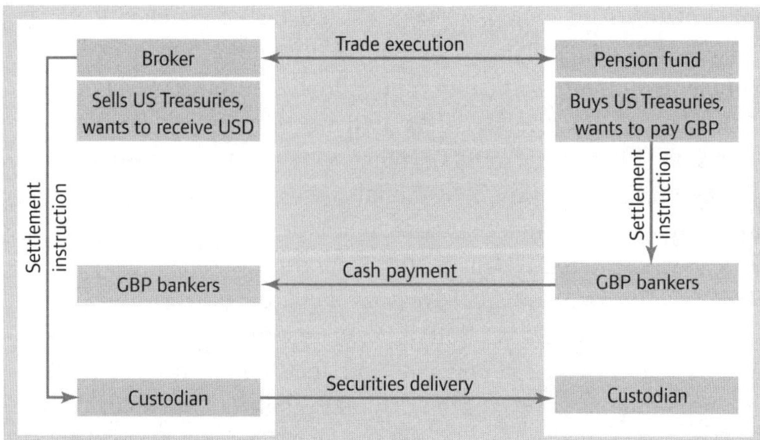

FIGURE 8.5 Free of payment settlement

The primary content of a securities settlement instruction is represented in Table 8.5.

TABLE 8.5 Content of securities settlement instruction

From **To**	**Name of the issuing firm** **Name of the custodian**
Depot account no.	The firm's securities account number over which movement is to be effected
Nostro account no.	The firm's cash account number over which movement is to be effected
Trade reference	The firm's processing system unique trade reference number
Deliver/receive	Whether securities are to be delivered or received
Settlement basis	DvP or FoP
Value date	The due date of settlement (the earliest date that settlement is to be effected)
Quantity	The quantity of shares, or quantity of bonds to be delivered/received
Security reference	The security identifier code, e.g. ISIN

Settlement currency	ISO code for the settlement currency (e.g. USD, EUR, GBP)
Net settlement value	The cash value to be paid or received
Counterparty depot	The counterparty's (securities) custodian details, including account number
Counterparty nostro	The counterparty's (cash) custodian details, including account number

Source: *Securities Operations: A guide to trade and position management* by Michael Simmons, John Wiley, 2002.

Note that in Table 8.5, the term **Depot** refers to a securities account, the term **Nostro** refers to a cash account.

Of vital importance is the method of transmission of settlement instructions. Firms that trade in securities must be aware of the risks associated with settlement instructions and the potential for fraudulent removal of assets. It is therefore essential to issue settlement instructions by a method that allows the receiver to authenticate fully the origin of such instructions; the account holder should only issue instructions by a method that can be authenticated, likewise for the custodian accepting instructions. Before automation, the account holder would issue each settlement instruction with a secret code attached (based upon a unique set of codes known only to the particular account holder and the particular custodian), and upon receipt of an instruction, the custodian's first step would be to prove (or disprove) authenticity of the instruction. This procedure was/is a control measure designed to guard against attempts at fraudulent removal of assets by third parties.

Today, the most popular method of issuing settlement instructions is by SWIFT. These settlement instructions are highly structured in format, requiring each component of the instruction to be placed in pre-specified fields. This structure allows a securities trading firm to automate the generation and transmission of settlement instructions, and the receiving custodian to automate the upload of the instruction into its own systems. Furthermore, SWIFT instructions use very high levels of encryption to prevent fraud. Use of SWIFT requires subscription by sender and receiver.

Custodians usually stipulate later deadlines for settlement instructions received electronically (e.g. via SWIFT) as these can be processed automatically within the custodian's internal systems, and earlier deadlines for those received by non-electronic means because these require human intervention.

Note that SWIFT communications are not limited to securities settlement instructions, as (for example) securities trade confirmations, statements of securities holdings, cash payments and statements of cash balances can be issued and received via SWIFT.

Pre-settlement statuses

It is essential that buyers and sellers of securities achieve matching instructions before value date, as settlement will not occur unless instructions are matched. Pre-settlement statuses are the mechanism by which an account holder becomes aware of the matching status of a settlement instruction at the custodian.

Once an account holder has issued a settlement instruction and the custodian has received it, the account holder is eager to know whether their instruction is matched by the counterparty's instruction, or not. A status of 'matched' is of course the status the account holder hopes for, and the trade can proceed to settlement. A status of 'unmatched' requires investigation and resolution, and until resolution occurs (and a status of 'matched' is achieved), the trade cannot settle.

An example of 'matched' instructions is given in Table 8.6. It shows that all the components of the seller's instruction (headed 'Account holder's instruction') are matched by the equivalent components of the buyer's instruction (headed 'Counterparty's instruction'):

An example of 'unmatched' instructions is given in Table 8.7. It shows that most of the components of the seller's instruction are matched by the equivalent components of the buyer's instruction, but do not match for 'quantity' and 'net settlement value'.

Once an account holder is informed of an unmatched instruction, it must be investigated urgently as the 'clock is ticking' towards value date. However, priority must be given to those instructions having

TABLE 8.6 An example of matched instructions

Account holder's instruction		Matched?	Counterparty's instruction	
Depot account no.	ABC0017769	√	LMN890347X	Depot account no.
Nostro account no.	ABC0017769	√	LMN890347X	Nostro account no.
Trade reference	Prin501677	n/a*	XX003768bb	Trade reference
Deliver/receive	Deliver**	√	Receive**	Deliver/receive
Settlement basis	DvP	√	DvP	Settlement basis
Value date	18th March YYYY	√	18th March YYYY	Value date
Quantity	600,000	√	600,000	Quantity
Security reference	US123456789	√	US123456789	Security reference
Settlement currency	USD	√	USD	Settlement currency
Net settlement value	43,404,000.00	√	43,404,000.00	Net settlement value
Counterparty depot	LMN890347X	√	ABC0017769	Counterparty depot
Counterparty nostro	LMN890347X	√	ABC0017769	Counterparty nostro

* Trade reference is unique to each firm and is therefore a non-matchable item

** The only item that differs validly is the direction of the securities delivery, where one party delivers and the counterparty receives

TABLE 8.7 Two components of the instruction do not match

Account holder's instruction		Matched?	Counterparty's instruction	
Depot account no.	ABC0017769	√	LMN890347X	Depot account no.
Nostro account no.	ABC0017769	√	LMN890347X	Nostro account no.
Trade reference	Prin501677	n/a	XX003768bb	Trade reference
Deliver/receive	Deliver	√	Receive	Deliver/receive
Settlement basis	DvP	√	DvP	Settlement basis
Value date	18th March YYYY	√	18 March YYYY	Value date
Quantity	600,000	x	660,000	Quantity
Security reference	US123456789	√	US123456789	Security reference
Settlement currency	USD	√	USD	Settlement currency
Net settlement value	43,404,000.00	x	47,744,400.00	Net settlement value
Counterparty depot	LMN890347X	√	ABC0017769	Counterparty depot
Counterparty nostro	LMN890347X	√	ABC0017769	Counterparty nostro

imminent value dates (otherwise cash loss and/or **reputation loss** may occur). Responsibility for investigation is normally the domain of the operations department.

In Table 8.7, the reason for the instruction being unmatched is that the securities quantity differs. Trade quantity is the trader's (rather than operations) responsibility, so the discrepancy must be reported to the relevant trader without delay. The trader will decide whether 'we' are correct, or not:

- If 'our' trader states that our quantity is correct, operations must communicate this to the counterparty's operations department, who should communicate with its trader; if the counterparty's trader agrees, an amended settlement instruction should be issued by the counterparty, which should then match 'our' instruction.
- If 'our' trader states that our quantity is incorrect, the trader must urgently amend the original trade in the trading system, which should automatically update the equivalent trade in the processing system, in turn generating an amended instruction to replace 'our' original instruction, which should then match with the counterparty's instruction.

Regulatory bodies demand that traders' phone conversations are recorded. In situations where the two traders cannot agree, the actual conversation can be played back to determine who is correct.

Traders are responsible for resolving 'economic' discrepancies (such as quantity, price, buy/sell, counterparty), but other discrepancies are the responsibility of the operations department. For example, an unmatched settlement instruction caused by the counterparty's SSI (counterparty depot/nostro details) not matching is usually investigated and resolved within the operations departments of the buying and selling firms, because SSIs are regarded as within the province of operations.

Statuses are also applied to matched instructions that have reached value date, at which point the trade will have either settled or failed. Where a trade has failed, the custodian will indicate the reason for failure, namely that the seller is insufficient of securities, or the buyer does not have the cash. These failures are explored in the following section.

Failed trade management

A failed trade is a securities trade that has not settled on its due date. It is important to note that settlement will be delayed; equity and bond trades are not automatically cancelled because the trade did not settle on time. Remember that a contractual agreement exists between buyer and seller and the contractual commitment of each party (the seller must deliver the securities, the buyer must pay) must be fulfilled, unless both parties agree to cancel the trade.

In some markets, there is a strict regime where fines are imposed for failing to settle on value date; consequently in such markets failed trades are rare. In other markets, failed trades are a fact of life, and have financial implications for sellers and buyers.

> in some markets, there is a strict regime where fines are imposed for failing to settle on value date

Failed trades are usually caused by the seller having insufficient securities to deliver, occasionally caused by the buyer having insufficient funds to pay.

Failure caused by seller's lack of securities

Consider Firm F's sale of £20,000,000.00 Bond X to counterparty P for a net cash value of £19,500,000.00, value date 21 March; let's assume that settlement instructions are matched before value date. On value date, Firm F's account at the custodian holds none of the bonds, and so the trade fails to settle because the seller does not have the securities; Firm F's custodian will communicate to Firm F the fact that the trade has failed due to insufficient securities, via a settlement instruction status update.

Immediately, Firm F will suffer from a failure to receive £19,500,000.00 cash into its bank account. The repercussions may include:

- If Firm F's bank account had a zero cash balance, Firm F has lost the opportunity of lending £19,500,000.00 and earning interest on that loan.
- If Firm F's bank account was overdrawn by (say) £32,000,000.00 on which overdraft interest was being charged at 6 per cent, Firm F has lost the opportunity of reducing its overdraft and saving 6 per cent on £19,500,000.00.

Such damage on Firm F's cash position will continue until the sale is settled.

But what is the underlying cause of settlement failure in this example? One of two situations cause a seller to have insufficient securities:

- Firm F has bought £20,000,000.00 Bond X from counterparty Q, but this trade has failed because counterparty Q does not have enough securities. The fact that this purchase has not settled means Firm F has no securities to deliver.
- Firm F has **sold short**, it has sold securities it has not yet purchased meaning that Firm F has no securities to deliver.

So what action can a seller take to settle a sale? The choices for a seller are either to take no action or to borrow securities. If no action is taken by Firm F, the detrimental effect on its bank account will continue until purchased securities are settled and those incoming securities are used to satisfy delivery of the sale to counterparty P, at which point Firm F will receive £19,500,000.00 (assuming DvP settlement). The following section provides an overview of securities borrowing.

Securities lending and borrowing

Many of the larger securities trading firms make maximum use of securities borrowing, to settle sales on (or shortly after) value date, so as to maximise cash benefit and minimise cash losses. Some investors choose to lend their securities for a fee to enhance income earned on their investments in equity and bonds.

A seller of securities that wishes to borrow securities to settle a sale will attempt to borrow from a securities lender; however the potential borrower must first locate a potential lender that:

- has the particular security;
- has an adequate quantity of those securities;
- is willing to lend the securities for an agreed period;
- agrees to the borrowing fee.

Assuming agreement is reached, the lending/borrowing trade must be settled without delay, so the securities arrive within the borrower's account at its custodian and those same securities are used to satisfy the sale, at which point the seller will receive the sale proceeds from the buying counterparty. This is represented in Figure 8.6. There are four stages:

1. A trade is executed between seller and buyer.
2. The seller does not have the securities available for delivery, so the seller arranges to borrow the securities from a securities lender, and the lender delivers the lent securities to the seller's custodian account.
3. The seller delivers the securities to the buyer.
4. Simultaneously, the buyer pays the purchase cost to the seller.

Note that after the final step, the seller has an outstanding commitment to return to the securities lender equivalent securities to those borrowed, at an agreed future date.

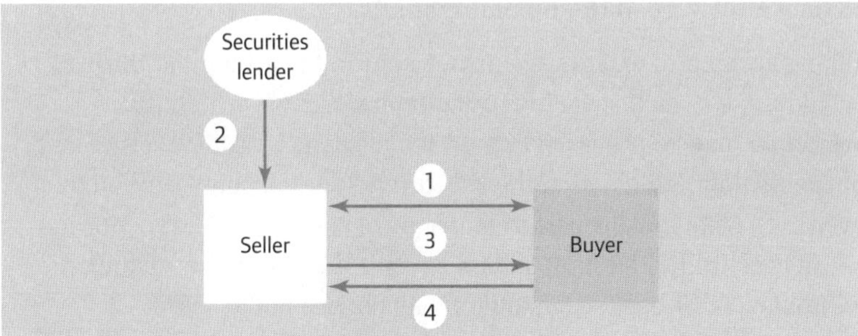

FIGURE 8.6 Securities lending and borrowing

For the securities borrowing to be viable financially, the borrowing fee must be less than the benefit derived within the bank account; for example, if a securities borrowing fee is (say) 1.50 per cent, but the cash that can be saved by settling the sale amounts to 6 per cent, then securities borrowing is viable.

A securities borrower must return the borrowed securities to the securities lender at an agreed future date. However, if the securities borrower wishes to continue borrowing the securities, the securities lender may agree, providing the securities lender has not sold the securities. If the securities borrower wishes to continue borrowing, but the securities lender wishes to discontinue its loan, the securities borrower could potentially find another securities lender.

Failure caused by buyer's lack of cash

Occasionally, failed trades are caused by the buyer having insufficient funds to pay. It is the buyer's responsibility to ensure that its custodian account has adequate means to settle purchases. It is dangerous for an account holder to assume that a custodian will allow the account holder to go overdrawn in cash without the custodian having a guarantee of repayment; custodians do not entertain such risks. Quite simply, if the custodian cannot find adequate means for the account holder to pay for a purchase, that trade will be failed by the custodian. The typical options for an account holder to manage cash at a custodian are:

- Pay funds into the account at the custodian on value date (from an outside source), and issue a funds pre-advice to the custodian so they are aware of the incoming funds.
- Taking account of existing securities held in the account at the custodian, use such securities as **collateral** against which the custodian may be prepared to lend the necessary cash for settlement purposes, following which the account holder's account will be in overdraft. Note that, as part of managing a cash account, it is normal for an account holder to negotiate a credit limit with the custodian; without a credit limit, a custodian may choose not to settle purchases, even where adequate collateral exists.

Enforcing trade settlement

Ultimately, settlement of purchases and sales can usually be enforced in any market, by use of **buy-in** and **sell-out**; these are procedures defined by the stock exchange or market authority and which must be followed by buyers and sellers. These procedures normally involve the appointment of an agent to either effect delivery of securities purchased, or effect payment for securities sold, with any additional costs charged to the original (defaulting) counterparty.

Trade settlement

Trade settlement is the act of exchanging securities and cash, carried-out by custodians on behalf of buyer and seller.

Settlement actually occurs at the relevant central securities depository (e.g. CHESS, DTCC, Euroclear UK & Ireland), where successful settlement requires:

- matched settlement instructions;
- value date to have been reached;
- seller to have adequate quantity of securities;
- buyer to have adequate cash/collateral/credit line.

If these conditions are met, settlement will occur. This is represented in Figure 8.7. The stages here are:

1. The seller's objective is to settle on value date whenever possible, so as to receive sale proceeds at the earliest opportunity and therefore to maximise cash earning opportunity. To achieve this objective, two situations are possible:

   (a) the seller must have an adequate quantity of securities (available for delivery to the buyer) within its depot account at the custodian; or

   (b) borrow securities from a securities lender to have an adequate quantity of securities (available for delivery to the buyer) within its depot account at the custodian.

   Note that if the seller cannot or does not meet either of these situations, the trade will fail to settle on value date, the seller will not receive its sale proceeds at the earliest opportunity and will therefore miss an opportunity to earn cash.

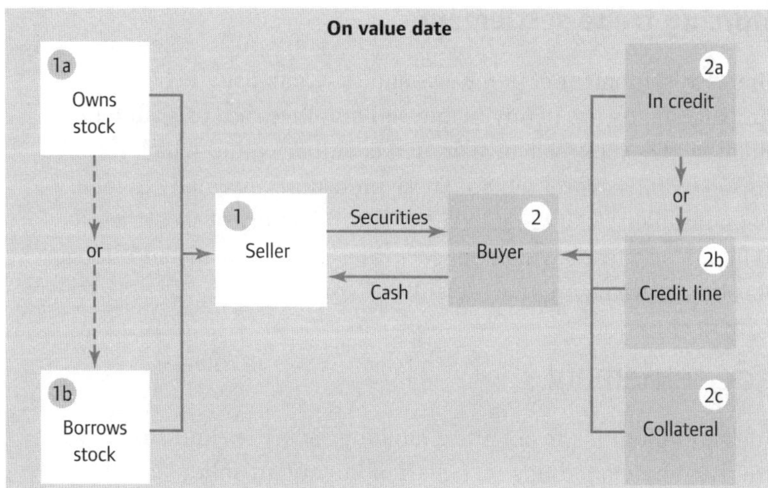

FIGURE 8.7 Enabling trade settlement

2 The buyer's objective is to settle on value date whenever possible (fundamentally involving the payment of the cash cost to the seller), so as to receive securities at the earliest opportunity. To achieve this objective, three situations are possible:

(a) the buyer must have an adequate cash balance (available for payment to the seller) within its nostro account at the custodian or;

(b) have a pre-arranged credit line (overdraft facility) with the custodian against which funds can be borrowed; and in addition

(c) have existing securities in the buyer's depot account at the custodian to act as collateral, against which the custodian will allow the purchase cost to be borrowed

Note that if the seller is not in a position to deliver the securities on value date, the trade will fail to settle and therefore the buyer will not be required to make payment (until such time that the seller is able to deliver). Furthermore, if the seller is in a position to deliver the securities, but the buyer does not have cash available for payment (as in steps a, b and c), the trade will fail to settle on value date. However, the seller will be able to claim loss of cash interest (known as an **interest claim**) from the buyer.

In a modern CSD, DvP settlement is reflected by:

- For the seller: debiting the securities account, crediting the cash account.
- For the buyer: crediting the securities account, debiting the cash account.

This process is known as **electronic book entry**, as more than 99 per cent of settlements require no physical movement of securities or cash.

Once the custodian's securities and cash accounts at the depositary have been updated, the custodian will in turn reflect settlement over the account holder's securities and cash accounts. Furthermore, the custodian will issue to the account holder an advice of settlement for each settled instruction, and updated statements of securities holdings and statements of cash balances.

Partial settlement

Normally, trade settlement occurs for the full quantity of securities against the full cash value. However, where the seller has only some of the securities available for delivery, the seller may choose to contact the buyer to ask if the buyer will accept a **partial delivery** (against a pro-rata cash amount). The buyer is not obliged to accept the offer of a partial delivery, but the partial delivery may suit the buyer, particularly where it enables the buyer to deliver a larger sale quantity that otherwise could not be delivered.

Net settlement

In the interest of settlement efficiency, settlement of several trades with the same counterparty in a single settlement is regarded as highly efficient; this is known as net settlement. This can be practised by a trading firm by agreement with an individual counterparty (**bilateral netting**). Net settlement within a central counterparty is known as **multilateral netting**. This topic is explored in Chapter 9.

Updating internal records

Updating internal records is the process of bringing into line the details held within a trading firm's internal books and records, as a result of settlement at the custodian. This step within the trade lifecycle is important because, without ensuring internal books and records are aligned, serious and costly mistakes can easily occur.

Within internal books and records, following trade capture and before settlement, an individual trade should appear as 'open with counterparty', reflecting the fact that the trade is outstanding and still to be settled. For the risk managers within the firm to be certain they are viewing factual information, it is essential that all trades not yet settled (i.e. future value dated trades and currently failing trades) are represented in this way. Table 8.8 provides an example of how a trade not yet settled should appear within a firm's internal books and records.

TABLE 8.8 How internal books and records should show a trade that has not been settled

Trade component	Trade example	Status
Trade reference	Prin501677	
Trade date	15 March YYYY	
Trade time	08:13	
Value date	18 March YYYY	
Operation	Buy	
Quantity	600,000	Open
Security	IBM Corp common stock	
Price	USD 72.34	
Counterparty	Counterparty T, Hong Kong	
Net cash value	USD 43,404,000.00	Open

Conversely, once a trade has settled externally at the custodian and an advice of settlement has been received from the custodian, it is essential that the individual trade is updated without delay to reflect the fact that settlement of securities and cash has occurred, on the actual date of settlement (known as the **settlement date**). By so doing, the trading firm's internal books and records will be a truthful statement of the firm's assets. Table 8.9 gives an example of how a settled trade should appear in the internal records.

Additionally, such records must reflect the fact that 600,000 shares are now held within the firm's specific securities account at the particular custodian, and that $43,404,000.00 has been debited from the firm's specific cash account at the particular custodian.

Passing such entries accurately and in a timely fashion will bring internal records into line with the reality in the outside world, and allow successful reconciliation to occur (see next section).

Updating of settled trades is normally achieved by linking the unique trade reference number (sent to the custodian as a component of the settlement instruction and which appears on the custodian's advice of settlement) to the same trade reference number within internal books and records.

TABLE 8.9 How internal books and records should show a settled trade

Trade component	Trade example	Status
Trade reference	Prin501677	
Trade date	15 March YYYY	
Trade time	08:13	
Value date	18 March YYYY	
Operation	Buy	
Quantity	600,000	600,000 received on 19 March YYYY
Security	IBM Corp common stock	
Price	USD 72.34	
Counterparty	Counterparty T, Hong Kong	
Net cash value	USD 43,404,000.00	USD 43,404,000.00 paid on 19 March YYYY

Reconciliation

Reconciliation is the comparison of one set of records with another, to ensure that internal books and records are accurate. The subject of reconciliation is arguably the single most important control within a financial services firm, as it provides proof of accuracy and integrity of financial assets. Some of the most effective types of reconciliation within a securities trading/operations environment are shown in Table 8.10.

TABLE 8.10 Effective types of reconciliation

Number	Reconciliation title	Purpose
1	FoBo trade reconciliation	To ensure that all trades captured in the trading system have been captured in the processing system. Example: 1,000 trades captured today in front office system, has the same number been captured in the processing system?
2	FoBo position reconciliation	To ensure that traders' positions within the trading system, at individual security level, are the same as those within the processing system. Example: Trader A has a position in the front office system of 600,000 Security M. Is this the same as in the processing system?
3	Depot reconciliation	To ensure that settled securities positions held at custodians, at individual security level, are the same as those within the processing system. Example: Custodian C reports the firm's position of 4,500,000 Security F bonds. Is this the same as in the processing system?
4	Nostro reconciliation	To ensure that settled cash balances held at custodians, at currency and account level, are the same as those within the processing system. Example: Custodian C reports the firm's cash balance of USD13,750,000.00. Is this the same as in the processing system?

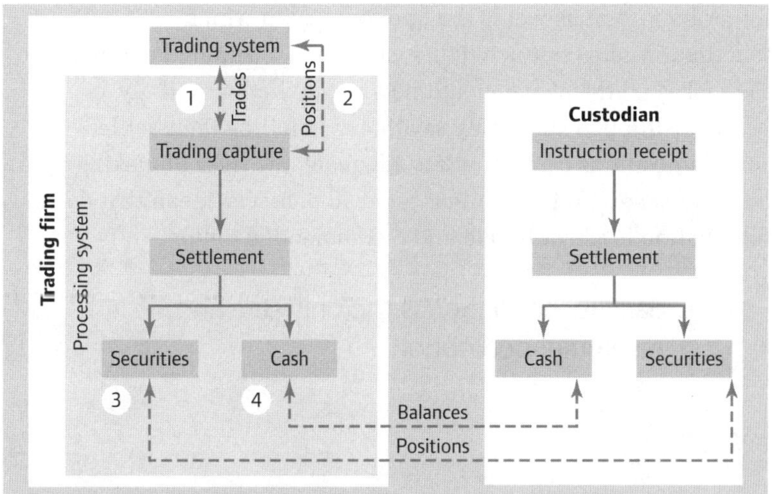

FIGURE 8.8 Types of reconciliation

Source: *Securities Operations: A guide to trade and position management* by Michael Simmons, John Wiley, 2002.

The numbers and reconciliation types listed in Table 8.10 are represented in Figure 8.8.

Reconciliation involves, for example in the case of a depot reconciliation, the simple comparison of the securities balances listed on the custodian's statement, against the equivalent list extracted from internal books and records (see Table 8.11).

Historically, reconciliation would have been conducted manually; a slow and time-consuming task. Because of the need to quickly identify whether there are any discrepancies and investigate and resolve any discrepancies, many firms today conduct reconciliation using dedicated systems.

TABLE 8.11 Reconciliation example

Internal books and records	Agreed?	Custodian's statement
1,000,000 Security A	√	1,000,000 Security A
5,500,000 Security B	x	5,000,000 Security B
2,750,000 Security C	√	2,750,000 Security C
8,500,000 Security D	x	0 Security D
1,300,000 Security E	x	13,000,000 Security E
25,000,000 Security F	√	25,000,000 Security F

Another important aspect is the frequency with which reconciliations are conducted; the value of assets traded and held today makes all the above mentioned reconciliations a daily necessity. Although some may say that reconciling their settled securities positions each month is adequate, the risks of making genuine mistakes and fraudulent removal of assets, mean that daily reconciliation is the only safe and recommended option.

> daily reconciliation is the only safe and recommended option

ANECDOTE

A firm that daily traded securities on a proprietary basis made a number of securities-only movements on an FoP basis, between two accounts that belonged to it. The processing system lacked the capability to generate such settlement instructions; consequently instructions would be manually generated. For many years, such movements were made without a problem. On one particular day, bonds with a market value of $5,000,000 were erroneously delivered from one of the firm's accounts, to another firm's account (with whom it did not trade), FoP. After the event it was discovered that the recipient account on the settlement instruction was written one digit different from the correct account number, and all subsequent checks had failed to identify this error. The incorrect delivery was identified the same day as the delivery occurred, the lucky recipient of the bonds was contacted immediately and were politely asked to return the bonds. Not much sleep was had awaiting the return of the bonds! Fortunately, the bonds were returned the following day. Under such circumstances, there was/is no guarantee that the recipient would return the bonds of his own volition. How was the error spotted? Daily reconciliation of the two custodian accounts. What might have happened had the firm reconciled monthly? I'd rather not think about the possible outcomes!

Summary

Traders and salespeople within a firm generate profits through the quality of trading and the client contacts that they nurture. But, just as in sport, the goals scored and the touchdowns made by your team will not count for much if the same are conceded; scoring five but conceding six leads to an exciting match but will not win you the game! To prevent 'own goals' and to realise the profits made in the front office, the operations area within a financial services firm must be very knowledgeable, well organised and be willing to learn from mistakes. The front office, middle office and back office must be tightly aligned with no barriers to communication.

In the past twenty years there has been a much greater appreciation globally of the importance of the operations role, exemplified in some firms by the head of operations being appointed to the board of directors.

As time goes by, firms will continue to require the services of excellent operations personnel, as trading volumes increase and settlement cycles reduce to T+1 or even T+0. Correct decision-making and fast action will become increasingly important; this can only occur through the use of eager and knowledgeable staff who can appreciate and visualise the implications of certain actions.

Further reading

Securities Operations: A guide to trade and position management by Michael Simmons, John Wiley, 2002.

9 Key stages in the lifecycle of an OTC derivatives trade

Bill Hodgson

The OTC derivatives market has been unfairly described as a 'dark market' without any visibility to the public nor any supervision by regulators.

- Introduction
- Process overview
- Trade capture and validation
- Tie-out
- Confirmation and affirmation
- Asset servicing
- OTC collateral management
- Central counterparties
- Settlement
- Legal background
- Systems overview
- Market size

Introduction

This chapter is an insight into the world of processing OTC derivatives trades, the processes, systems and risks involved, and the reasons why the various procedures occur. Chapter 2 introduces the products mentioned in this chapter including interest rate swaps and credit default swaps.

At the end of this chapter is background material which will help you understand the how and why of OTC processing, including the importance of a legal framework. It is worth keeping Figure 9.1 in mind so you can place yourself as one **party** in an OTC derivative contract, with your **counterparty** as the other firm you did the **trade** with. The point is that each contract has someone else as a signatory to the contract, referred to as the counterparty in this chapter.

Process overview

Before going into the details, it helps to have an overview of the processes and the order in which they take place. This chapter is concerned with the steps that take place after trading in the front office (Figure 9.2):

1. Capture the details of the trade from the trader for the electronic systems of the bank.
2. Check that the trade details accurately represent what the trader agreed.
3. a: Agree full details of the trade with the counterparty.

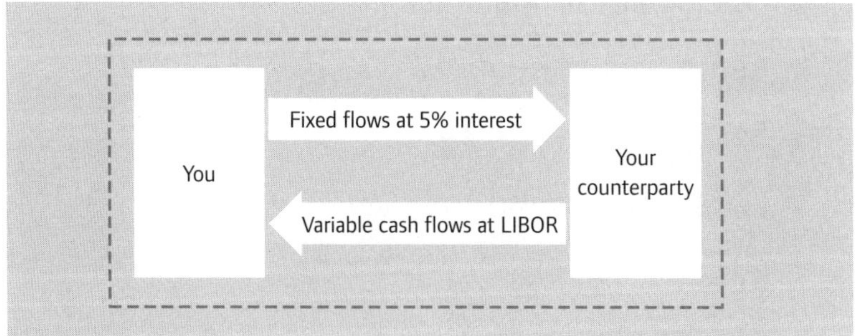

FIGURE 9.1 Example OTC derivative contract, an interest rate swap

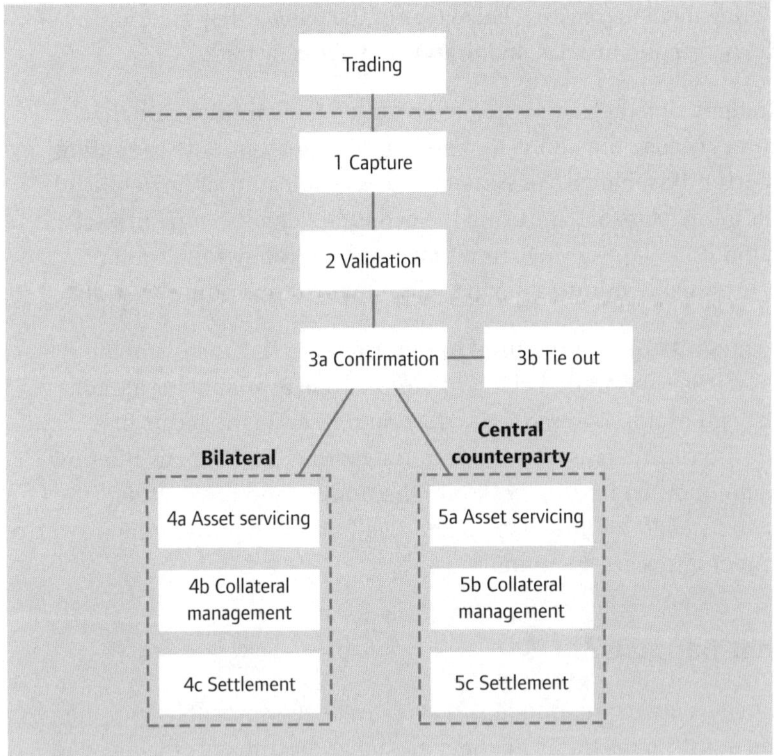

FIGURE 9.2 Process overview

3 b: If needed, agree a rough check of the number and type of new trades executed today.

4 a/b/c: Process the trade through to the scheduled termination date using a firm's own systems and making payments direct to and from the counterparty.

5 a/b/c: Process the trade through to the **scheduled termination** date using a **central counterparty (CCP)** to make all payment calculations and carry out any actions on the trade.

Trade capture and validation

The trading environment is a world apart from the rest of any bank. If you've ever seen a trading floor of a large global bank you will have seen masses of people with huge numbers of computer screens in front of them, bombarded with numbers, graphs and software screens, enabling them to track the behaviour of the market they face, and quickly respond to price enquiries leading to new trades.

A trader's time horizon tends to be only a few minutes into the future, because the aim is to respond minute-by-minute to trading opportunities, hence the systems they use to capture the details of each trade focus on capturing the economic details using pre-set templates and quick keyboard entry and not require the trader to waste valuable minutes keying in the many terms of the contract.

The quantity of data required to represent the fine details of an OTC derivatives trade is larger than the time available for a trader to key all of it into a trading system, and often many terms of a trade are regarded as 'standard' in the market. This means the flow of data from the trading desk into the middle and back office systems needs careful checking and validation to be sure the contract terms are accurate.

What happens?

All traders are required to record every trade they execute. Once the trade is within the trading system, the other departments that need to act upon that trade must receive a copy of the details. There is no easy way to detect missing trades that are agreed on the phone but not recorded. However, the downstream processes including tie-out and confirmation are a way to validate the existence of trades with counterparty and back office staff ensuring data are valid.

Various methods are used to ensure that the trade details entered by the trader make sense, and agree with other records of the trade:

- Population reconciliation: compare the list of trades in the front office, with the list of trades in the middle and back office. There should be a direct correspondence between the two, so wherever the lists don't match, someone needs to investigate and resolve the problem.
- **Valuation** reconciliation: every trade is worth something economically, often called the '**mark-to-market**' or valuation. The valuation is derived from the cash flows, market price sources and any special features of the trade. By calculating a valuation

independently in the front office and back office systems, and comparing this value, a complex set of data can be represented by a single amount of money, and quickly compared between the front and back office, enabling any issues between the two systems to be researched and resolved.

- Cash flow reconciliation: all trades have at least one cash flow, and often many more. Comparing the cash flows for a trade between the front and back office systems is another way to spot differences in the data.
- **Sales desk** versus **trading desk**: Any trades executed by the sales desk must match up with trades executed on their behalf by a trader. Until these trades are paired up, they are not usually sent to the back office for processing.

What can go wrong?

> without careful controls the safety of the firm is at risk

Without careful controls on trade capture and validation the safety of the firm is at risk. Consider these scenarios:

- **Booking** error: trader executes a trade and accidently adds a zero to the **notional** value of the contract, therefore the payment becomes ten times bigger. The firm makes a fee payment to the counterparty for the ten times bigger amount, and then has to use legal and commercial means to recover the excess payment.
- Booking omission: a trade involves paying a fee to the counterparty but it fails to reach the back office, so the counterparty fails to receive the fee, causing a claim against the firm for the payment plus interest.
- Fraud: someone with access to the trading systems executes trades that are not known to the supervisors of the trading desks, with the intention of stealing for themselves or paying an accomplice.

Summary

Goals for a front trade capture include:

- Capture as much detail as possible about the terms of each trade in the firm's back office **books and records** – the official record of trades for that firm.
- Make sure all trades executed by the trading and sales desks are held in electronic systems, and none are missed.
- Make sure the terms of the trade in the back-office books and records systems are the same as those in the front office systems.

Risks include:

- A trade in the front office doesn't get recorded.
- The terms of the trade in the front office are different from those in the back office.
- Payments are missing or incorrect.

Tie-out

The section above describes the various internal controls intended to ensure accurate trade capture and validation. This section describes an additional method, which uses external help to add another layer of security.

Tie-out means agreeing with the counterparty that a trade exists, including the key terms of the trade, such as who the buyer and seller is. A tie-out is an intermediate step, to be completed by the end of each trading day, in parallel with full confirmation. The tie-out doesn't aim to achieve full agreement on every term of the trade but would at least agree the following:

- who the buyer and seller is (or the fixed payer for an interest rate swap);
- the size or notional of the trade;
- currency;
- price;
- **effective date**;

- scheduled termination date;
- any fees to be paid, and by whom.

Once a trade has been 'tied out' you have an increased level of legal and operational certainty that any payments due on the trade should be made or received, even if full confirmation takes more time to achieve.

What happens?

There are three ways to achieve a tie-out, depending on how sophisticated each firm is:

- Telephone: you wait until a preset time marking the end of your trading day, let's say 17:00, and then call each counterparty with the list of new trades you executed, and talk through each data item.
- Spreadsheet: similar to telephone, but using a spreadsheet with the list of trades and data items, you then agree to the list using email and telephone.
- Fully electronic: an example of this is the Markit tie-out service, where you enter the details of the trades and use Markit's web-based screens to achieve a tie-out in a fully controlled environment.

What can go wrong?

Tie-out isn't a precisely defined process in the OTC market. Each firm has its own opinion on how much data is required to tie-out an OTC contract, and how much value from a legal perspective this adds. Depending on the method chosen above, different risk and errors can occur:

- You use a different cut-off time from your counterparty so have a different list of trades with missing items that you can't resolve.
- You mumble on the telephone leading to misunderstanding on one detail such as the direction of the trade (buy versus sell).
- Your counterparty requires data from you that you can't or won't supply to complete the tie-out and vice-versa.

The OTC industry doesn't regard tie-out as a high priority compared with achieving full electronic confirmation. As you will see later, full electronic confirmation is the only way to be sure you both have recorded the same trade in your respective systems, so tie-out is of limited value if a dispute goes to court.

Summary

Tie-out goals include:

- Make sure that at the end of each day you agree with your counterparty the number and type of trades done today.
- Make sure the details of the trade you booked agree with those your counterparty booked.

Risks include:

- Missing a trade that you or your counterparty executed.
- Not having any evidence a trade exists.

Confirmation and affirmation

Trade confirmation (or affirmation) achieves full and precise legal agreement to the rights and obligations between the two parties for the contract executed between them.

It is worth comparing the process of trading using an **exchange** with that of trading OTC, to understand why confirmation occupies the importance it does for OTC products (Table 9.1).

TABLE 9.1 Comparison of exchange-based and OTC trading

Process	Exchange-traded	OTC-traded
Trading	Within the exchange systems, centralised	Via many methods including telephone and electronic, decentralised
Contract terms	Fully standardised, published in advance of trading, only modified by the exchange	Hybrid, some terms are standardised, many are flexible and provide choices to suit the parties to the trade

Trade capture	Carried out within the exchange systems. Each firm takes a copy of the trade data electronically from the exchange, which holds the official record of the trade	Carried out in parallel within each of the two parties using whatever standards are applicable. Each firm regards its own books and records as the primary source of trade details
Confirmation	Not needed	Happens after trade capture, see below
Reconciliation	If needed, back to the exchange records, generally not likely to find issues because the trade feed from the exchanges is fully automated	Happens between each party to a trade using confirmations, cash flows, valuations and credit exposure amounts

Data formats

The OTC market has been through three phases of technology in carrying out the confirmation process, described below. The goal in all cases is to exchange details of the trade with your counterparty and ensure you both have the same records of the trade.

- Facsimile: OTC parties bought enough fax machines and paper to enable them to prepare confirmation documents, often using MS Word templates, to then send a fax of the trade to the counterparty. Figure 9.3 shows an edited and simplified example of an ISDA long form confirmation, the way OTC trades were confirmed before the arrival of electronic matching services. A full confirmation would have additional legal pages at the top and bottom, and depending on the complexity of the contract take up many pages to fully describe.
- MT3xx: SWIFT operates a matching service called **Accord**, which uses a data format called the MT3xx series. Firms would prepare an MT3xx message containing the terms of the OTC contract, which would be sent electronically via the SWIFT network to Accord. Accord would compare the MT3xx message from you with the one from your counterparty. Both parties can view matching results on computer screens and then confer on the telephone on how to resolve mismatches. The two most common uses of Accord have been for interest rate swaps using an MT360

Megabank Inc.
Swap Transaction – 15th March 2009 – with
Small and Tiny Bank, 1 High Street, Any Town

Dear Sir/Madam,

The purpose of this facsimile (this 'Confirmation') is to confirm the terms and conditions of the Swap Transaction entered into between us on the Trade Date specified below.

The definitions and provisions contained in the 2006 ISDA Definitions, as published by the International Swaps and Derivatives Association, Inc., are incorporated into this Confirmation. In the event of any inconsistency between those definitions and provisions and this Confirmation, this Confirmation will govern.

This Confirmation constitutes a 'Confirmation' as referred to in, and supplements, forms part of and is subject to, the ISDA Master Agreement dated as of [date], as amended and supplemented from time to time (the 'Agreement'), between [Megabank Inc] ('Party A') and [Small and Tiny Bank] ('Party B'). All provisions contained in the Agreement govern this Confirmation except as expressly modified below.

(a) The Office of Party A for the Swap Transaction is Number 1 Prestigious Building, London; and

(b) The Office of Party B for the Swap Transaction is 1 High Street, Any Town

Please confirm that the foregoing correctly sets forth the terms of our agreement by executing the copy of this Confirmation enclosed for that purpose and returning it to us or by sending to us a letter substantially similar to this letter, which letter sets forth the material terms of the Swap Transaction to which this Confirmation relates and indicates your agreement to those terms.

Yours sincerely,
Signed by :

____

Name: Harold Bodgson
Title: VP Confirmations

Confirmed as of the date first above written:

By: ____________________

Name: Ms Freda Bloggs
Title: Head Clerk

Additional Provisions for a
Confirmation of a Swap Transaction that is a
Rate Swap Transaction or Cross-Currency Rate Swap Transaction

1. The terms of the particular Swap Transaction to which this Confirmation relates are as follows:

Notional Amount:	100,000,000 USD
Trade Date:	15th March 2009
Effective Date:	16th March 2009
Termination Date:	15th March 2019

Fixed Amounts:	
Fixed Rate Payer:	Party A
Fixed Rate Payer Payment Dates:	Semi annually (meaning every 6 months)
Fixed Amount:	5.324%
Floating Amounts:	
Floating Rate Payer:	Party B
Floating Rate Payer Payment Dates	Semi annually (meaning every 6 months)
Floating Rate Option:	USD-LIBOR-BBA
Designated Maturity:	6Months
Spread:	None
Floating Rate Day Count Fraction:	ACT/360
Business Days for:	London & New York
Business Day Convention:	Modified Following

FIGURE 9.3 Example of long confirmation form sent by fax

Source: Reprinted with permission of ISDA © 2008 International Swaps and Derivatives Association Inc.

message and **FX options** using an MT305 message. An example portion of an MT360 message is hown in Figure 9.4.

- Financial products Mark-up Language **(FpML):** The MT3xx series of messages has been superseded by data formats defined within the XML standard. The OTC community has been developing FpML since 1999 to represent the full detail and richness of OTC trades across all asset classes including rates, credit, equities, FX and commodities. An example portion of an FpML document is shown in Figure 9.5.:

Block	MT360 Tag	Field name	Example
Fixed Leg			
	37U	Fixed Rate	4.1234
	37N	Details of Interest Rate	Free text
	17F	Period End Date Adjustment Indicator	Y
	14D	Day Count Fraction	ACT/360
	14A	Business Day Convention	MODF
Financial Centres			
	18A	Number of Repetitions (Centres)	1
	22B	Financial Centre	USNY
Payments			
	18A	Number of Repetitions (Payments)	10
	30F	Payment Date	05 Jun 06
	32M	Currency, Payment Amount	USD 4,123,400

FIGURE 9.4 MT360 message portion

```
<calculationPeriodAmount>
  <calculation>
    <notionalSchedule>
      <notionalStepSchedule>
        <initialValue>10000000.00</initialValue>
        <currency>USD</currency>
      </notionalStepSchedule>
    </notionalSchedule>
    <fixedRateSchedule>
      <initialValue>0.04123</initialValue>
    </fixedRateSchedule>
    <dayCountFraction>ACT/360</dayCountFraction>
  </calculation>
</calculationPeriodAmount>
```


FIGURE 9.5 Example portion of an FpML document

Confirmation versus affirmation

In 2000, **SwapsWire** was created with the intention of providing a new way to achieve confirmation of OTC interest rate swap contracts. SwapsWire differed from the SWIFT Accord platform by introducing the concept of affirmation. Figures 9.6 and 9.7 illustrate the two methods.

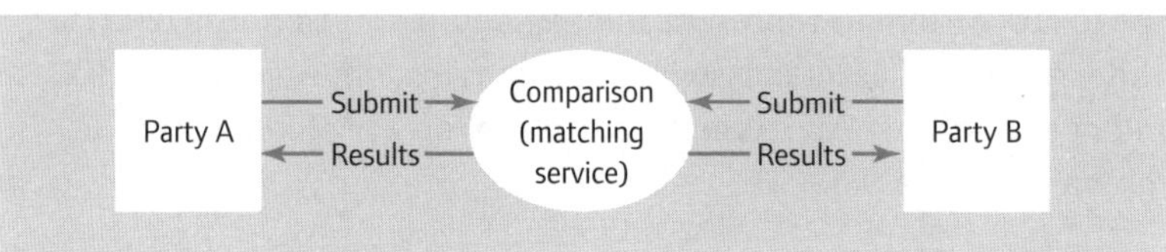

FIGURE 9.6 Traditional confirmation approach typified by SWIFT & DTCC

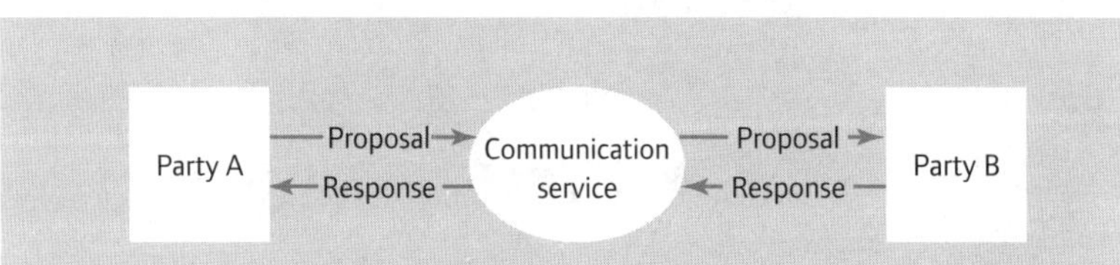

FIGURE 9.7 Affirmation method of achieving confirmation, typified by SwapsWire

The matching method of Figure 9.6 involved both parties making a submission to a central comparison service, which delivered back to each party details of differences between each party's submission. SWIFT Accord and the **DTCC Deriv/SERV** systems work this way.

The SwapsWire affirmation approach did not provide central comparison, but required the buyer of the contract to propose a fully detailed trade **ticket** to the seller, who could then respond by accepting the proposal, or replying with a modified proposal, and then repeating the cycle until both parties agree (Figure 9.7).

SwapsWire was attempting to avoid the problem of each firm's systems having a different approach to standardising certain terms of the trade, and representing differences in a central place. The SwapsWire approach did two things. First, it made it the buyer's obligation to express the exact terms of the contract they wanted to enter into, and second, made it the trader's responsibility to agree exact contract terms, before sending the trade for back-office processing.

In 2003, DTCC launched its Deriv/SERV subsidiary, who provided confirmation for credit derivatives trades. The Deriv/SERV system supported both methods in one system albeit with subtle differences in how the user interacted with the system.

The stages in confirmation

1. Data preparation. Depending on the technology, prepare a spreadsheet, or an FpML message containing the details of the trade you did, using data from your back office systems.
2. Submission. Upload the spreadsheet file, or FpML message into the confirmation system, or manually key in the details to a 'new trade' entry screen.
3. Results:
   - Matching: the system compares your submission with those from your counterparty and using a scoring mechanism recommends which is the 'best match' for your trade, and how it differs from your counterparty's submission.

   - Affirmation: you review the proposed trade and mark any proposed changes for the other party to review.

4. Resolution of inaccurately matched trades. Via telephone or email, discuss and resolve the detailed differences between the data you both submitted. Usually, one or both parties have to modify their data and re-submit to the confirmation or affirmation service.

What can go wrong?

- You submit but your counterparty doesn't. Without a submission from the other party, your trade cannot be confirmed and so is not legally a complete trade. (All firms record the phone lines of traders but these don't contain the exact details of what was agreed, only the main terms).
- Your submissions are different. As described above, you have to resolve the differences. In most cases this is relatively simple, but can sometimes mean referring back to the trader who executed the deal and asking for her opinion on what the details really should be.
- Other problems are combinations of the above, due to errors in your own books and records, timing issues, misunderstood 'standards' and wider industry issues on how to confirm a trade.

Summary

The goal of confirmation is to make sure the details of the trade you booked agree with those of your counterparty.

The risks include:

- Slow response from your counterparty.
- Inaccurate processing by your counterparty.
- No use of electronic systems by you or your counterparty.

Asset-servicing

Almost all OTC trades have to be serviced through their life due to events that occur within the contract. Some of these events and how they get processed are described below:

- Fixings and resets. A typical interest rate swap must make a payment every three or six months, where the parties calculate and pay to each other the fixed amount and the variable amount. The variable amount is calculated using an industry published variable rate of interest, the most common of which is LIBOR. A few days before making the variable (or floating) payment, each party will note the relevant LIBOR rate for their swap, and use it to calculate the payment.
- Coupons. The payment referred to above on an interest rate swap is often referred to as a coupon, using the older terminology from the bond market, when the coupon was a tear-off slip of paper entitling the holder to receive an interest payment on their bond. Most payments (coupons or cashflows) on OTC contracts settle with a regular frequency, often three months, sometimes six and sometimes annually.
- Exercise. The buyer of a call option on foreign exchange rates (called an FX option) has the right to buy currency (let's say USD) at a pre-agreed exchange rate, referred to as the **strike**. A **European style** option allows the buyer to exercise this right (if they choose to) on a single specific day in the future. When that day arrives, the buyer must tell the seller by a deadline that day (often 11am) that they wish to exercise the option, so the seller can pay to the buyer as required by the option, this process is known as **exercise**.
- Corporate actions. This category is a list of the many things that can affect an OTC contract other than the terms of the contract itself. Examples that became all-too-familiar in 2008 include bankruptcy (e.g. Lehman), mergers (e.g. JP Morgan and Bear Stearns), credit events (such as banks in Iceland), and changes to shares where you have an option on them such as a **split** or **redemption**.

What happens?

In almost all cases the generic sequence is:

- Ensure you have a precise definition of the event, what occurred, and when it took place (or will take place).

- Prepare a list of affected trades.
- Review the list to be certain, and if necessary agree with your counterparty which trades are affected by the event.
- Apply the event to the trades (on a pre-agreed date) and make any modified payments resulting from the event.

What can go wrong?

> the rules for capturing and applying the LIBOR rate can be misinterpreted

- The rules for capturing and applying the LIBOR rate each day are defined by the BBA, and can sometimes be misinterpreted. The BBA publishes each day's LIBOR rates at 11am UK time, but reserves the right to make a correction up until noon UK time. After noon no changes will be made. However it is possible for a correction to LIBOR to pass the cut-off time, in which case the rate published at noon still stands. Any firm that isn't precise about following these rules may take the rate published just after 12:00 and therefore apply the wrong rate, resulting in a wrong payment.
- Calculating interest for each coupon payment relies upon both firms being precise about the number of days in the period, any adjustment to the beginning and end period days, and the day-count fraction in use for that trade. Should either firm miscount the days in an interest period the resulting payment will be wrong. If either firm mis-applies the precise calculation rules, including the day-count fraction, the payment will also be wrong.
- Payments. Assuming you can calculate the correct amount of money, the next problem is making sure you pay it on the right day, to the right bank account. Many banks hold several accounts for each currency, so, for example a USD account for the Japanese division, a USD account for the New York division, and another for London. Each account is used by different divisions of the same bank. From your perspective you don't care which account you send it to, because they are all legally the same. However, if the money is sent to the Japanese account but expected to be received in New York, your counterparty is going to claim against you for a

late payment when the money doesn't arrive in New York, plus interest. Of course, you will dispute such a claim, and time will drag on while you argue about what should have happened.

- Calendars. Most trades are designed to make a payment on a day when the central banks for the relevant currencies are open, and you have staff in the office. Firms subscribe to services that provide carefully checked non-working-day data, an example would be www.financialcalendar.com. If your counterparty takes data from a different supplier, or you've not set up your trade with the relevant currency calendars, your payment timing will be wrong compared with your counterparty.
- Exercise. When you are the buyer of a call option, the only reason you would exercise your option is when it will make you a profit. In all other cases your option is worthless. It therefore matters a great deal to the trader that any option which will make him a profit is exercised on the right day at the right time. This function is sometimes carried out by the back office and if an exercise opportunity is missed, the trader will lose money. The way to avoid this is to implement internal procedures to verify exercise dates on trades that are coming up, and in some cases get the traders to check that the dates are correct.
- Corporate actions. These can have such wide-ranging effects on trades that a list of what could go wrong is too long for this chapter. Suffice it to say that if you and your counterparty don't agree on the effect of an event, you're going to get problems. Most firms will carry out an event by verifying the population of trades with your counterparty first, before making the necessary changes. An example of a corporate action would be a merger, a bankruptcy, a credit event or any other non-financial event that has an effect on your trades.

Summary

The goals of asset servicing are:

- Carry out the terms of the trade as agreed.
- Calculate any necessary payments.
- Carry out any events on the trade.

Risks include:

- Inaccurate numbers leading to bad payments.
- Missing exercise events mean missed profits.

OTC collateral management

In simple terms, if someone owes you £100 but isn't due to pay for six months, would you feel happier if they gave you something worth £100 (collateral) to hold on to until they pay? Throughout the banking industry this principle has been adopted in more complex ways to protect against the possibility that the firm who owes you money can't pay.

To make such a process workable, firms sign legal agreements that describe in detail the process of calculating the amount of collateral due, what assets are acceptable to provide as collateral, and the timing and mechanisms for delivering the collateral. In the OTC markets the agreement they sign is an ISDA **credit support annexe (CSA)** which sets out all those points. The details to agree are:

- Which OTC trades are included in the CSA? Does it include rates, credit, equities, FX and commodities?
- Are securities such as bonds and equities acceptable as collateral? If so, precisely which bonds (usually government and occasionally other **AAA** issuers). It assumed that cash in most currencies is always eligible.
- How often is the value of your portfolio of trades recalculated? Should be daily but could be less frequent.
- What rate of interest is paid on cash when provided as collateral?
- Is any amount of debt (or exposure) allowed without providing any collateral? (referred to in the CSA as a threshold).
- Is there any add-on amount of collateral to give even more protection with a high-risk counterparty such as a hedge fund? This add-on would ensure you received not just the amount the other party owes you, but a higher amount using some formula you jointly agree.

- Is the agreement symmetrical? Sometimes the CSA can require more stringent terms for a high-risk party in the agreement.

What happens?

To carry out a typical phone call to a counterparty for collateral, you follow these steps:

1. Gather together details of all the trades included in the CSA.
2. Collect for each trade, today's valuation for that trade:
   a. If the valuation is positive, you are making a profit.
   b. If the valuation is negative, you are making a loss.
3. Add together the valuations for all the trades, arriving at a single number in a single currency, called your **exposure**:
   a. If the value is positive, the other party may owe you collateral.
   b. If the value is negative, you may owe them collateral.
4. Compare your exposure with the current collateral holdings:
   a. If the exposure is higher than your collateral holdings, call the other party for a top-up of collateral.
   b. If the exposure is lower than your collateral holdings, you need to repay some collateral, if the other party requests it.

Figure 9.8 shows some example collateral calculations.

What can go wrong?

This area of OTC derivatives is still an opportunity for better automation. It suffers from the fact that many OTC contracts are still confirmed using PDF files and paper, causing issues when carrying out the collateral procedure above. Among the main issues are:

- Each of the parties collects the list of trades included in the CSA. This is harder than it sounds, as so many systems and non-standard trades can be involved. You both arrive at different lists of trades, causing the calculations of exposure to be different.

Example 1: they owe you

Trade ref	**Trade type**	**Valuation**
TR1	FX option	25
TR2	Interest rate swap	–10
	Net mark to market	*15*
You:	Collateral holding	10
	Shortfall	5
Your action:	Call for 5 top-up	

Example 2: you owe them

Trade ref	**Trade type**	**Valuation**
TR1	FX option	–25
TR2	Interest rate swap	5
	Net mark to market	*–20*
You:	Collateral pledged	10
	Shortfall	–10
Their action:	They call you for a top-up of 10	

Example 3: return of collateral

Trade ref	**Trade type**	**Valuation**
TR1	FX option	20
TR2	Interest rate swap	–10
	Net mark to market	*10*
You:	Collateral holding	20
	Shortfall	–10
Their action:	They ask for a repayment of 10	

FIGURE 9.8 Collateral calculations

- Even if you both agree on the list of trades included, the valuation for some trades can rely on manual procedures and verification by other departments. If you both disagree on a valuation, the calculations will also be different.
- If your systems don't run to a similar time schedule as your counterparty, capturing data at similar times, these timing differences will lead to both the problems above.

> the fallback is to undertake a portfolio reconciliation

Disputes happen frequently in the market. This is allowed for in the CSA, and in general means one party disagrees with the collateral calculations from the other. The fallback is to undertake a portfolio reconciliation, which means each side exchanging electronic files of data (often spreadsheets) listing the trades and valuations concerned. It is then up to each party to compare its data with the counterparty's data and try to find the reasons for different calculations.

Five companies that offer a centralised automated service for this process are:

- TriOptima;
- Markit;
- Euroclear;
- Lombard Risk;
- Omgeo/Allustra.

A number of other companies supply software to reconcile the two data sets. The underlying problem to all these services is exchanging data in a format both parties can process. An Excel spreadsheet is inadequate for this purpose, and ISDA has been working hard to develop FpML to expedite a better data format.

Summary

The goals of collateral management include:

- Reduce net exposure to a party by collecting collateral assets.
- Measure the health of a party by their ability to deliver collateral.
- Provide portfolio valuation statements to a party.

The risks include:

- Late delivery of collateral means benefits reduced.
- Inability to respond to a margin call can indicate financial or operational problems.
- Failure to escalate problems can mean missing a default.

Central counterparties

In 2009 the OTC industry was in a competition to build and operate a central counterparty (CCP) for OTC credit derivative contracts, such as credit default swaps. Regulators and politicians wanted more controls in the OTC credit market and believed a CCP would provide additional stability. The only existing CCP for OTC products is the **SwapClear** service run by **LCH.Clearnet**, which accepts OTC interest rate swaps from banks.

How does it work?

If you think back to the section on collateral, a CCP is the best way to eliminate credit risk from the capital markets using a sophisticated collateral calculation. What that means, is that by **clearing** your trades through a CCP, they provide protection from the effects of your counterparty being declared bankrupt. A CCP cannot prevent bankruptcy but will ensure that you suffer minimal or zero loss should this occur.

To do this:

- A CCP will interpose itself between you and your counterparty from a legal perspective and become the party to the trade for both of you, as in Figure 9.9.
- Each of you modifies your records of the trade to show the CCP as your counterparty.
- The CCP has a set of rules and regulations, which include complex collateral calculations.
- You both pay to the CCP amounts of collateral they calculate.
- Should either party in the trade go bankrupt, the collateral held by the CCP is used to compensate the other for any losses.

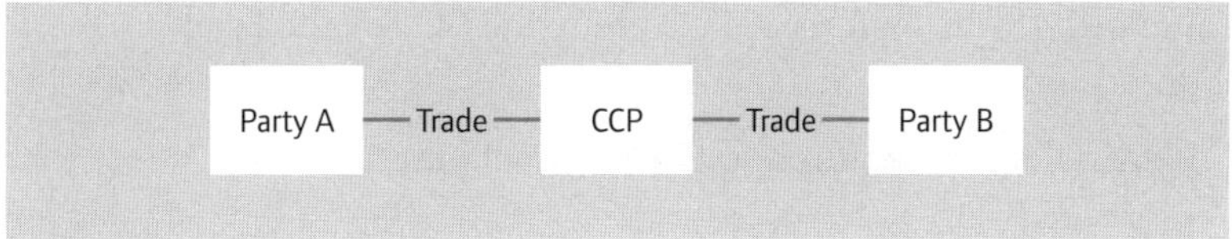

FIGURE 9.9 CCP overview

The collateral calculations involve several layers of protection, which are usually described like this:

- Variation margin. The change in the daily mark-to-market of the trade, very similar to the collateral calculation described above for an ISDA CSA.
- Initial margin. An amount recalculated every day to protect against volatility in your portfolio of trades. In other words, if the market conditions move against you, how bad could your losses be?
- Default fund. A fund common to all members of the CCP calculated using extreme market scenarios.
- Insurance. A final amount of protection, only used if the other layers of protection are used up for compensation.
- Capital. If things went really bad, the share capital of the CCP itself would be sold and the cash used to compensate members. If things got this bad, the CCP would itself be bankrupt, and the world banking system probably in meltdown.

What happens?

- Well before you need it, join a CCP and sign up to its rules and regulations.
- Every day, match or confirm your trades with your counterparty.
- Submit the trade to the CCP via a central service such as MarkitWire.
- The CCP checks carefully that your trade is eligible for the service:
  - If so, it is ‘registered’ and you are notified.
  - If not, it is rejected, and you are notified why.

- You modify your own records to show the CCP as the legal counterparty.
- Pay the collateral required to the CCP each day.

What can go wrong?

Using a CCP is generally a highly automated process. Trades for LCH.Clearnet SwapClear are delivered direct via an electronic link from MarkitWire to SwapClear and the steps above almost fully automated. Becoming a member of SwapClear also involves meeting membership rules. These measure the number of IRS trades you have open, plus the credit rating and regulatory capital holdings of your firm. The effect of these criteria is to restrict membership to highly experienced professional firms, meaning the procedures are well understood by those firms, and the daily settlements with LCH.Clearnet free of errors, as they are also highly automated.

The SwapClear service faced a test in Autumn 2008 when Lehman Brothers was declared bankrupt, and a complex process was carried out to re-allocate the Lehman trades to the remaining members of SwapClear. LCH.Clearnet announced that it had completed this process and that the amounts of collateral collected were sufficient to compensate member firms for any losses without any adverse effects on LCH.Clearnet.

So why doesn't the industry put all OTC contracts through a CCP? Reasons include:

- Collateral. The level of collateral required by the CCP to protect the members will increase as the population of members moves into the 'riskier' categories of firms. There is a point where allowing any firm to join a CCP makes the collateral requirements for the individual firm, and the membership as a whole, too costly.
- Risk calculations. Calculating the above amounts of collateral for complex OTC products is not straightforward. The more complex the products, especially anything involving an option, the more complex and costly the margin calculations become. In addition, more complex products are harder to find sufficient market data for, to drive the calculation models.

- Product flexibility. A CCP has to be a stable and well managed service, meaning any addition or change to cleared products needs careful planning, especially if the product has never been cleared before. There is an argument that many OTC derivatives contracts have become a de facto standardised product and could therefore be brought into a cleared environment, leaving newer and less developed products in the pure OTC space.

Summary

CCP goals include:

- Register trades for clearing.
- Reconcile cleared trades versus your own books and records.
- Achieve credit line and regulatory capital savings.
- Provide required collateral to the CCP.

The risk is that:

- failure to deliver collateral to CCP can cause a default.

Settlement

Regardless of how complex an OTC contract becomes, they all result in payments of one sort or another. Given that the OTC market has no central infrastructure, there is no single service for settling payments on OTC contracts, but there are three methods in the market:

- Direct payment from one party to another.
- Payment using central payments infrastructure.
- Centralised net settlement via a service provider, in this case CLS Bank.

In each case below the following example payment will be used:

Payer:	Birmingham Builders (BB)
Payer's bankers:	Barclays Bank plc

Receiver:	Archway Artists (AA)
Receivers bankers:	Citigroup Inc
Amount:	$200,000
Due date:	20 December (assume this is a day when US banks are open)

Direct payment

In this model, the banks use payment messages provided by SWIFT to instruct their bankers to move the money (Figure 9.10) The stages in the process are:

1. (BB) sends a SWIFT MT103 instructing its bank account holder to pay funds to the receiver (AA).
2. Barclays sends an MT202 to Citigroup informing it of the upcoming payment.
3. Barclays uses its access to the payments service to debit $200,000 from BB's account, and provide the funds to Citigroup.
4. Citigroup receives the funds in the payments service and credits them to the account of AA.
5. Citigroup then notifies AA that the funds have been received.

Payment using central bank infrastructure

This method of settlement applies to banks that are direct members of the central bank settlement systems such as **FedWire** or **CHIPS** in the US, or **CHAPS** in the UK. This replaces the bottom part of Figure 9.10 and is shown in more detail as Figure 9.11.

FedWire, CHIPS and CHAPS have wide membership, and are how large or urgent payments are settled within each country. For a UK bank to pay dollars to a US bank (Barclays to Citigroup in this example), they must both hold accounts at the same service, in this case FedWire, for the money transfer to take place. These services are accessible via **SWIFTNet**.

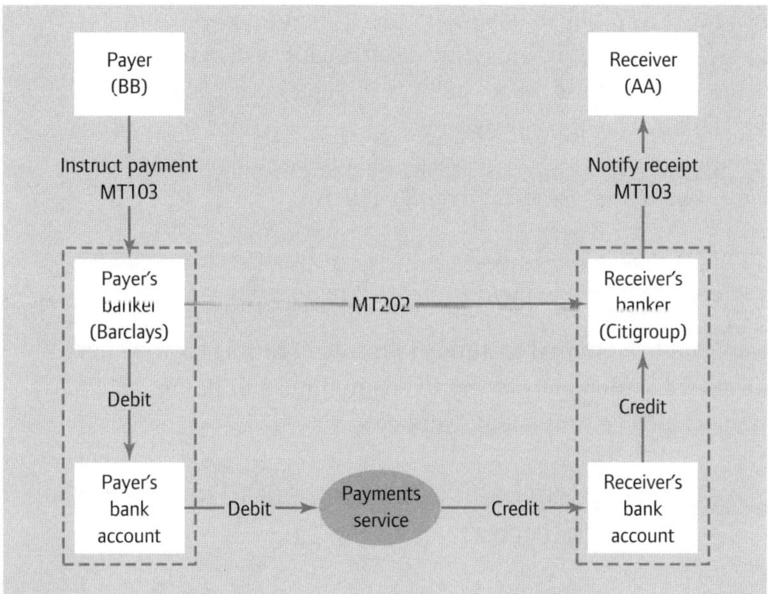

FIGURE 9.10 OTC settlement

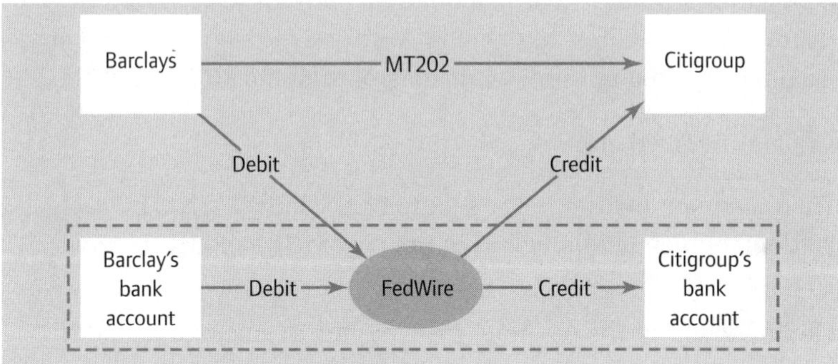

FIGURE 9.11 Central bank settlement

Payments using CLS Bank

The term Herstatt risk follows from an incident on 26 June 1974, when the German Herstatt bank was closed due to insolvency during German banking hours, but before the start of US banking hours. As a result, the bank failed to make payments on the US dollar legs of foreign exchange transactions even where it had received the Deutschmark payments on such transactions. A number of ways of preventing this problem have been tried, the most recent and successful is the continuous linked settlement system (CLS). CLS took ten years to build, and went live in September 2002. By 2009, it served 61 settlement member banks, plus, 3,336 third-party users, and settled daily over 1.5m gross payment instructions for FX spot and forward trades valued at over $8 trillion.

Settlement at CLS takes place multi-laterally, so each settlement member makes one payment (in or out) per currency a day.

The system has internal methods to resolve funding 'circles' and has a staged settlement process to ensure liquidity in the system during each day's settlement cycle.

the system has internal methods to resolve funding 'circles'

CLS also has a direct link to the DTCC Trade Information Warehouse for OTC credit derivative trades. In December 2007, 340,000 gross payments worth about $14.5 billion were netted in the warehouse down to 123 payment instructions to CLS valued at approximately $288 million; 14 dealers participated (Figure 9.12).

The stages involved are:

1. Each payment instruction is sent to CLS via SWIFTNet by each settlement member on behalf of the payer (BB) and the receiver (AA).
2. CLS matches up the payment instructions to ensure both sides agree a payment and a receipt are taking place.

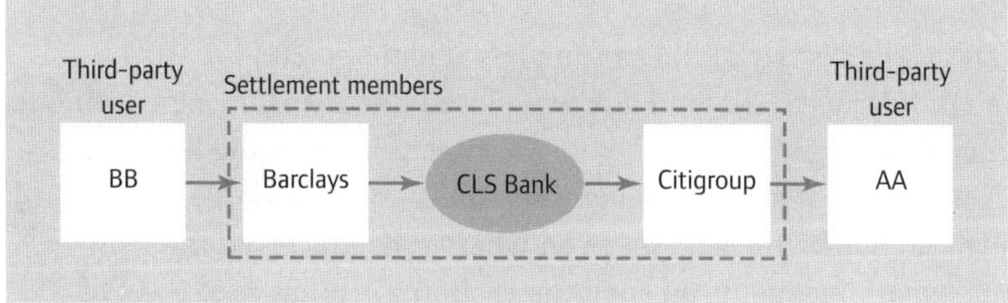

FIGURE 9.12 CLS overview

3. CLS collects these instructions from all settlement members up until a hard deadline at midnight Central European Time (CET), the day *before* the payment is due (just after 23:59:59 the day before you receive your payment).
4. After the cut-off time, a pay-in-schedule is calculated, which nets all payments in each currency for each settlement member. This means each settlement member will only make one payment per currency into CLS or receive from CLS, on each settlement day.
5. Between 00:00 and 06:00 CET, settlement members can enter additional payment instructions to balance out large balances in one currency with shortfalls in another.
6. From 07:00 CET, CLS begins the settlement process, by collecting in-flows from the settlement members first, then making the payment outflows.

What can go wrong?

In all the scenarios above, you need to state carefully:

- were the money is going to;
- were the money is from;
- how much;
- what currency;
- when.

If any of these are mis-stated, incorrect, or mis-directed, the obvious problem is that the wrong amount goes to the wrong place at the wrong time. The resolutions to the problems are:

- Wrong receiver: ask nicely for your money back.
- Missing payment: contact the payer and chase the payment, demand interest on the missing money, which might have caused you overdraft charges.
- Unwanted payment: either hold on to the money until the payer decides to ask for it back (and potentially earn interest on it), or automatically send it back because you didn't expect to receive it.

Summary

The goals of settlement are:

- Build a big list of payments to be made and received.
- Apply any netting rules.
- Reconcile bank statement with expected payments and receipts.
- Chase failed receipts and claim interest.

The risks are:

- Pay the wrong amount.
- Pay to the wrong party.
- Don't pay at all.
- Don't receive at all.

Legal background

An OTC derivative is a contract between two parties, setting out the rights and obligations of each party. Whilst an OTC contract is concerned with pure financial obligations, in law it is similar to that of any other contract. Many OTC derivatives contracts last for many years, and so must have a comprehensive framework to cover all eventualities.

Anyone who has negotiated a contract involving large amounts of money will know how complex, time-consuming and detailed the process can be. The OTC market started out many years ago by hand-drafting the contract for each trade, including all the details on who paid whom, why and when. It soon became apparent that much of the detail in each OTC contract could be agreed in advance between parties, reducing the size and complexity of the documentation for each OTC trade. At the same time, a trade association was formed which became the means to developing a standardised legal framework for OTC trading, and enabling expansion into trading in many countries.

Legal framework

Figure 9.13 sets out how a single OTC trade fits into an overall legal framework, the components are:

- An **ISDA** master is negotiated before trading takes place, and only occurs once between any two parties. The master has a number of benefits, including reduction of credit risk by enabling a collateral agreement. It provides a way to terminate trades under certain circumstances such as bankruptcy: it sets out how to carry out a **liquidation** of the whole agreement; and gives each party rights to offset transactions in a default and numerous other necessities. An ISDA master and the documents related to it are written to operate under a specific national law. Given that the majority of OTC trading happens in the UK or the US, the parties can elect to use an English law master or sometimes Delaware law in the US for different corporate treatment when in bankruptcy or for tax reasons.
- The **trade confirmation** contains the main terms agreed to by the two traders involved for a single specific trade/contract. For instance, you need to write down the fixed interest rate agreed on an interest rate swap, or the strike price for an equity option. Nowadays, this takes place electronically using services provided by DTCC Deriv/SERV, MarkitWire and T:Zero, where the terms of the trade are represented using FpML.

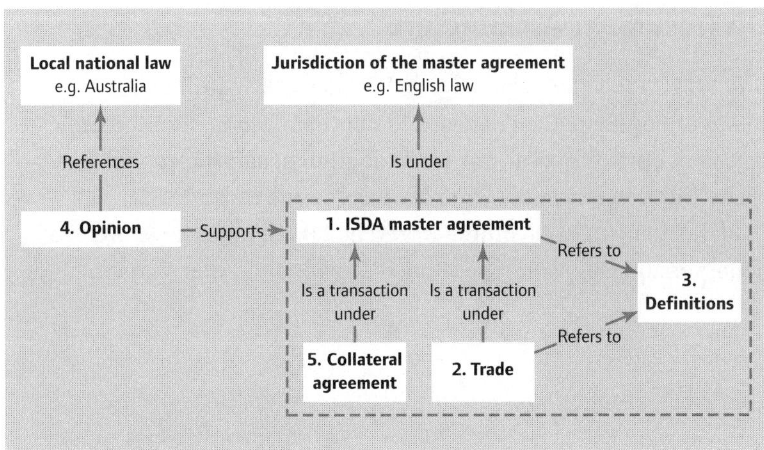

FIGURE 9.13 Legal framework for an OTC trade

- The **ISDA definitions** are a short-hand way of defining terms used in the trade confirmation, which don't require any negotiation but must be precisely understood by both parties for consistent and accurate use. For example, 'trade date' means, in respect of a swap transaction, the date on which the parties enter into the swap transaction.
- An **opinion** is a document written by a law firm, which seeks to provide the party to a trade with an assessment of the likelihood of success should you attempt to enforce your rights under the ISDA master in a court, usually in the country where your counterparty was declared bankrupt. So, for example, you have a trade with a firm in Bermuda, 'Beach Co.', where it is declared bankrupt. Using the method laid out in the ISDA master to calculate the money Beach Co. owes you, you apply to the court in Bermuda to recover your losses. The opinion (which you receive by being an ISDA member), provides you with guidance before you even agreed to the original trades, that you can recover your losses in a Bermudan court.
- A collateral agreement or in ISDA terminology a credit support document, is an additional optional agreement you negotiate and sign between you and your counterparty, which gives both of you rights to calculate and call for collateral to reduce the credit risk between the two of you.

ISDA Document Architecture

Figure 9.14 shows the complete legal framework within which OTC derivatives contracts fit. This book is not the place to describe each component or its function, but without all this, and the continuing work by ISDA to tackle the complex legal needs of the OTC derivatives market, none of this would be taking place now. Some of the components below are mentioned elsewhere in this chapter.

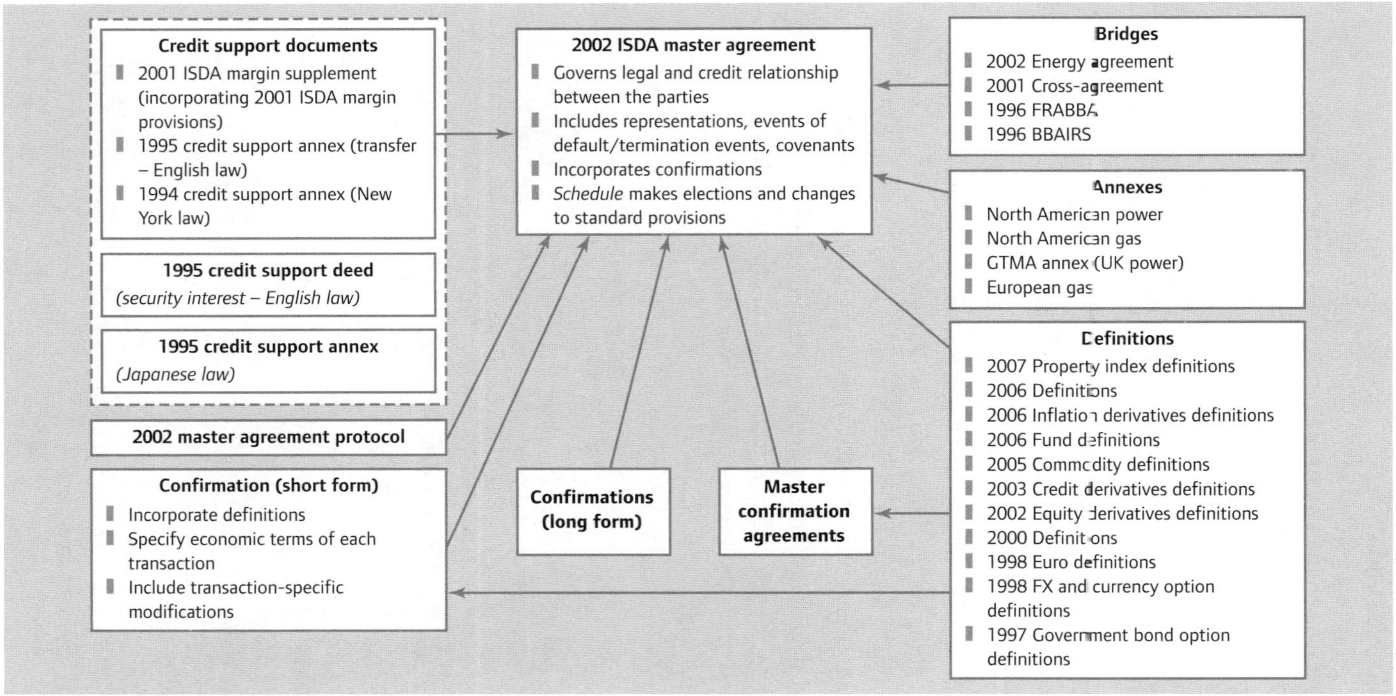
Credit support documents
2001 ISDA margin supplement (incorporating 2001 ISDA margin provisions)
1995 credit support annex (transfer – English law)
1994 credit support annex (New York law)
1995 credit support deed
(security interest – English law)
1995 credit support annex
(Japanese law)
2002 master agreement protocol
Confirmation (short form)
Incorporate definitions
Specify economic terms of each transaction
Include transaction-specific modifications
2002 ISDA master agreement
Governs legal and credit relationship between the parties
Includes representations, events of default/termination events, covenants
Incorporates confirmations
Schedule makes elections and changes to standard provisions
Confirmations (long form)
Master confirmation agreements
Bridges
2002 Energy agreement
2001 Cross-agreement
1996 FRABBA
1996 BBAIRS
Annexes
North American power
North American gas
GTMA annex (UK power)
European gas
Definitions
2007 Property index definitions
2006 Definitions
2006 Inflation derivatives definitions
2006 Fund definitions
2005 Commodity definitions
2003 Credit derivatives definitions
2002 Equity derivatives definitions
2000 Definitions
1998 Euro definitions
1998 FX and currency option definitions
1997 Government bond option definitions

FIGURE 9.14 ISDA legal structure

Reprinted with permission of ISDA © 2008 International Swaps and Derivatives Association, Inc.

Systems overview

OTC derivatives are more complex to process than most other products in the capital markets, mainly because they are contracts with many negotiable terms. This gives rise to complexity within an organisation, and the systems it needs to support the OTC business. Figure 9.15 is an example of the way a large OTC trading firm might assemble systems to focus on the specialised areas of OTC processing.

Main points

- The front office will have its own systems to carry out the trading activity, along with pricing and risk management systems. These are specific to the speed at which trading takes place, and give each trader their own personal view of their trading activity.
- The middle and back office are is more concerned with accuracy and independence from the front office, to ensure each trade is processed as accurately as possible, meeting any legal or regulatory requirements.

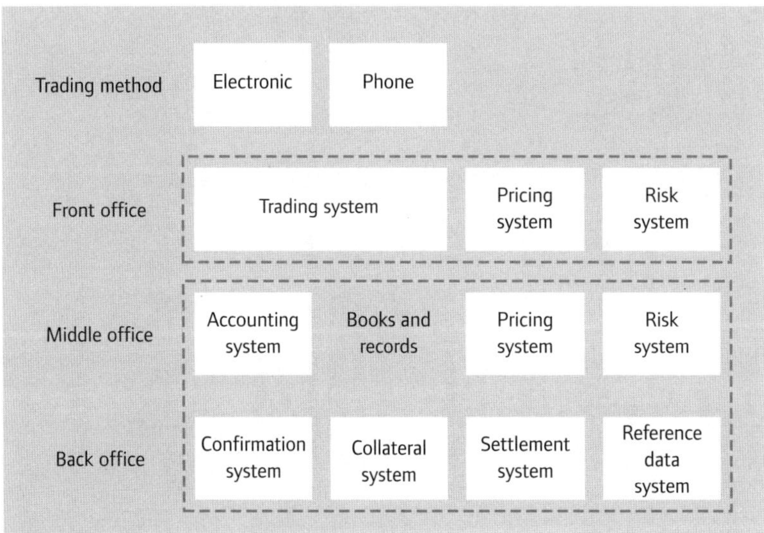

FIGURE 9.15 Systems overview

Market size

The OTC derivatives market indicates the extent of economic activity across the globe, and how important the OTC market has become to the world financial system.

A notional is the number used in an OTC derivatives trade for calculation purposes. A $100m interest rate swap doesn't mean $100m has been loaned, only that payment calculations use $100m as the imaginary (or notional) amount for mathematical purposes.

In Table 9.2, the gross notional numbers for OTC derivatives are like the mileage on a car. If a car does a 100-mile return journey from A to B and back, the gross mileage is 200 miles, but the net mileage is zero, you end up back where you started. Hence, two OTC trades in opposite directions (a buy and sell) lead to a reduced net market risk, but a large gross notional.

TABLE 9.2 Economic activity and the OTC market

Example	Value	Scale
Typical notional trade size	$10,000,000	Tens of millions
Large notional trade size	$100,000,000	Hundreds of millions
Net credit payments on the Lehman default (2008)	$6,200,000,000	Billions
Value of Bear Stearns before its value crashed (2008)	$18,000,000,000	Billions
Value of JP Morgan Chase (2008)	$140,000,000,000	Billions
Value of UK government bank bail-out plan (2009)	$350,000,000,000	Billions
Value of US banking money markets support (2009)	$900,000,000,000	Billions
Nominal gross domestic product of the USA (2007)	$13,807,550,000,000	Trillions
Gross notional size of the OTC credit derivatives market	$42,000,000,000,000	Trillions
Nominal annual gross domestic product of the entire world (2007)	$64,903,314,000,000	Trillions

TABLE 9.2 continued

Example	Value	Scale
Gross notional size of the OTC interest rates derivatives market	$389,000,000,000,000	Trillions
Gross notional size of the OTC derivatives market	$596,000,000,000,000	Trillions
Level of financial settlements at DTCC in 2004	$1,000,000,000,000,000	Quadrillion

10

Key rules of business behaviour

Sue Cooper

These are not the sort of rules they teach you in business school, but break them and it will destroy your career.

Author's note

This chapter, aims to explain the legal and regulatory environment and most commonly found workplace policies that provide the everyday 'rules' of workplace behaviour.

As the reader, you should be aware of the following:

1. This is not legal opinion in any sense. Whilst it is current at the time of writing and accurate to the best of our knowledge, readers should not rely on the legal consequences in any jurisdiction, but should rather take independent legal advice.
2. The chapter is written on the basis of the current legal and regulatory position in the UK. Similar laws and regulations exist in most countries but the specifics may be different.
3. Practical examples of breaches of the 'rules' and their consequences are illustrative only. The vagaries of human behaviour are such that different situations will probably result in significant differences in outcomes. The advice given here cannot be used 'off-the-peg' without checking carefully the laws, regulations and workplace policies that are applicable to your own environment.

Introduction

We are now going to look at the best practice 'rules' of business behaviour. I'm not talking here about the 'be-the-first-to-grab-the-flip-chart-pen-at-the-assessment-centre exercise' type of behavioural rules taught at business schools and universities. I am talking about the sort of best practice to adopt if you:

- intend to operate ethically and with integrity;
- want to avoid any questions about your behaviour in the workplace;
- wish to build a strong reputation as a finance professional;
- don't want to be sacked for gross misconduct or otherwise disciplined;
- want to stay out of jail or avoid heavy fines.

Break the rules here and the best you can hope for is disciplinary action and a big question mark over you that can last for the whole of your career. These best-practice rules include respecting diversity, avoiding discriminatory and bullying behaviour or harassment of others, adhering to the protocols relating to insider dealing, operating ethically and knowing if or when to become a whistleblower. Best practice in these areas is usually clear, backed by company policies and, in many cases, by the law.

To re-iterate:

- I am not giving you legal opinion. Apart from any other considerations, the sheer amount, scope, complexity and frequency of updates to these laws, regulations and company policies, plus all of the vagaries of human behaviour, mean that it is not a practical possibility.
- Any references made to law are from a UK perspective. The legal position in your environment might well be different, but the 'rules' are undoubtedly similar.
- All financial institutions have (or should have) policies covering each of these areas. These should be your first port-of-call if you need guidance. If you need further help or advice you should consult a suitably-qualified professional.

Respect at work: diversity

Imagine this: you arrive at your desk one morning to find a letter stating that a complaint of sexual harassment has been made against you. With a sinking feeling, you remember an incident that occurred a couple of weeks ago. You thought you were having a bit of fun, the recipient obviously thought differently. You are asked to attend an interview with your boss in an hour's time. At the interview, you are told the nature of the complaint (and your hunch was right). You are suspended immediately, pending an investigation. On your way out, everyone avoids your gaze. You realise that your office friends have probably been called as witnesses. You realise that in your absence, every email you ever wrote, every joke you ever told and any other related incidents are now under review. You realise that your office life has become an open book. You suspect you may well have flushed your career down the toilet.

Up to the 1970s, the workplace was pretty well homogenous (most people confirmed to a type). The fundamental premise of workplace life was that to succeed in (or, in some cases, even to join) this semi-exclusive club, you had to:

- be male (straight or not openly gay);
- share the same race or ethnicity as the bosses;
- have the same religion as the bosses;
- be a suitable age for the job, reaching a career peak in your mid fifties;
- Not have any noticeable physical disability or mental health issues.

The rules and behaviours of the workplace evolved or were designed to keep this long-accepted system in place. These included: strict hierarchy, a mandatory respect for anyone above you in the pecking order and a toleration of aggression, bullying, intimidation and threats as a necessary part of 'firm management'. And woe betide anyone who did not fit the above criteria and believed they too had a right to succeed!

Today, the fundamental premise of workplace life is different and is based on two fundamental human rights:

- Equality of opportunity for everyone, solely based on their talent and ability.
- The right of anyone to work in a respectful environment without fear of bullying or harassment.

Thanks to the heroic efforts of campaigning groups and, I hope, a real shift in social attitudes, there are now laws that underpin these rights at work. By law now you cannot be disadvantaged, for example, because of your gender or ethnicity. Even the health and safety legislation has been broadened in scope to extend the duty of care of employers to include protection for individuals from exposure to 'unreasonable stress'.

The trouble is that in spite of all of this, and despite the fact that some of this legislation is as much as thirty years old, far too many workplaces are operating from the rule-set of the pre-1970s. Discrimination, harassment and bullying are still rife in many organisations but now the penalties for these archaic practices can be huge. In the UK, we are now seeing Employment Appeal Tribunal settlements of millions of pounds (there is no upper limit to compensation by law). In a global marketplace, business can be severely damaged if, for example, an organisation has a reputation for consistent racism. Organisations with a record of punitive settlements against them for harassment and bullying find that they are no longer the first choice for the best candidates. These facts have been a harsh wake-up call for many organisations in the last fifteen to twenty years and have galvanised them into action both in the creation of policies and their reinforcement in the workplace. The financial community has, unfortunately, been one of the worst culprits in terms of both the number of settlements awarded against it and the monetary size of those settlements.

> far too many workplaces are operating from the rule-set of the pre-1970s

Best practice rules to keep yourself out of hot water

So, what are the rules or guidelines for you as an individual in the workplace? I'll start by appealing to your better nature. *I* would like to think about the myriad laws and regulations that exist as a kind of sad safety net. In a world where people treated one another with reasonable dignity and respect, you would not need rules to remind people not to discriminate or bully. Where do you stand on these issues? Take a good look at yourself: what are your beliefs and values relating to this? How do you see yourself in relation to other people? Where are your strengths and weaknesses in this area? How does this, or will this, influence your workplace behaviour? Do you behave in a way that is consistent with your beliefs or are your beliefs compromised by your actual behaviour? Second, think about career and reputation: what sort of work colleague, manager or chief executive do you intend to be? It takes a great deal of self-awareness to acknowledge our own prejudices and courage not to condone or join in behaviour that offends basic values.

If that is too 'fluffy' for you, or your better nature has temporarily eluded you, consider the following practical information and advice:

- Read and understand the policies on diversity, discrimination, bullying and harassment for your own organisation. Be aware that they are also backed by law and the penalties for offences can be severe.
- Remember that if you bring your personal prejudices or bullying style to work with you, they will bite you back eventually. At the least, it will earn you a terrible reputation that will almost definitely cost you dearly, particularly if and when you become a manager and others have scores to settle. At worst, it could get you sacked, make you unemployable or land you in jail.
- Remember that if as a result of a complaint made against you, a financial settlement is imposed, you share the liability with the organisation. That is to say, as well as any disciplinary action or a dismissal to cope with, you will probably also be faced with a bill for tens of thousands of pounds in damages.
- Your view of the world is up to you, but remember that if you want to have rights yourself, you need to accept that everyone else does too. As the lottery says, 'it could be you' – in this case one day it will be you who is abused or disadvantaged simply because you are the wrong gender or age.

The following two sections examine the law and the workplace rules on discrimination, bullying and harassment in greater depth.

Avoiding discrimination

Are you prejudiced? Of course not...well, maybe. Try finishing these sentences:

- People born rich tend to be...
- Fat people are usually...

- Footballers never seem to…
- People who like cricket…
- Women alone in bars are most often…
- Politicians never…
- People who talk with regional accents are…
- Small men are nearly always…
- People who drive 4X4s are usually…

We all have a tendency to group people and to generalise about them. The laws around workplace discrimination are designed to ensure equality and respect and to stop people coming to work to express their own particular prejudices.

What the law says

The law in the UK and many other countries forbids discrimination on the grounds of:

- race or ethnic origin;
- gender (male or female);
- disability (including physical constraints and mental health issues);
- sexual orientation (whether someone is gay or straight);
- religious belief;
- age (considering that someone is too old or too young).

I will briefly sketch in the scope of these laws, which are very broad and apply to all aspects of workplace behaviour, and point out some of the common pitfalls.

First, these laws apply from 'cradle to grave' in terms of employment. That is to say from advertising and selection of candidates, throughout the work relationship in terms of any discretionary awards: promotion, development opportunities, pay and other benefits and also beyond, when an employee has left the organisation for another job or to retire.

Second, discrimination laws apply to both direct and indirect discrimination. Most people can spot direct discrimination, (denying someone an opportunity or benefit because they are X or Y). Indirect discrimination can be rather more subtle and may include:

- jokes aimed at members of a particular group (e.g. homophobic jokes);
- office banter (e.g. sexist or racist comments, whether aimed at people present, or not present, e.g. clients);
- comments relating to newspaper articles or world events that generalise about a particular group or race of people on the back of a specific act;
- creating or circulating emails of dubious content;
- excluding certain types of people, for example from a project team, and favouring others;
- setting up social activities that are likely to exclude others consistently (such as 'male' sports contests and alcohol-fuelled parties).

it can even apply if workplace behaviour affects someone's life at home

Finally (but not exhaustively), discrimination laws also apply beyond the workplace: when travelling on company business, at a client's premises and at any work-related social events. It can even apply if workplace behaviour affects someone's life at home e.g. offensive homophobic jokes when someone has a gay family member.

How the law and workplace rules operate in practice

You need to be aware of three principles here:

- If you offend someone else, *you* have the responsibility. This applies *even if you were not aware of giving offence*. The law says that we all have the right to set our own limits (within reason) – we all have the right to draw the line for ourselves.

Therefore, when complaints of discrimination are judged, it is not the intent of the perpetrator but the effect on the victim that is assessed.

EXAMPLE

Karen was secretary to Charlie. Charlie had suggested to Karen that sex was good exercise, to which Karen made no response. Charlie made an attempt to look up Karen's skirt and, when she angrily left the room, he laughed. Charlie showed Karen and others a newspaper cartoon depicting an affair between a boss and secretary. He frequently stood behind Karen when telling other colleagues dirty jokes. After a year of this, Karen complained.

EXAMPLE

Bill and Fred frequently try to gather together drinking parties and football tournaments 'for the lads' after work. If someone refuses, it is inferred that they must be gay. Unbeknown to them, there are two gay men and one lesbian in the work group, none of whom are 'out' at work. One of these people makes a complaint.

In each of these cases, the complaint is legitimate and the perpetrators liable, even though they might have defended themselves by saying they did not know they were giving offence or that they were merely joking. The rule here is to think before you open your mouth. Is what you are about to say potentially offensive to someone else? If so, is it worth risking your career for a cheap laugh?

- The second principle is that the law applies irrespective of corporate culture. You cannot use as a defence the excuse that 'that's just how we are around here' or that this type of behaviour is custom and practice.

EXAMPLE

Sarah and Alison have been working together on a trading floor for three years. They are in the habit of making sexist jokes and specific remarks about the male members of the team, all of whom tolerate this behaviour to varying degrees. A new analyst, Henry, joins the team and complains about the banter. Alison and Sarah say that theirs is a high-pressure environment, the others do not mind and he will just have to get used to it.

EXAMPLE

The complainant was working as a broker in a leading city firm. There was a practice on the trading desks that if any employee was late in to work on Friday morning they would be given a costume to wear as a forfeit. The complainant, who is Jewish, was given a Second World War German uniform to wear. He refused to wear the costume and later resigned after an alleged attempt to demote him. The bank denied wrongdoing, arguing that the incidents were part of the office culture the complainant had previously joined in with. (This is based on an actual Employment Appeals Tribunal case between Laurent Weinberger and Tullett & Tokyo.)

Once again, in each of these cases, the complaint is legitimate and the perpetrators liable, even though they tried to defend themselves by saying that the behaviour was simply part of corporate culture. As the law sees it, an organisation is never allowed to set up or tolerate a system of behaviour proscribed by law. The rule here? Consider the potential effects on others and, if in doubt, don't join in.

- When judging behaviour, tribunals are likely to consider your whole style of behaviour. Even if the individual offences you commit are small and relatively trivial, the accumulation of a number of small acts in context can be added together to decide on your guilt.

In the case of Karen and Charlie above, a tribunal would find that although Charlie's actions towards Karen varied in severity (from circulating a cartoon to trying to look up her skirt), the combination of actions meant that his unwanted sexual attentions towards this woman should be taken particularly seriously.

Keeping yourself out of hot water

As well as the rules outlined above, here are some guidelines for damage limitation should the need arise. These are the most sensible best practice rules to adopt should someone complain directly to you about something you have done or said:

- Listen carefully and show that you have heard, if necessary by summarising and reflecting back (e.g. 'you are complaining to me about the incident when I…').
- If the complaint is factually correct or a possible interpretation of meaning, apologise sincerely (e.g. 'I understand that that was offensive to you and I am really sorry. It won't happen again').
- Don't discount what you hear or become defensive (e.g. 'I was only joking' or 'Aren't you a bit sensitive?'). Remember, it is the victim's perception, not the perpetrator's intent that is judged. You may make the situation worse if you appear not to take the complaint seriously.
- Ensure no repetition. Consider this a warning shot across the bows and adjust your behaviour. The powers that be take a dim view of repeat offences.
- Report if necessary. If the complaint is serious, or untrue, or in any way likely to escalate, it makes sense to let someone in authority know. Better to risk a bit of embarrassment now than burying a ticking time bomb in your desk drawer.

better to risk a bit of embarrassment now than burying a ticking time bomb

Bullying and harassment

The fastest-growing category of recorded complaints in the workplace in the past few years is about bullying or harassment. A recent analysis of the number of calls to the TUC helpline revealed that about a third were about bullying – outstripping those on pay, safety or any other category. It is also becoming a focus of attention in schools. Does this mean that bullying and harassment is on the increase? I doubt it. Does it mean that people are no longer suffering discrimination? Certainly not. From my experience, I believe it means two things: first, that people working in twenty-first century institutions are less likely than their predecessors to accept the right of bullies to bully and are more likely to challenge bullying behaviour and harassment. Second, when someone is the victim of a bully, they do not always know what to do and need all of the advice they can get.

Defining bullying and harassment

Bullying and harassment are usually separated in the following ways:

- Bullying: (Intentional) offensive, intimidating, malicious, insulting behaviour and abuses of power.
- Harassment: Unwanted conduct that violates a person's dignity or creates an intimidating, hostile, degrading, humiliating or offensive environment, having regard to all circumstances including the perception of the victim.

Workplace bullying occurs when an individual singles someone or a small sub-section of people out for his or her malicious attention. Indications of bullying are things such as:

- misuse of power or position;
- verbal insults;
- undermining by overloading or criticism;
- unfair treatment;
- overbearing supervision;
- exclusion;
- spreading malicious rumours;
- blocking promotion or training opportunities;
- threats about job security;
- unwelcome sexual advances;
- physical intimidation or violence.

There are many theories about why bullies demonstrate this compulsive need, but why people bully is not the concern here. We are more interested in identifying bullying behaviour and being clear about the behavioural rules that this throws up – plus the implications should you become a bully yourself.

There seem to be four types of workplace bully:

- 'Look at me' types. These are the ones who love to single out someone in public (open plan office, internal meeting, with a client) and shout at or otherwise abuse their subject purely for the sense it gives them of their own importance and power.
- 'Driven' types. These bullies, often experts in their fields, have few interests in life other than their work. They drive everyone else to work excessive hours, are ridiculously perfectionistic and are likely to scorn the efforts of others.
- 'If only' types, people with a losing script in life but who have achieved a tiny bit of power that they then misuse, e.g. an administrator whom you have to 'treat nicely' or they will put your work to the bottom of the pile.
- 'Just because I can' types. These are the most dangerous bullies of all. They only do their stuff behind closed doors, seeming to latch on to a target and taking great pleasure in the harm that they do to the victim, but who are usually very plausible externally. The danger is that people find it very hard to believe that this person is bullying.

I have had dealings with all of these types, ranging in severity from the woman who fiercely guarded the entrance gate at the university where I once worked (an 'If only' bully) to a senior manager who worked for me (a 'Just because I can' type) who committed covert acts of serious sexual assault.

Harassment may take many different forms, but is most often discrimination by another name. Examples include sexual and racial harassment.

Sexual harassment is unwanted conduct of a sexual nature or other conduct based on sex, e.g.:

- subjecting someone to insults or ridicule because of their gender;
- sexually provocative remarks or jokes;
- suggesting that sexual favours may in some way further someone's career or that refusal may have career consequences;
- offensive comments about dress or appearance;
- the display or distribution of sexually explicit, or pornographic or sexually suggestive pictures or written material;
- unwelcome sexual attention, advances or physical contact.

Racial harassment is offensive conduct related to race, e.g.:

- jokes about, or gratuitous references to, a person's colour, race, religion or nationality;
- offensive remarks about dress, culture or customs that offend an individual or foster hatred or prejudice;
- commenting unfavourably on racial characteristics;
- subjecting someone to insults or ridicule because of their race;
- not co-operating with someone because of race or encouraging others to behave in a similar way;
- the display of written or printed material related to race that causes offence to an individual.

Similar indicators exist for the other discrimination categories. Harassment of people with disabilities can take the form of individuals being ignored, disparaged or ridiculed because of mistaken assumptions about their capabilities. Their disability rather than their ability becomes the focus of attention. Harassment can include inappropriate personal remarks, jokes or inappropriate references to an individual's appearance. Harassment on the grounds of a person's sexual orientation is usually experienced by gay men and lesbians, transsexuals or bisexuals. Examples include homophobic remarks or jokes, offensive comments relating to a person's sexuality, threats to disclose a person's sexuality to others or offensive behaviour relating to HIV or Aids status. Harassment of people because of their age usually involves individuals being excluded from social events or groups, disparaged or ridiculed because of mistaken assumptions about their capabilities based on age, or being denied development opportunities.

How the law and workplace policies operate in practice

The three principles we explored in the previous section on discrimination apply equally to bullying and harassment:

- If you offend someone else, you have the responsibility and this applies *even if you were not aware of giving offence.*
- The law or workplace rules apply irrespective of team or corporate culture.
- When judging behaviour, tribunals are likely to consider your whole pattern of behaviour, even if the individual offences you commit are small and relatively trivial.

Best practice rules to keep yourself out of hot water

Once again, refer to the best practice rules outlined in the section on discrimination:

- listening and acknowledgement;
- apologising sincerely;
- not discounting or becoming defensive;
- ensuring no repetition;
- reporting if necessary.

If you are the victim

Hopefully, you will never need this advice, but if as a result of discrimination, harassment and bullying, you need to make a complaint on your own behalf, here are some best practice guidelines:

First consider approaching the perpetrator, preferably in person. If the issue is not too serious and has occurred either by ignorance or lack of awareness by the perpetrator, it can be resolved simply. If the issue is more serious than this and you wish to make a formal complaint:

- Read your organisation's grievance procedure. It will tell you the right steps to take and how you can expect your issue to be dealt with.
- Keep records including time, date, incident and any evidence or witnesses.
- Make a formal complaint to your manager or human resources department (depending on your organisation's policies).
- Be prepared to be interviewed and to put your complaint in writing.
- Expect a formal response on the outcome.
- Support and counselling is often provided if wanted.

There will be a formal hearing and you will be informed of the outcome or decision made. You have the right to be represented or supported throughout the proceedings. Should you not be satisfied with the outcome, you have the right of appeal both internally via the grievance procedure and externally via the Employment Appeals Tribunal system. Do note, however, that you are required to have exhausted your organisation's internal procedures before you can take your complaint to a tribunal.

should you not be satisfied with the outcome, you have the right of appeal

Reviewing your own behaviour and impact

Some final thoughts. When I am teaching courses on diversity, discrimination, harassment and bullying, the most common question is: 'if it all hangs on the perception of the victim, how can I know if I am giving offence?' My answer is this: most people know if they are crossing a line in terms of their behaviour on a common sense basis. There are no absolutes, but here are three 'killer' questions you might like to ask yourself when reviewing your own behaviour:

- Would you treat your child, partner, neighbour in this way? Many people would be outraged if someone close to them had to tolerate the sort of daily behaviour they are happy to dole out to someone else's loved one or close friend.
- How would your behaviour look summarised at a tribunal? Sometimes, jokes and actions don't sound quite so hilarious when played back by a prosecuting barrister.
- Would you be ashamed if everyone knew this about you? If you ever had to explain to those at home that a complaint had been made against you, could you do so without feeling a bit guilty or ashamed?

Insider dealing

Henry is a trainee banker and is away from the office on business one week. On a conference call on the Tuesday of that week, he and his fellow trainees are asked to clear their schedules and report back to the London office on Friday for a special assignment. On arrival at the office, they are told that their bank, First Federal International, will be acquiring a competitor bank. The announcement of this is to be made first thing Monday morning. The job of the trainees is to call each of the First Federal Branch managers and brief them in the strictest confidence. Henry has a regular monthly 'date' on a Friday lunchtime, lunch with his fiancée's father in the City (with whom he has a 'tricky' relationship), which he must now cancel. He calls to cancel lunch and receives a frosty reception. Flustered, Henry hints at the nature of his special assignment to give a good reason for cancelling. Henry now has two problems in his life: his future relationship with his prospective father-in-law, who takes a dim view of unreliability; and the fact that he has broken the laws, regulations and bank policy relating to insider dealing.

Insider dealing is usually thought of in terms of the major cases (Tyco, Martha Stewart, etc.), where senior executives or famous people are charged or found guilty of attempts to manipulate the market for personal or corporate gain, or act improperly on inside information, but the protocols can affect everyone at whatever career stage and the penalties are severe.

Definition of insider dealing

Insider dealing is the dealing in stock or other securities (e.g. bonds or stock options) by someone who has access to 'inside' or non-public information about a company. The laws and regulations are designed to protect the markets. You may not often stop to consider this, but as a finance professional, particularly working in the capital markets, the work that you do and actions you take can have a profound effect on the market and thereby affect the lives of many people and so strong protection is needed. Just about all countries have laws on this, plus a regulatory body to oversee them and ensure good practice. In the UK, this is the Financial Services Authority (FSA). The FSA regulates the financial services industry and has four objectives:

- maintaining market confidence;
- promoting public understanding of the financial system;
- securing the appropriate degree of protection for consumers;
- fighting financial crime.

See www.fsa.gov.uk.

Legally, inside information is 'information relating to particular securities or a particular issue of securities which, if it were made public would be likely to have a significant effect on the price or value of any securities'. The law and regulations cover everyone who is an officer (is employed by) of the company and also anyone on the 'outside' (like Henry's potential father-in-law) who may attempt to benefit from inside information.

How the law and workplace policies operate in practice

Insider dealing rules are strictly enforced. Information that may materially affect the market price of stock or other securities should be made public as soon as it is practical. Until that is done, anyone dealing in that stock or security on the basis of inside information is committing a criminal act, which carries a range of severe punishments, including imprisonment.

The types of information that may influence the market include the obvious ones such as:

- Pending mergers or acquisitions. These are particularly market-sensitive.
- Company results and any updates along the way, e.g. trading statements.

Less obvious but also potential nuggets of inside information could be knowledge about a company's performance or prospects such as:

- A decision to re-structure the business (divesting a division for example or entering new markets).
- The gain or loss of a major contract.
- A sudden crisis in the business (a warehouse burned down, a ship sank, etc.).
- A change in the leadership of the business (board re-shuffle or the senior executive team has been poached en masse by a rival).

Offences against the insider dealing laws can be both 'sins of commission' and 'sins of omission'. In a 'sin of commission', an individual knowingly breaks the law. This person knows the rules and their duties and responsibilities but nevertheless seeks to benefit personally or benefit another or the organisation, through the use of inside information. 'Sins of omission', refer to someone who, for whatever reason, fails to think about the potential sensitivity of inside information and discloses it to a third party, or makes inside information available to others through negligence.

In response to this, most financial institutions have tightly enforced policies and procedures that cover the following:

- That you be made aware of the scope of and penalties for insider dealing, probably as part of your general, contractual agreement on confidentiality when you begin your employment. Your responsibilities to maintain confidentiality remain, even after you have left the firm.
- That you adhere to strict rules on personal dealing. It is assumed that most people will have their own share portfolio and will

want to maximise their return from it. Workplace rules on personal dealing usually require transparency, e.g. you must disclose your holdings regularly to your employer. They may also forbid dealing in the shares of client companies. They may further require you to gain your line manager's permission when dealing in certain circumstances or at certain periods. These rules also apply to your immediate family.

- Inside information that is particularly market-sensitive should only be shared on a strictly 'need to know' basis. If your boss excludes you from a meeting, is suddenly not copying you in on memos, or has started closing the door whenever his or her phone rings, this does not necessarily mean that you have fallen out of favour or that she/he has become power-crazed and secretive. They are probably just fulfilling their responsibilities regarding inside information. You will need to do the same if you are in charge of others.
- You must be fully aware of your responsibilities to protect information in whatever form. This applies to documents left on your desk or binned rather than shredded, failing to store information securely to prevent unauthorised access, all aspects of IT security and any phone calls made or received.

Best practice rules to keep yourself out of hot water

The law, regulations and workplace rules relating to insider dealing in terms of 'sins of commission' are clear and relatively unambiguous. If you are ever unclear about whether information in your possession meets the criteria of inside information, or you are unsure about your personal dealings or those of your family, seek help immediately. This is not the sort of stuff you can brush under the carpet.

> this is not the sort of stuff you can brush under the carpet

Regarding 'sins of omission', you may wish to think through the following to avoid unwittingly disclosing inside information:

- What information do you possess or have access to that could be market-sensitive? This includes reports and data that routinely come your way as well as things that happen by chance (an overheard conversation, coffee-time gossip, a document that was left on view at a client's, etc.) What are you doing with it and are there any areas where you may be at risk?
- Who is in your wider network? With whom do you regularly or occasionally exchange work chat? This may include work colleagues; friends in other institutions and your wider circle of friends and family (see the case or poor Henry earlier). What are your 'rules of engagement' when discussing business matters? Can you maintain them at all times? Sometimes people are clear about their responsibilities to protect information in the everyday but slip in particular circumstances – when trying to impress someone, when it is 'just a good gossip' between friends, after a few drinks, 'pillow talk'. This is not about being poe-faced, but rather about maintaining a reputation, protecting your career or even keeping yourself out of jail.

  How are you protecting information from unauthorised access? If you can hand-on-heart confirm the following, you are taking reasonable steps to prevent unauthorised disclosure of inside information:

  - I take care to secure all potentially sensitive information in my workspace including locking away documents, shredding anything sensitive immediately and keeping my desk clear.
  - I am the only person who has access to the information stored on my computer and anything sensitive is specifically protected. This also applies to my home PC and any storage media I am using (Blackberry, memory sticks, discs, etc.).
  - When away from the office, my laptop and storage media are in my possession at all times, unless they are locked away securely.
  - I rarely take sensitive documents outside the office. If this is ever necessary, those documents never leave my sight (they are not in check-in baggage, left in a briefcase during a 'natural break' on client premises, left at a friend's house when we go clubbing, left in a car overnight, etc.).

- I am extremely careful about the use of phones, including my mobile phone. I never talk about business matters where anyone else could overhear (trains, planes, car, bars, hotel foyers, etc.).

Operating ethically

All the sections in this chapter involve workplace ethics. This section explores ethical issues not covered elsewhere.

Consider the following: Bill is at a client meeting with his boss Mary. In the first part of the meeting, Mary is advising the client. Bill is concerned that she is proposing a route that will lead to disastrous consequences for the client. In the second part of the meeting when Bill is presenting on another topic, Mary constantly interrupts Bill and provides an interpretation of information based on a sketchy understanding of the particular issues involved. What are the ethical considerations here?

There are two main types of ethical issues that you may face:

- the ethics of business operations;
- the ethics of business behaviour.

In the case above, in the first part of the meeting, if Mary was wrongly advising the client because she was unaware of the full implications of what she was proposing, the ethical considerations would be about the ethics of business operations and ethical requirements to explain the downside risk of a course of action. In the second part of the meeting, the ethics are around business behaviour – when is it right or ethical to contradict your boss? At any number of points in your career, you are likely to be faced with similar ethical dilemmas.

The ethics of business operations

In terms of the ethics of business operations, all financial institutions will have policies in place to which you can refer. In addition, individuals who are regulated by the FSA in the conduct of investment business also comply with their statements of principle including:

- Acting with integrity.
- Acting with 'due skill, care and diligence'.
- Observing 'proper standards of market conduct'.

In the financial markets, there are conventions on ethical standards. Some have become accepted best practice over time; others have the backing of the law. For example, it is a legal requirement in the UK that financial service providers make clients aware of the risk as well as the opportunity from any investment or derivative product, especially in the case of complex structures (see Mary and Bill at the beginning of this section). There was a US case, where the client was able to gain a multi-million dollar settlement after a derivatives strategy went badly wrong. Internally recorded tapes of telephone conversations were discovered at the seller's office. These conversations were recorded between two individuals laughing at the fact that the clients did not understand the possible consequences of the deal they had done.

Some other ethical issues regarding business operations can be more tricky.

EXAMPLE

You are asked to loan money to Unilateral Defence Inc. This company is an armaments manufacturer. It needs the loan to finance increased production caused by the escalation of the civil war in an African country. Their activities are perfectly legal, but you are aware that many civilians have been caught up in the fighting.

EXAMPLE

You are asked to loan money to Value Megastores Ltd, an international chain of discount clothing stores. A recent TV documentary has exposed that their value price positioning is achieved by buying their products from factories with unsafe working practices and employing children as young as ten as machinists. Again, their activities are perfectly legal.

Many financial institutions have clear ethics policies, designed for situations such as in these two examples. Providing the task that you are asked to perform is legal and within the policy rules of your organisation, your job as an employee is to maximise return for your organisation and to act in the best interests of your clients, not to exercise your personal moral judgment. This may sometimes include working with a client of whose business you disapprove. If the ethical stance of your organisation means that you are constantly being asked to do this, you may be working for the wrong outfit and might be happier or more comfortable elsewhere. It is never appropriate to compromise the business of a client or the profit of your institution because you do not agree with what they do. If you do so, you are breaking the ethical rules governing your duty to your employer and its clients.

In addition to staying within the law, the regulations and the policies and practices of your organisation, there will be times, however, when you need to decide on your own ethical stance on business operations. The line is a continuum and here are some samples along it.

- At the extreme end are individuals who will flout the rules with reckless abandon. They believe firmly that 'the end justifies the means' and may even be prepared to operate illegally for short-term gain or kudos. Their immediate results may be spectacular but equally spectacular usually is the sudden end to their careers.
- Next along are the people who abide strictly by the letter of the law or the policy, which offers them a defence should their behaviour ever be challenged, but will put results ahead of broadly ethical operations and exploit every loophole.
- Further along still are people with a strong internal compass when it comes to business ethics and who would never flout either the spirit or the letter of the law or workplace policies. They may be creative in terms of their dealings, but always within a framework. They work hard and are committed to results, but would not 'sell their grandmother' to achieve them.

The ethics of business behaviour

As well as your workplace behaviour with regard to diversity, discrimination and harassment and bullying covered above, just about everyone faces some ethical dilemmas at work. Typical dilemmas include relatively mild 'everyday' ones such as:

- Taking home office stationery for your own use.
- Dealing with a situation where someone keeps taking credit for your work.
- Being asked to recommend a workmate or subordinate that you may like but not particularly 'rate' as an operator.

However, they might be more troublesome such as:

- Being aware of harassment or bullying and wondering whether to blow the whistle on behalf of someone else.
- In a redundancy situation, having to choose who stays and who goes.
- Becoming aware that your boss is acting unethically in business dealings.

Once again, in addition to staying within the law and the policies of your organisation, you have to choose your ethical position, based on the need to protect or enhance your reputation and your personal or business values. In terms of ethical business behaviour, there is a range of action. This includes:

- People with no apparent ethical standards who do not seem to feel any need to treat others with respect but ruthlessly pursue their own agenda.
- People who will espouse ethical standards when it suits them or appears to be required but will equally happily leave them behind when it suits them or when under pressure.
- People with strong personal values and who are consistent in behaving accordingly, striking a careful balance between the requirements of the job and the 'how'.

The choice is yours.

Whistleblowing

Whistleblowing is when an individual raises concerns or provides information of wrongdoing to an employer or a regulator. Usually, the alleged wrongdoing affects others (e.g. other employees or shareholders). The whistleblower may or may not be affected by the wrongdoing, but may be vulnerable to reprisals because of their actions. The term whistleblowing is a throw-back to police officers on the beat who, making best use of the technology of the day, would blow their whistle to attract attention or gain help, on discovering a crime. Here are two famous whistleblowers who demonstrated great persistence and personal courage in highlighting wrongdoing. Their actions did result in huge loss to many people, but had they never spoken up, the consequences would have been even more disastrous and far-reaching.

> whistleblowers may be vulnerable to reprisals because of their actions

Cynthia Cooper was vice-president of the internal audit department at the US telecommunications company WorldCom. In March 2002, she learned of accounting irregularities to the tune of $400 million. When she questioned this, she was told it was not her problem. When she persisted, she was told to back off. On investigation, she found a huge hole in the books amounting to billions of dollars that was wildly inflating company results. Battling on despite all efforts of the finance chief to delay her investigation, Cooper's findings were proved to be all too true. In August 2002, the finance chief was indicted on charges of securities fraud. WorldCom filed for bankruptcy. Some 17,000 employees were made redundant around the globe. Shareholders lost an estimated $3 billion, including the largest state pension fund in the US, which lost $600 million it had invested in the company.

Harry Templeton worked as a printer on the Scottish Daily Record and the Sunday Mail, newspapers owned by Robert Maxwell's Mirror Group. In 1985, he was appointed as a trustee of the group's pension scheme. He became uneasy about how the pension fund was being administered. Despite his relatively junior rank, he persisted in questioning the apparent transfer of funds to other Maxwell businesses, but often found himself isolated on the pensions committee. Eventually, he was dismissed from his job and told by Maxwell that he would never work in the print industry again. Only after Maxwell's death a couple of years later was it revealed that Maxwell had robbed the pension scheme of £400 million of staff pension money.

Two different people, one senior, one much more junior, but sharing similar experiences. Along with Sherron Watkins at Enron, Cynthia Cooper and Harry Templeton are two of the best-known whistleblowers of the recent past. You may never uncover another Enron, but there may be a point in your career when you are faced with other, perhaps much smaller issues and have to make the call: am I prepared to become a whistleblower?

What the law and regulations say

Whistleblowers are protected by UK law from personal reprisals because of their actions, provided they have behaved within guidelines. These are outlined below. You may not be punished or disadvantaged if, as an employee, you reveal information of the right sort (a 'qualifying disclosure'), in the right way (a 'protected disclosure').

Qualifying disclosures can only be allegations of:

- criminal acts;
- lack of compliance with a legal or regulatory obligation;
- miscarriages of justice;
- a threat to people's health or safety;
- serious environmental damage.

You also need to demonstrate 'reasonable belief' that the misconduct has occurred, is occurring or is about to happen. The rules also contain penalties for people who are aware of misconduct but deliberately attempt to cover it up. You may not break another law in blowing the whistle; for example, if you have signed the Official Secrets Act as part of your contract of employment.

A protected disclosure is a qualifying disclosure made to the right person in the right way:

- Made in good faith (you honestly believe it to be true).
- Not made maliciously or for personal gain.
- To your employer or relevant person (i.e. the person responsible for the area in question).
- Using the policies and procedures of the organisation.

In certain circumstances, it is also permitted to make disclosures to a regulator or your legal representative.

Keeping yourself out of hot water

If you have reasonable grounds for believing that wrongdoing is happening or about to happen, check your organisation's policies for guidance on how to proceed. Usually these policies share a similar format with those on grievance procedures (see the section on discrimination). The first port of call is usually your line manger. If you make your disclosure official, you can usually expect a formal response within a prescribed period. If you are unhappy with the response, you have the right to escalate your concern to more senior management. The Charity Public Concern at Work (PCaW) is the independent authority on public interest whistleblowing (www.pcaw.co.uk). It offers free guidance to people with whistleblowing dilemmas. The following lists expand on PCaW advice.

Do

- Keep calm. Ensure you are acting in a considered and not hasty way – it is not because you have a score to settle. Make sure that your concern is covered as a qualifying disclosure (see above) and is delivered to the right person.
- Think about the risks and outcomes before you act. What are the consequences for everyone involved should your suspicions turn out to be incorrect? Are you in breach of any contractual confidentiality issues?

- Remember you are a witness, not a complainant. You do not need to make the case, just have reasonable grounds for your disclosure.
- Phone for advice. In serious cases, you may wish to call a helpline such as the PCaW's.

Don't

- Forget there may be an innocent or good explanation. However convinced you are, you may not have all the facts.
- Become a private detective. You may set hares running unnecessarily or break other laws in the process.
- Use a whistleblowing procedure to pursue a personal grievance. You may well not be legally protected if you do so.
- Expect thanks. While you may not be victimised by law, you can expect a strong response on the part of others whose alleged wrongdoing is being investigated.

Glossary

AAA or triple A Triple A: a rating issued by a rating agency indicating the 'risk' of the company. AAA is the highest rating, usually allocated to governments, and rarely otherwise, indicating almost zero risk that you will not be paid what you are owed. In 1998 the Russian government defaulted on bond payments, breaking the assumption that governments always pay.

Abandon Where an option holder chooses not to exercise his option.

ABS Asset-backed security. A security collateralised by loans, leases, unsecured receivables or instalment contracts on personal property, cars or credit cards. The cash flows generated by the underlying obligations are used to pay principal and interest to the ABS holders.

Absolute risk The volatility of total returns.

Acceptance Short-term debt instrument, drawn on a bank for future payment.

Accord A trade-matching service run by SWIFT.

Accreting loan A loan where the principal increases in stages as capital is required.

Accrued interest Interest that has been earned but not yet paid.

Actuary A statistician who calculates risk. Usually employed by an insurance company.

ADR American Depositary Receipts. See *Depositary receipts*.

AIM Alternative Investment Market. For small, young and growing companies; opened by the London Stock Exchange in June 1995.

Algorithmic trading The use of complex computer programs built into computer trading models to trade financial instruments in electronic markets. Huge numbers of trades can be executed simultaneously across many platforms, much faster than humans can do. Also known as 'black box' trading.

Alpha Additional return above that expected by a stock or portfolio; often generated by exposure to foreign exchange.

American style An option that may be exercised into its underlying instrument on any business day until expiry.

Amortising loan A loan where the principal reduces in stages as capital is repaid.

Annual general meeting (AGM) A mandatory yearly meeting that allows shareholders to stay informed and involved with company decisions and workings.

Arbitrage The purchase or sale of an instrument and the simultaneous taking of an equal and opposite position in a related market, for profit.

Arbitrageur A trader who takes advantage of profitable opportunities arising out of pricing anomalies.

At-market An order to buy or sell at the current trading level.

At-the-money option (ATM) An option with an exercise price at the current market level of the underlying. For example, this could be ATMF – at the money forward.

Audit Inspection of a company's books by independent accountants.

Average rate option An option where the settlement is based on the difference between the strike and the average price of the 'underlying' over a predetermined period. Also known as Asian options.

Backwardation When the spot or near-term price of a commodity is higher than the forward price.

Banker's acceptance Bill of exchange accepted by large banks. A BA bears interest for periods of three to six months. It constitutes an irrevocable primary obligation of the drawer and of any endorsers whose names appear upon them. BAs primarily serve to finance imports and exports.

Basel II Published in 2004, by the Bank for International Settlements, Basel. This is a set of recommendations on banking law and regulations, with specific reference to the amount of capital the banks need to set aside to guard against financial and operational risk.

Basis point One hundredth of 1 per cent (0.01%).

Basis risk When relationships between products used to hedge each other change or break down.

BBA British Bankers' Association. Represents UK banking industry and sets LIBOR rates.

BC Base currency.

Bear market A falling market.

Beauty parade Investment banks in competition, pitching for a large corporate issuer's business.

Best The broker can buy or sell at the 'best' price available at his/her discretion.

Bid An order to buy.

Bid-offer spread The difference between the buying price (bid) and selling price (offer) as quoted in the market. In the US, the term is bid-ask.

Big Bang 27 October 1986, the London Stock Exchange's new regulations were introduced and the automated price quotation system.

Bilateral netting Movement of a single quantity of securities and payment/receipt of a single cash amount, in settlement of multiple trades with one counterparty. See *Multilateral netting*.

Black and Scholes The original option pricing model used by many market practitioners, written by Black and Scholes in 1972 (see *Scholes-Merton*).

Blue chip Large established company, in China known as 'red chips'

Bond A debt security that represents a temporary cash borrowing by a bond issuer, from investors. Typically issued with a fixed interest rate (coupon), and capital repayable on a specified maturity date.

Bond rating A rating given to a bond as the likelihood that the borrower will default on the interest and principal payments.

Booking Recording the terms of a trade into a firm's official record keeping systems, as in 'booking the trade'.

Books and records Most firms have many systems holding trade details. For audit and accounting purposes one system has to be regarded as the company's primary source of information.

Brady bonds Eurobonds issued by the government of a developing country refinancing its debt to foreign commercial banks, under a Brady-type agreement. The agreement is characterised by the introduction of an IMF plan and the opportunity for the creditor to exchange its debt against a set of instruments that comprise various original financial solutions aimed at satisfying both counterparts of the deal. Brady bonds' main features are collateralisation, debt reduction, debt-equity conversion, underwriting against new money and options on oil revenues.

Broken date A value date that is not a regular forward date.

Broker An individual or a firm that acts as an intermediary, putting together willing sellers and willing buyers for a fee (brokerage).

Bull and bear bond Fixed interest bond, whose value at maturity is dependent on the performance of a stock market index. The issue is divided into two parts: a bull bond and a bear bond. The bull bond's redemption value rises if the market index increases and declines if the index decreases. Conversely, the bear bond has a higher redemption value if the stock market weakens and a lower value if stock prices rise.

Bull market A rising market.

Buy-in Procedures laid down by a stock-exchange or market authority for a buyer to enforce settlement of a purchase from the selling counterparty.

Buy-side Collective term for market participants that have a requirement to buy financial services and products. Typically, these could be private and institutional investors, hedge funds and corporates.

Call option An option that gives the holder (buyer), the right but not the obligation to buy the underlying instrument at a pre-agreed rate (strike rate) on or before a specific future date.

Callable bond The issuer has the right to redeem the bond at a specified earlier date than the one originally fixed as the final maturity.

Capital growth bond Issue price at par (100 per cent) with redemption at a multiple of that amount.

Capitalisation issue An issue where funds from a company's reserves are converted into shares and offered free of charge to the shareholders.

Capped FRN FRN with a maximum interest rate.

CaR Capital at risk.

Cash settlement Where a product is settled at expiry, based on the differential between the fixed/guaranteed price and the underlying instrument.

CCP Central counterparty, a service provided by a clearing house to provide the highest level of certainty that a trade will settle over its life, and that all parties are protected from the consequences of one another going bankrupt.

CD Certificate of deposit. A tradable deposit issued by banks and building societies.

CDO Collateralised debt obligation.

CDS Credit default swap, used to protect against or take credit risk.

Central securities depositary (CSD) The ultimate location of securities within a marketplace, where CSD participants hold securities and cash accounts. The assets are held securely by the CSD, and settlement of securities trades are effected electronically.

CFD (equity) Contract for difference. A derivative product to trade the price differential over an indefinite time period of a specified number of shares.

CFD (oil) Contract for difference. A derivative product used to manage the price risk between 'dated Brent' and the first front month.

CHAPS Clearing House Automated Payment System: bank-to-bank payment system in UK.

CHIPS Clearing House Interbank Payments System: electronic payments system in US.

Choice price Where the buying and selling price is the same, and there is no bid/offer spread.

Clean/dirty price The clean price of a bond is the price traded in the market which ignores accrued interest/coupon. Upon settlement, final payment is made using what is known as the dirty price, which has been adjusted for accrued interest.

Clearing A way of processing trades using a central counterparty (CCP).

Clearing house A provider of CCP services for particular markets, e.g. LCH.Clearnet, once known as the London Clearing House.

CLS Continuous linked settlement: a way to settle FX and currency trades through CLS Bank and minimise Herstatt risk.

CMO Collateralised mortgage obligation: a debt security based on a pool of mortgages.

Collateral Usually cash and sometimes bonds, provided by one party to another, to offset debts in the event the other party goes bankrupt. For example, you are owed $10m by your counterparty. Using a collateral agreement, you can ask for that $10m to be paid up front, and held by you, in case your counterparty is declared bankrupt. You will be obliged to pay interest on that amount of cash back to your counterparty, and to adjust the amount of cash you hold each day, as the total debt increases or decreases.

Compound option An option on an option. The holder (buyer) has an option to purchase another option on a pre-set date at a pre-agreed premium.

Contract Same as a trade.

Convertible bond Bond/note, which can be converted for newly, issued shares or bonds at predetermined prices during specified periods of time.

Convertible rate FRN An issue, which carries the option to convert either from an initial floating rate note into a fixed rate bond, or from a fixed rate bond into a floating rate note. This provides ways in which investors and borrowers can speculate and/or hedge against the future course of interest rates.

Corporate actions Collective term for a change to the structure of an existing security. Including (for equity) stock splits, buy-backs, takeovers, (for bonds) early redemption, conversion, final maturity.

Counterparty The opposing entity with whom a firm executes a trade. From a buyer's perspective, the selling entity; from a seller's perspective, the buying entity.

Counterparty risk When counterparties are unwilling or unable to meet their contractual obligations.

Coupon Interest payment on a bond.

Coupon rate The fixed rate of interest on a bond.

Covered warrant A warrant issued by a party other than the originator or issuer of the underlying asset.

Covered writing Where an option is sold against an existing position.

CP Commercial paper: an unsecured IOU issued by large companies and banks.

Credit risk Uncertainty associated with the financial condition of a company.

CREST The paperless share settlement system. CREST is operated by CREST Co and was introduced in 1996.

Cross rate The exchange rate for one non US dollar currency against another non US dollar currency, e.g. EUR/JPY.

CSA Credit support annex: part of ISDA documentation.

Custodian A firm that is a participant of a CSD, which holds securities and cash on behalf of its clients and which facilitates settlement of its clients' purchases and sales.

Dated Brent A physical oil cargo becomes dated when it has been allocated a loading date.

Day count/convention A system used to determine the number of days between two interest payments. For example, a 30/360 day-count convention assumes there are 30 days in a month and 360 days in a year. An actual/actual day-count convention uses the actual number of days in the month and year.

Day trade A position opened and closed within the same trading day.

Deep discount bond This is a bond with issue price significantly below maturity price, due to lack of coupon or a coupon below market rate.

Default Failure to perform on a foreign exchange transaction or, failure to pay an interest obligation on a debt.

Default risk The uncertainty that some or all of an investment may not be returned.

Delivery versus payment (DvP) Method of settling securities trades, whereby the seller's securities are delivered to the buyer, and the buyer's cash is paid to the seller, simultaneously. The simultaneous nature of DvP minimises risk for both seller and buyer. See *Free of payment*.

Depositary receipts Certificates that represent ownership of a given number of a company's shares, which can be listed and traded separately from the underlying shares, e.g. ADRs and GDRs.

Depot account Account held at a CSD or custodian in which securities are held. See *Nostro account*.

Derivatives Risk management instruments that are 'derived' from the underlying markets (e.g. equity, bonds, FX, commodity). The main derivative instruments are futures, options and swaps.

Deriv/SERV A provider of automation services for the post trade OTC derivatives market.

Discount The margin by which the purchase price is cheaper than the redemption price.

Disintermediation Generally, removing the middleman or intermediary. A bank, rather than being the principal lender of capital will act as a middle man between issuers (raising funds) and investors (buying securities).

Dividend The part of a company's profits which is distributed to shareholders, usually expressed in pence per share.

DMO Debt Management Office. An executive agency of the UK Treasury, responsible for issuing Gilts to fund the government's borrowing.

DOL Daily official list. The daily record setting out the prices of all trades in securities conducted on the London Stock Exchange.

Drop-lock (DL) bond The drop-lock bond (DL bond) combines the features of both a floating and a fixed rate security. The DL bond is issued with a floating rate interest which is reset semi-annually at a specified margin above a base rate, such as six-months LIBOR. This continues until such time as the base rate is at or below a specified trigger rate on an interest fixing date or, in some cases, on two consecutive interest fixing dates. At that time the interest rate becomes fixed at a specified rate for the remaining lifetime of the bond.

DTCC The main clearer in the US for all debt and equity trades.

Dual currency bond A hybrid debt instrument with payment obligations over the life of the issue in two currencies. The borrower makes coupon payments in one currency, but redeems the principal at maturity in another currency in an amount fixed at the time of the issue of the bonds. The price of the bonds in the secondary market is indicated as a percentage of the redemption amount.

ECP (Euro commercial paper) An unsecured general obligation in the form of a promissory bearer note, issued on a discount or interest-bearing basis by large commercial and industrial organisations. Maturities of ECP range from a few days up to one year, with most 182 days. ECP provides a flexible alternative to short-term finance credit lines with commercial banks and the rate for prime issuers is usually set at a small margin above that offered by prime bank money market securities of comparable maturities.

EDR (Euro depositary receipts) A certificate representing ownership of the issuer's underlying shares. The EDR is denominated and quoted in euros.

Effective date A date on which the trade 'enters into force', most commonly the date on which some OTC trades begin calculating interest. In almost all cases this occurs one or two days after trade date.

Electronic book entry Method of holding securities and transferring securities between participants in a CSD. Matched securities quantities (and cash amounts) are transferred from one participant to another electronically; no physical movement of securities occurs.

End/end A transaction for settlement on the last business day of a month against the last business day of a future month.

Equity Ownership interest of shareholders in a company. Equity is issued following receipt of cash from investors. Synonymous with 'shares'.

ETF (exchange traded funds) Known in the US as index shares. Stock exchange quoted fund portfolios designed either as index trackers (index funds) or as managed stock baskets (actively managed funds).

Eurobond Bond issued by a borrower in a currency which is not his own, e.g. US borrower, issuing in yen, underwritten and sold by an international syndicate of financial institutions.

Euronote A short-term, negotiable bearer promissory note usually issued at a discount with maturities of less than one year. (Issued in bearer form; may be held as a global certificate.)

European style An option which may only be exercised on the expiry date. See *American style*.

Eurozone The euro is the sole currency in Austria, Belgium, Cyprus, Finland, France, Germany, Greece, Ireland, Italy, Luxembourg, Malta, the Netherlands, Portugal, Slovakia, Slovenia and Spain. These 16 countries together are often referred to as the eurozone or the euro area, and, more informally, 'euroland' or the 'eurogroup'.

Exchange A place where parties meet (whether electronically or in person) to negotiate and execute trades. Regulated exchanges include, Euronext-Liffe, CME and ICE.

Exchangeable bond A bond or note that can be exchanged for existing shares or bonds of a third party at, predetermined prices during specified periods of time.

Exchange-traded A transaction where a specific instrument is bought or sold on a regulated exchange, e.g. futures.

Execution/executed The point at which a trade becomes legally binding between the two (or sometimes three) parties.

Exercise The conversion of the option into the 'underlying'.

Exercise price/strike price The price at which the option holder has the right to buy or sell the underlying instrument.

Exotic options New generation of option derivatives, including look-backs, barriers, baskets, ladders, etc.

Expiry The date after which an option can no longer be exercised.

Expiration date The last date on which an option can be exercised.

Exposure Amount of money a party is owed by another party.

Extendible bond The investor has the option at one or several fixed dates to extend the maturity.

Extraordinary general meeting (EGM) A meeting other than the annual general meeting between a company's shareholders, executives and any other members. An EGM is usually called on short notice and deals with an urgent matter.

Failed trade Securities trade that has not settled by close-of-business on value date (but which is still expected to settle in the coming days).

Fair value For options, this is calculated by an option pricing model such as that developed by Black and Scholes. For futures, it is the level where the contract should trade, taking into account cost of carry.

Fannie Mae Federal National Mortgage Association (FNMA) in the US.

FedWire Payment system used by US Federal Reserve banks to transfer large or time critical US dollar amounts internationally or domestically.

Fixed-interest securities Securities that attract a fixed rate of interest each year.

Flip-flop FRN Combines an FRN with a very long final maturity, or even a perpetual issue, and an investor option to convert after a specified period into a short-dated FRN, which typically pays a lower margin over LIBOR than the original issue. The investor further has the option at a later date to convert back into the initial issue before redemption of the short-dated note.

Flotation When a company's shares are issued on an exchange for the first time.

Foreign bond Securities, for example Yankee, Samurai, Bulldog and Matador bonds, issued by a borrower in a domestic capital market other than its own, usually denominated in the currency of that market, underwritten and sold by a national underwriting and selling group of the lenders' country. (Usually issued in bearer or registered form.)

Forward foreign exchange All foreign-exchange transactions with a maturity of over two business days from transaction date (see *premiums/discounts*).

Forward/forward Calculation uses information known now to infer where an asset will trade in the future.

FpML Financial products mark-up language. A way of representing the terms of an OTC contract electronically, suitable for automated processing. See www.fpml.org.

Free of payment (FoP) Method of settling securities trades, whereby the seller's securities are delivered to the buyer, and the buyer's cash is paid to the seller, non-simultaneously. The non-simultaneous nature of FoP means that one or both parties will go on risk when settling trades. See *Delivery versus payment*.

FRN (floating rate note) FRNs are medium to long-term debt obligations with variable interest rates, which are adjusted periodically (typically every one, three or six months). The interest rate is usually fixed at a specified spread over one of the following specified deposit rates:

- LIBOR: London interbank offered rate.
- LIBID: London interbank bid rate.
- LIMEAN: London interbank mean rate (average of LIBOR and LIBID).

FSA (Financial Services Authority) Regulates the financial services industry under the Financial Services and Markets Act 2000.

Futures A contract to buy or sell a standardised amount of an underlying instrument at a future date at a pre-determined price. Trading at a recognised exchange (e.g. NYSE Liffe).

GDR (global depositary receipt) See *Depositary receipts.*

GEMMs Gilt-edged market makers.

Gilt Gilt-edged securities, debt instruments issued by the UK government.

Ginnie May Government National Mortgage Association (GNMA) in the US.

Global bond International issue placed at the same time in the euro and one or more domestic markets with securities fungible between the markets.

Global custodian Organisation that provides a single point of contact for its clients, and which has a network of sub-custodians in several financial centres. See *Custodian.*

Gross redemption yield (GRY) See *Yield to maturity.*

Guaranteed bond Guaranteed bonds have their interest, principal or both guaranteed by another corporation. A parent company commonly guarantees bonds issued by subsidiaries.

Haircut When they are used as collateral, securities will generally have a haircut imposed to allow for volatility. It is a margin imposed on collateral sellers.

Hedge A transaction that reduces or mitigates risk.

Historical volatility An indication of past volatility in the market place.

Holder The buyer/owner of an option.

Herstatt risk The failure to settle one side of an FX trade by value date. Named after the bank where this failure occurred in 1974. See *CLS*.

Implied volatility The volatility implied by the market price of the option.

Index A relative expression of the weighted value of a group of securities used as a performance indicator.

Index multiplier Monetary amount used to value an index futures contract.

Indication only Quotations that are not firm.

Initial public offering (IPO) The first sale of stock by a private company to the public.

Insider dealing The purchase or sale of securities (or other financial instruments) by someone who possesses 'inside' information, likely to affect the price of the instrument in the market. In the UK, such deals are a criminal offence.

Institutional investor Generic term for organisations wishing to buy and sell securities, including pension funds and investment companies, mutual funds and insurance companies.

Interest claim A written communication made by one party on its counterparty, claiming recompense for cash interest lost where the latter failed to make a cash payment at the scheduled time. This concept is applicable across all financial instruments.

Intermediary An institution that acts as the middleman between investors and firms raising funds. Often investment banks.

International bond Bond issued by a borrower in a foreign country. International bonds include foreign bonds, parallel bonds and eurobonds.

In-the-money option (ITM) An option with an exercise price more advantageous than the current market level of the underlying.

Intrinsic value One of the components of an option premium. The amount by which an option is in-the-money.

Investment trust A collective investment fund in the form of a listed company that holds a portfolio of securities on behalf of its shareholders.

Investor An individual or organisation who wishes to buy and sell securities and other assets for investment purposes. See *Institutional investor*.

Investor relations The process by which a company keeps its investors informed. Good investor relations will support the share price.

ISDA International Swaps and Derivatives Association. Many market participants use ISDA swap documentation.

ISIN International Securities Identification Number. A method of coding securities to make them uniquely identifiable.

Issuer A legal entity that develops registers and sells securities for the purpose of financing its operations.

Junk bond High risk, low rated speculative bonds.

LCH.Clearnet London Clearing House. A central counterparty set up to remove credit risk on exchange-traded transactions.

LIBOR The London inter-bank offered rate. The inter bank rate used when one bank borrows from another. It is also the benchmark used to price many capital market and derivative transactions. Other countries have their own forms (EURIBOR, TIBOR), but LIBOR is the global benchmark.

LIBID The London inter-bank bid rate. The rate where one bank will lend to another.

Limit order An order given at a certain price.

Liquid market A market-place where much selling and buying occurs with minimal price concessions.

Liquidation The closing of an existing position.

Liquidity The ease with which an item can be traded on a market.

Listed company A company whose securities are admitted to the daily official list in London.

Listing particulars A prospectus which details what the London Stock Exchange requires a company to publish about itself and its securities before they can be admitted to the main market.

Long More purchases than sales.

LSE London Stock Exchange.

LYON Liquid yield option note. Combines the features of a zero-coupon bond with those of a convertible bond. The zero coupon bond pays no interest until it is redeemed at or before maturity; the difference between the issue price and the redemption price represents the accrued interest. In addition, the LYON bond may be converted by the holder into the stock of the issuing corporation within a specified period and at a specified conversion price.

Mandatory quote period The time when market-makers on the LSE's SEAQ and SEAQ international computers are obliged to make firm two-way quotes for the securities in which they are registered.

Mark to market A process whereby existing positions are revalued each day.

Market maker An authorised trader, obliged to make firm two-way quotes in financial instruments during trading periods.

MarkitWire More recent name for SwapsWire.

Mezzanine finance See *Subordinated debt*.

Mine Where a dealer takes the offer that has been quoted by a counterparty. It must be qualified by the amount.

Mini-max (or collared) FRN FRN with a minimum and a maximum interest rate.

Mismatch FRN FRN having a coupon structure re-fixed more often and for different maturities than the interest periods, e.g. the interest rate is based on six-month LIBOR but adjusted every month.

Momentum A mathematical method of measuring the rate of change in ascending or descending prices. Many trading models use momentum to trigger buy and sell signals automatically.

Monoline A business that focuses on operating in one specific financial area, bringing specialised skills and expertise, in contrast to firms providing a wider range of financial services.

Mortgage-backed security (MBS) Debt security backed by a pool of mortgages.

Moving average A trend following indicator used in technical analysis to generate buy and sell signals.

MTN Medium-term note. An unsecured note issued in a euro-currency with a maturity of three to six years.

Multilateral netting Movement of a single quantity of securities and payment/receipt of a single cash amount, in settlement of trades amongst several counterparties. See *Bilateral netting*.

Naked option An option position taken without having the underlying.

New issue An issuer coming to the market for the first time.

Nominated advisor Compulsory, exchange-approved advisor for AIM companies.

NMS Normal market size. Calculated for each security, based on a percentage of daily turnover. The percentage is set at 2.5 per cent and intended to represent the normal institutional bargain.

Nostro account Account held by some other party on your behalf, cash or securities.

Notice of exercise Notification by telex, fax or phone which must be given irrevocably by the buyer to the seller of the option before, or at the time of, expiry.

Notional An amount of money used in an OTC contract, from which cash flow calculations are made. The notional isn't necessarily an amount of money that is paid by one party to another.

OASYS An electronic trade affirmation mechanism that allows subscribers to match details of securities trades.

OEIC An open-ended investment company governed by a trust deed or memorandum with specific investment objectives. The funds are pooled under management and the price of units is based on net asset value.

Offer An order to sell.

Offer for sale A method of bringing a company to the market. The public can apply for shares directly at a fixed price. A prospectus giving details of the sale must be published in a national newspaper.

Option An agreement between two parties that gives the holder (buyer), the right but not the obligation to buy or sell a specific instrument at a specified price on or before a specific future date. On exercise the seller (writer) of the option must deliver, or take delivery of the underlying instrument at the specified price.

Order book Otherwise known as SETS (stock exchange trading system). Introduced on 20 October 1997, the electronic order book automatically executes orders when bid and offer prices match.

Orders Firm order given by a dealer to a counterparty to execute a transaction under certain specified conditions, e.g., limit order, stop loss order, etc.

Ordinary share The most common form of share. Holders may receive dividends on the recommendation of directors. Known in the US as 'common stock'.

Out-of-the-money option (OTM) An option with an exercise price more disadvantageous than the current market level of the underlying. An out-of-the-money option has a time value but no intrinsic value.

Outright The purchase or sale of a currency for delivery on any date other than spot.

Over the counter (OTC) A bilateral transaction between a client and a bank, negotiated privately between the parties.

Overnight Transaction for settlement tomorrow, taken out today.

Par Where the price is the same at purchase and redemption.

Partial delivery Settlement of a quantity of securities (versus a proportionate cash amount) which is less than the full quantity of the shares (and cash amount).

Party A legal entity empowered to enter into OTC Derivatives trades e.g. JP Morgan Chase & Co.

Perpetual bond These are bonds, that are due for redemption only in the case of the borrower's liquidation. Usually the terms and conditions provide a call option at a premium. The interest rate can be fixed for the whole maturity or only for an initial period (e.g. ten years). For each subsequent period the interest is reset as provided in the terms and conditions.

P/L Profit/loss.

Point/pip The last decimal place of the quotation.

Portfolio A collection of securities owned by an investor.

Post-trade event A modification to a trade agreed between the parties some time after the original trade is executed. An example would be an assignment (sometimes called a novation), where an original party to a contract transfers its role to another party in exchange for a fee.

POTAM Panel on Takeovers and Mergers. UK regulatory body.

Preference shares Normally fixed income shares, where holders have the right to receive dividends before ordinary shareholders. In the event of liquidation, preference shareholders rank above ordinary shareholders. Participating preference shares have further rights, which are normally linked to the relevant company's profits or dividend payment on ordinary shares. Other preference shares will have the rights of standard preference shares, but may also be:

- Cumulative: income arrears are carried forward to the next payment date.
- Convertible: into ordinary shares.
- Redeemable: at a fixed date or contingent on a special event.
- Permanent: not redeemable except at issuer's option.
- Callable: can be repurchased by its issuer at a specified price.
- Protected: has its dividend guaranteed in the event that the company does not earn a profit.
- Participating: allows its holders to receive dividends in addition to the fixed amount in years when the ordinary dividend exceeds a certain level.
- Prior preferred: has senior rights over other classes of stock.

Premium The margin by which the purchase price is more expensive than the redemption rate.

Premium on options The cost of the option contract. It is made up of two components, intrinsic value and time value.

Premiums/discounts (FX forwards) A forward FX price is calculated using interest rate differentials between currency pairs over a given time period. This interest rate adjustment is expressed as 'forward points' and either taken off the spot rate (premiums), or added on (discounts) to give an 'outright forward price'.

P/E ratio Price/earnings ratio. A measure of investor confidence, normally the higher the figure the higher the confidence. Current share price divided by earnings per share.

Price transparency Where a transaction is executed on the floor of an exchange, and every participant has an equal price.

Primary market The function of a stock exchange in bringing securities to the market for the first time.

Private company A company which is not a public company and cannot offer its shares to the public.

Privatisation Conversion of a state-run company to public limited liability status.

Put option An option that gives the holder (buyer), the right but not the obligation to sell the underlying instrument at a pre-agreed strike rate (exercise rate) on or before a specific future date.

Puttable bond The investor has the right to require redemption of the principal at a specified earlier date than the one originally fixed as the final maturity.

PvP Payment versus payment. Typically used in FX markets where one currency is used to pay for another, resulting in simultaneous currency payments being swapped between buyer and seller. See also *Delivery versus payment* (DvP), and continuous linked settlement (*CLS*).

Redemption Where the issuer of shares decides to buy back shares from investors.

Registrar An organisation responsible for maintaining a company's share register.

Repo Sale and repurchase agreement. Used by many central banks as a method of managing liquidity in the money markets. Banks trade repos and reverse repos in many products but mainly bonds.

Reputation loss Damage caused to a firm's image that may adversely affect its future trading capability.

Resistance level A high price level where selling interest has historically been seen, resulting in the asset price falling. If historical resistance levels are broken then it signals that the market can move to much higher levels.

Retractable bond Issue carrying the option (for both the issuer and the investor) for early redemption at one or several fixed dates.

Reverse convertible bonds Convertible bond that may be redeemed at the issuer's decision against existing shares of an underlying company which has no economic relation with the issuer or the guarantee of the bonds.

RIE Recognised investment exchange, in the UK that meets FSA requirements.

Rights issue An invitation to existing shareholders to purchase additional shares in the company, normally at a discount.

Risk The volatility of expected outcomes.

RNS Regulatory News Service. To ensure that price sensitive information from listed, AIM and certain other bodies, is disseminated to all RNS subscribers at the same time.

Rollercoaster loan A loan with both accreting and amortising elements. See *Accreting* and *Amortising*.

RUF Revolving underwriting facility, sometimes called a note-issuance facility (NIF). This is a medium to long-term finance instrument, which allows the borrower, by issuing short-term paper, to benefit from cheaper short-term funds.

Sales desk A team of people who sell trading solutions across many products to solve problems for the customers of a bank. Sales people do not quote prices, they must request one from a trader.

Scheduled termination date The date on which a trade ceases to be economically or legally active.

Scholes-Merton Nobel prize-winning revision of the Black-Scholes option pricing model.

SEAQ Stock Exchange Automated Quotation system for UK securities. A continuously updated computer database containing price quotations and trade reports for UK securities.

SEAQ international Stock Exchange Automated Quotation System for international securities.

SEATS plus Supports the trading of all AIM and listed UK equities whose turnover is insufficient for market makers or SETS.

Securities Generic term referring to financial instruments (specifically equity and bonds) issued following the issuer's receipt of capital from investors.

Sell-out Procedure laid down by a stock exchange or market authority for a seller to enforce settlement of a sale to the buying counterparty.

Sell-side Collective term for firms (such as brokers and investment banks) that service the needs of buy side firms such as institutional investors.

SETS Stock Exchange Trading Service. Otherwise known as the order book.

SETSmm SETSmm is a SETS-style order book supported by market makers for FTSE 250 securities not trading on SETS, all UK FTSE Eurotop 300 securities and exchange-traded funds (ETFs).

Settlement (securities) The exchange of securities and cash, between buyer and seller.

Settlement cycle The default/standard number of days between trade date and value date, within a securities market.

Settlement date The date that settlement of a securities trade actually occurs. Also known as actual settlement date. See *Value date.*

Settlement instruction A communication issued by a buyer or seller of securities to its custodian, to initiate settlement.

SFA Securities and Futures Authority. The self regulating organisation (SRO) responsible for regulating the conduct of brokers and dealers in securities, options and futures. Now included within the FSA.

Shares UK term commonly used for equity.

Short More sales than purchases.

Short dates Foreign exchange deals for a broken number of days up to the one month date.

Short selling The practice of firstly selling securities without owning those securities, with the intention of buying the same at a later point in time (at a lower price).

SICAF Société d'investissement à capitale fixe. An SICAF share represents one part of ownership in a fixed capital investment company.

SICAV Société d'investissement à capital variable. An SICAV share represents part of ownership in an open-ended investment company with a variable capital.

Sinking fund Regular payments made by the borrower to a special account to set aside the necessary funds for the redemption of its long-term debt. In the euromarket, borrowers can meet their requirements through purchases in the open market or through drawings by lot.

SMF Securities masterfile provides up-to-date information on securities traded on UK and international markets.

Sold short Someone who has sold a commodity without previously owning it (short sell).

Split Where the issuer of shares decides to divide each share into two or more parts to increase the number of shares, with an adjustment to the price of each share.

Spot foreign exchange A transaction to exchange one currency for another at a rate agreed today (the spot rate), for settlement in two business day's time.

Spot/next Swap transaction for settlement on the second business day against the third business day after the transaction date.

Spread The difference between buying and selling rates.

SSN Stock situation notices contain extensive details of action by companies.

Standing settlement instructions (SSIs) Details of a firm's custodian accounts within each market in which it conducts securities trading. Such instructions are held within the firm's static data repository, allowing automation of the trade enrichment process.

Step-up/step-down bond Rate will go up or down as indicated in the terms and conditions of the notes.

Stock Bonds in the UK; equity in the US.

Stockbroker An exchange member firm which provides advice and dealing services to the public and which can deal on its own account.

Stop-loss order Becomes an order at best after a certain rate has been reached or passed or dealt, depending upon the specified conditions previously agreed between the parties.

Strike The price or level at which an option begins to make a profit or loss.

Strike price/exercise price The price at which the option holder has the right to buy or sell the underlying instrument.

Subordinated debt Sometimes called mezzanine finance. Has many of the characteristics of both debt and equity. A subordinated creditor agrees to rank after senior creditors but before ordinary shareholders in a winding-up. For regulatory purposes certain forms of subordinated debt issued by financial institutions may be treated, like equity, as primary capital.

Support level A historical level where the price of an asset (share, commodity, etc) finds buying interest. The more times this support level is reached, the more significant it becomes.

Swap A derivative risk management tool.

SwapClear Central clearing service for OTC interest rate swap contracts, run by LCH.Clearnet in London.

Swaption An option into a predetermined swap transaction. Options can be 'payers' or 'receivers' on the swap which itself can be American or European.

SwapsWire A provider of automation services for the post trade OTC derivatives market. Now called MarkitWire.

SWIFT Society for Worldwide Interbank Financial Telecommunication. Global organisation providing secure message transmission and structured message formats for a variety of financial communications, for firms that subscribe.

SWIFTnet The private network operated by SWIFT to enable secure electronic messaging amongst the worlds financial institutions.

Syndicated loan A loan offered by a group of lenders (called a syndicate) who work together to provide funds for a single borrower.

TechMARK Market launched in November 1999 that groups together technology companies from across the main market. It has its own indices, the FTSE techMARK 100 and FTSE techMARK Allshare.

Technical analysis A graphical analysis of historical price trends used to predict likely future trends in the market. Also known as 'charts'.

Tick Unit of movement on a futures contract.

Ticket Jargon for a paper or electronic presentation of the trade details. A computer screen showing the details of a trade might be referred to as 'the ticket', or else a printed sheet with the trade details could also be regarded the same way.

Theoretical value The fair value of a futures or option contract. See *Fair value.*

Tie-out Agreeing with counterparty that a trade exists, including the main terms of the trade, such as the buyer and seller.

Time value The amount (if any), by which the premium of an option exceeds the intrinsic value.

Tom/next A transaction for settlement on the next business day after tomorrow.

Touch The best buying and selling prices available from market makers on SEAQ and SEAQ International in a given security at any one time.

Trade A contract between two or more parties. Many thousands of trades are done every day in the OTC market.

Trade confirmation A communication containing full details of an individual trade, issued to (or received from) the counterparty.

Trade date The date on which the trade is executed between the parties.

Trade enrichment The process of automatically adding essential information to the basic trade details captured by the trader.

Traded option An option contract bought or sold on a regulated exchange.

Trading desk A team of people who focus on a particular trading market or product, who quote prices for trades they are prepared to execute a trade at.

Trading position (securities) The accumulated net quantity of securities owned on a trade date basis.

TRAX An electronic trade matching mechanism owned by the International Capital Market Association (ICMA)

Treasury bond Bond issued by the US Treasury; longer than ten years.

Treasury bill Short-term security issued by the US Treasury.

Trend The general direction of the market, which is either in an uptrend (bull market) or a downtrend (bear market). A market can also be in a non-trending or sideways trading phase.

Trillion One thousand billion (twelve zeroes).

TRUF Transferable revolving underwriting facility (TRUF). Similar to a RUF, but the underwriting bank's contingent liability (back-up line) to purchase notes in the event of non-placement by the borrower is fully transferable.

UKLA United Kingdom Listing Authority. A capacity assumed by the FSA from the LSE, as the competent authority for a UK listing.

UK Treasury bill Short-term security issued by the UK Treasury.

Underlying An asset, future, interest rate, FX rate or index upon which a derivative transaction is based.

Underwriting An arrangement by which a company is guaranteed that an issue will raise a given amount of cash. Underwriters undertake to subscribe for any of the issue not taken up. They charge commission for this service.

Unit trust A collective investment in the form of a trust which holds a portfolio of securities on behalf of the investors who hold units in the trust. Known in the US as mutual funds.

USF Universal stock futures. Quoted on Liffe, single-share futures contracts covering a range of shares from a number of countries and sectors.

Valuation The monetary value of a trade at any point in time to you, either a profit, a loss, or occasionally zero.

Value date The intended date of settlement of a securities trade. Also known as contractual settlement date.

Value today Same day value.

Value tomorrow Value the next working day or business day.

Vanilla A nickname derived from vanilla ice-cream, for the simplest of OTC derivatives trades.

VaR Value at risk: a statistical measure used for risk management.

Variable-rate note FRN: where the margin over the reference rate is fixed by the issuer and the re-marketing agent several days before the following interest period. The holders, during a predetermined period of time, have the right to either bid for the new applicable margin over the reference rate or (under certain conditions) put the notes to the arranger (but not the issuer) on the following interest payment date.

Volatility One of the components of the option pricing model, based on the degree of 'scatter' of the underlying price when compared with the mean average exchange rate.

VWAP Volume-weighted average price, which is calculated by dividing the value of trades by the volume over a given period. A closing ten-minute VWAP is used to calculate set closing prices on the order book.

Warrant An option that can be listed on an exchange, generally longer than one year. Many capital market issues have warrants embedded in them.

Writer The seller of an option.

Yard One thousand million (billion).

Yellow strip The yellow band on a SEAQ screen that displays the highest bid and the lowest offered price that competing market makers are offering in a security. It is known colloquially as the 'touch' or 'yellow strip' price.

Yield The return earned on an investment taking into account the annual income and its present capital value. There are several types of yield, and in some cases different methods of calculating each type.

Yield curve A curve showing interest rates at a particular point in time for securities with the same risk but different maturity dates.

Yield to maturity The annualised rate of return if a bond is held to maturity, often known as gross redemption yield (GRY).

Your risk Quoted rates are subject to change at the risk of the receiver.

Yours Opposite to mine. The dealer gives at the bid which has been quoted by the counterparty. It must be qualified by the amount.

Zero-coupon bond This is a bond without a coupon providing interest payments. Zero-coupon bonds have an issue price well below 100 per cent with repayment on maturity at face value or par. The investors' return is the difference between the issue price and redemption value.

Index

Page numbers in *italics* denotes a table/illustration

Taylor Associates

Taylor Associates runs programmes and tutorials in the following areas:

Technical skills

- Derivatives: OTC and exchange-traded instruments
- Capital markets
- Corporate treasury
- Banking
- Foreign exchange
- Fixed income
- Securitisation
- Equities
- Technical analysis
- Wealth management
- Fund management
- Hedge funds
- Post-trade processes, both OTC derivatives and securities
- Clearing
- Portfolio management
- Credit evaluation
- Risk and risk management
- Mergers and acquisitions
- General finance and accounting
- Law

Management skills

- Diversity: combating sexual, racial, age, disability, sexual orientation and religious discrimination
- Diversity: combating harassment and bullying
- Team-building
- Strategy
- Sales and communication skills
- Presentation and writing skills
- Assertion and managing difficult staff
- Coaching: small groups and one to one

All programmes can work towards CPD points and are ACCA-accredited.

For details contact:

Francesca Taylor, B.Sc., MBA, AMCT
Taylor Associates (International) Ltd
Tel: +44 (0) 1372 841096
Mobile: +44 (0) 7776 146889
e-mail: info@taylorassociates.co.uk
web: www.taylorassociates.co.uk